"Jump, Damn It, Jump!"

"Jump, Damn It, Jump!"

Memoir of a Downed B-17 Pilot in World War II

EDWARD F. LOGAN, JR.

McFarland & Company, Inc., Publishers
Jefferson, North Carolina, and London

Frontispiece: 1st Lt. Edward F. Logan, Jr., June 1945 (U.S. Army Air Corps)

Library of Congress Cataloguing-in-Publication Data

Logan, Edward F., Jr.
    "Jump, damn it, jump!" : memoir of a downed B-17 pilot in World
War II / Edward F. Logan, Jr.
        p.   cm.
    Includes bibliographical references and index.

    ISBN-13: 978-0-7864-2572-3
    ISBN-10: 0-7864-2572-5
    (softcover : 50# alkaline paper) ∞

    1. Logan, Edward F.   2. World War, 1939–1945—Aerial
operations, American.   3. World War, 1939–1945—Personal
narratives, American.   4. Aircraft accidents—United States.
5. United States. Army Air Forces—Bibography.   6. B-17 bomber.
7. Fighter pilots—United States—Biography.   I. Title
D790.2.L64   2006
940.54'4973092—dc22   2006022235

British Library cataloguing data are available

Cover illustration by Mark Durr; *inset* 1st Lt. Edward F. Logan, Jr.,
October 1944

Manufactured in the United States of America

McFarland & Company, Inc., Publishers
  Box 611, Jefferson, North Carolina 28640
  www.mcfarlandpub.com

To my father and mother;
my wife, Betty;
and my instructors in the
Eastern Flying training Command
of the U.S. Army Air Force

Acknowledgments

I would like to begin these acknowledgments with some words about the people to whom this book is dedicated.

The first of those people are the ones most responsible for my early years of growth, and for my personal achievements during service in the Army Air Corps throughout World War II and in my early adult life afterward. These are the people who guided and nurtured me and supported my every effort to succeed. They stood solidly behind me with unflagging encouragement during almost two years of arduous Aviation Cadet School training and the demanding Army Air Corps training that followed. These people are, of course, my wonderful father and mother.

Words of dedication and praise go also to my lovely wife, Betty, for her valued assistance in the completing of this book. It would never have been finished without her tireless efforts in typing and retyping the manuscript. I deeply appreciate her help.

Finally, my dedication mentions the ground and flight instructors in the Eastern Flying Training Command of the U.S. Army Air Force who energetically and fastidiously trained me for the difficult tasks I would face in aerial combat. I owe them a deep debt of gratitude. I feel that I actually owe my many successes in that great war, and even my eventual survival, to the marvelous training provided by these dedicated people.

Other acknowledgments must include many people, government services, and organizations who provided immeasurable assistance to me in writing this book. They offered direction, sources of historical data, and factual information relevant to my 34th mission and my travels and associations while on the ground in Slovenia in March of 1945. In addition, I am grateful to those who supplied me with some of the pertinent recorded history of the 15th Air Force, principally its 5th Wing and the 483rd Bomb Group (H), during its period of operations in the Mediterranean Theater during World War II.

In view of their contributions, I offer acknowledgment and thanks to:

The Embassy of the Republic of Slovenia
  (Washington, DC)
General Viktor Krajnc, M.Sc.,
  Chief of the Slovenia Armed Forces;
  The Republic of Slovenia, Ministry of Defense,
  Ljubljana, Slovenia
Mr. Matija Zganjar, Curator, Museum of Modern History,
  Ljubljana, Slovenia
Mr. David A. Giordano, National Archives,
  College Park, Maryland
Air Force Historical Research Agency,
  Maxwell Air Force Base, Alabama
Bolling Air Force Base,
  Historical Records,
  Washington, DC
Mr. Jacob L. Grimm, Archivist (deceased),
  483rd Bomb Group Association
Air Forces Escape and Evasion Society;
  BritishForces.Com
The Library of Congress,
  Washington, DC
National Archives,
  Washington, DC
Fifteenth Air Force Association,
  March Air Reserve Base, California
Mr. Michael Lombardi,
  Historical Archives,
  Boeing—Seattle, Washington
John W. Leland,
  Deputy Command Historian,
  Department of the Air Force,
  Air Mobility Command Headquarters,
  Scott AFB, Illinois
Ms. Sue Knopf

Table of Contents

Preface

I was blessed with a patriotic and aviation-oriented family. My father, Edward F. Logan, in his leisure time, was a private pilot who regularly flew his two airplanes—a Kinner "Bird" biplane and a Loening "Commuter" amphibian, and I flew with Dad often when I was a boy.

My sister Mari, seven years older than I, was also a pilot. She received her student pilot's license at sixteen and regularly flew Dad's biplane. By age eighteen, she was flying one of O.M. Goodsell's Ford Tri-Motor airplanes. Shortly after her eighteenth birthday, she soloed the Ford Tri-Motor with chief maintenance supervisor Gil Minnic as her copilot. She was a maintenance instructor specializing in Allison liquid cooled aircraft engines for Embry-Riddle Aviation Schools during World War II.

My sister Jane, three years older than I, was an enlisted WAAC (Women's Army Auxiliary Corps) in a tank battalion and served as a map specialist during World War II.

My brother Bob, three years younger than I, was a tail gunner on a B-24 during World War II, and my brother Glen, ten years younger than I, also became a pilot and was popularly known in south Florida as the "Flying Fisherman." In 1976, in his early forties, he disappeared while flying a light twin-engine airplane from Port au Prince, Haiti, to Lantana, Florida.

My sister Patricia, five years younger than I, worked for an army tent fabrication company during World War II, and was an avid hunter and sports racing boat competitor in South Florida.

I was attracted to the Army Air Corps because I wanted to serve my country by actively defending freedom. I wanted to be a part of the very important role that American air power would play in World War II.

1

This book outlines my progression as a determined would-be pilot from the outset of my Army Air Corps career through my training, my journey to the air war's theater and eventually to my thirty-fourth combat mission, where "Jump, damn it, jump" became a stark reality. It also highlights the success of the sustained application of air power by the United States Army air forces in the Mediterranean theater of operations during World War II, as conducted by the Fifteenth Air Force, originally from its bases in North Africa and later from bases in Southern Italy.

It is interesting to review the evolution of World War II. In the 1940s Hitler continued his far-encompassing conquests and occupation of much of Europe, portions of Africa, many of the countries bordering the Mediterranean Sea and the large islands within it, as well as several mid-eastern European countries. Further conquests by the German military had to be halted and the existing occupations reversed. This reversal could be accomplished only by chasing the German military from the nations they occupied.

To accomplish the liberation of these nations from Hitler's grasp, second and third fronts of Allied military pressure had to be added to the fierce ongoing war in Europe proper. The most significant of these newly required battle fronts were in the Mediterranean area.

To be able to eclipse the German military presence at their back door, so to speak, these fronts first had to force the Germans out of Africa and occupied countries bordering the Mediterranean Sea ... all the way to Italy and Southern France. German military forces would then have to be pursued northward through Sicily, Italy, Yugoslavia and other occupied countries of southeast Europe to meet the advanced Allied armies fighting Hitler's military in northern Europe itself. To accomplish this gigantic task, large armies and masses of air power would be required. The purpose of the air power was to destroy every part of the German military's manufacturing and petroleum complexes, as well as its far-reaching transportation systems.

It was at this point that the Fifteenth Air Force came into existence. It would employ four-engine heavy bombers, twin-engine medium bombers, and several types of single-engine fighters to overpower the Germans. The B-17s and B-24s of the Fifteenth Air Force Heavy Bomber Command were responsible for destroying the German military strategic targets no matter where they were located within the bombers' flight range capabilities. Usually they were within a seven-hundred-mile radius of its center of operations in the Foggia Valley in southern Italy.

I was assigned to the Fifth Wing of the Fifteenth Air Force—composed entirely of four-engine B-17 Flying Fortresses—in October 1944.

The Fifteenth's ability to take advantage of the United States' upgrades in high- altitude and weather-obscured bombing techniques enabled its heavy bomber forces to become consistently precise in their target destruction effectiveness. This effectiveness was apparent as the war progressed: Each time we bombed them, the Germans required considerably more time to rebuild and restore factories, refineries, railroads, marshalling yards, bridges, and roadways to even a fraction of their normal functional levels.

Because of the tremendous damage the Fifteenth Air Force Aircraft inflicted, the Germans gradually pulled their troops out of the countries they occupied because delivering supplies to them became extremely difficult, and in some cases impossible. We heavy bomber pilots and our crewmen who flew strikes for the Fifteenth Air Force were very proud to be a part of the success of American air power. This proud heritage continues today through the 15th Air Force Association and the Air Force Association with their thousands of dedicated members who have continued to serve America since World War II.

On several occasions since the war I have been asked to write the story of my thirty-fourth mission. Doing so was impossible immediately after the war ended because sufficient unclassified material was not available; nor was I able to use the few notes I had written about the experience during and soon after it had transpired. A busy flying career further postponed writing the story for thirty-eight years (although I continually made additional notes and outlined recollections of people, places, events and chronology). Finally, in retirement, I now have the time and resources to tell this fascinating tale.

· · · ·

Introduction

During the World War II years of 1944 and 1945, my crew and I were assigned to the European Theater of Operations. We were based in the Foggia Valley of Southern Italy with the Fifteenth Air Force, Fifth Wing, 483rd Bomb Group (H), 817th Bomb Squadron. We were transferred to the Fifteenth Air Force from the Eighth Air Force Combat Crew Replacement Pool in England during the last week of September, 1944, via Africa. We arrived at the 483rd Bomb Group (H) on October 4, 1944. The very large tract of land which had been selected for the 483rd Bomb Group's air base was at Sterparone, which prior to the war years had been a tremendous wheat farming complex in the vast expanse of the Foggia Valley.

All of us who fought in World War II by flying airplanes can attribute our day-to-day progress, and perhaps even our eventual survival in the war, to our marvelous training and to our mental and physical health conditioning. At Sterparone my crew and I become a seasoned, well-tuned and extremely efficient combat bomber crew. We developed a tremendous cohesiveness and we always functioned as a team.

We were thoroughly familiar with all of the inner systems of our B-17, and each crew member was highly efficient at his duties. Perhaps this is one of the reasons we were given the nickname "the Wonder Crew" by the people in our squadron and group. Another is that we always came back from our bombing missions, even when damage to the bomber made return difficult. We always returned—that is, with the exception of our 34th mission, from which we could not return to our base with our airplane. This is the mission on which my story is based.

The damage caused by German fighter aircraft and anti-aircraft fire included hundreds of holes (some very large) in the airplane, engines shot out, systems destroyed, and a ball turret severely damaged, with the gunner trapped inside. We returned nine times with one of our four engines inoperative and three times with two engines inoperative. One of the two-engine returns was with two engines shot out on the same side of the airplane! Flying an airplane in that condition is a real feat.

All of our crew members shared the same simple desire—to destroy the Nazi war machine and return home when our tour of duty was completed. The normal tour of duty with the 15th Air Force was thirty-five combat missions. The crew approached each of these missions tremendously motivated, with high spirits and a great sense of confidence and ability.

1

The Training Story

The summary of my Army Air Corps pilot training is presented here to bring into view the almost two years of extensive curriculum which an aspiring Air Corps pilot was required to assimilate prior to graduating as a Commissioned Second Lieutenant and receive his "Silver Wings." In my case, I was assigned to the Eastern Flying Training Command for this long period of training, and it began with indoctrination training at the U.S. Army Air Corps basic training center at Miami Beach, Florida, on October 7, 1942.

The next phase of my training was a six month period at the Army Air Corps 63rd College Training Detachment at the University of Tennessee, Knoxville, Tennessee. The curriculum was intensive, both academically and physically, from December, 1942, through June, 1943. During this period at the University of Tennessee, we also completed the "Army Controlled Indoctrination Flight Course," conducted under the auspices of the C.A.A. War Training Service. This course consisted of a multi-subject aeronautical ground school and flight instruction in a Piper J-5 Cub airplane.

Crew Classification

From the College Training Detachment at Knoxville we were shipped to the U.S. Army Air Corps Classification Center at Nashville, Tennessee, during June of 1943, where we were processed through the U.S. Army Air Corps combat flight crew classification program. This classification program tested the individual cadet's mental, psychological and physical make-up and prowess. At the completion of this program, we were categorized for a

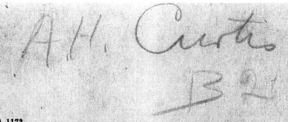

A.H. Curtis B-2

Form ACA 1173

U. S. DEPARTMENT OF COMMERCE
CIVIL AERONAUTICS ADMINISTRATION
WASHINGTON, D. C.

CONTROLLED INDOCTRINATION FLIGHT COURSE

PILOT RATING BOOK

Logan, Edward F. Jr.
(Name of trainee)

3848 Wood Avenue, Coconut Grove, Fla.
(Address)

14134949   *October 7, 1942*
(Enlistment No.)   (Certificate No.)

14134949   *OCTOBER 7, 1942*
(Class)

Woods Flying Service
(Flight operator)

Alcoa, Tenn.
(Address)

cockpit crew position and the type of airplane we would fly, with consideration given to the individual's choice of airplane he had requested to fly. In some cases, the cadet would be classified for navigational or bombardiers training, a classification which was often times requested by the cadet himself.

Aviation Cadet Pre-Flight School

Our next training assignment was at the U.S. Army Air Corps Cadet Pre-Flight School at Maxwell Field, Montgomery, Alabama. This two-month period in July and August was a rugged time for all of us upward-looking aviators. Preflight school consisted of rigorous aviation related courses, such as theory of flight, navigation, radio and Morse code, weather, map reading, aircraft engines, etc.

The physical conditioning training program was also intensive and exhaustive. We had bi-weekly ten mile jogs, seven mile "rough terrain" obstacle course timed runs, one mile high-density obstacle course workouts, calisthenics of every variety, and constant physical testing in these types of endurance exercises. We marched in formation and jogged in formation, and sang all the way. We learned to enjoy this.

On Sunday, the entire Aviation Cadet Corps—which consisted of literally thousands upon thousands of cadets in full dress uniform, all wearing white gloves—would parade in formation before the reviewing stand (the Commanding Officers and dignitaries) for an extended period of time. At the initial part of this "Sunday exercise" the cadets would all be standing at attention, or "parade rest," in Group and Squadron formations. Then, when the appointed time came, they would march from their positions across the field and past the reviewing stand. There were so many Cadets in the formations that it took an hour or so to march them through the parade grounds to the dispersing area. This business of standing at "attention" or "parade rest," while all the many formations ahead of your group paraded in review, was a demanding and disliked procedure. Actually, the entire Sunday Review was a very difficult military spectacle. However, after we were dismissed and back in our barracks, we were happy it was over, but proud to have been a part of the event.

Opposite: **Army controlled indoctrination flight course, CAA War Training Service, flight instruction and ground school—1942. Aircraft: Piper J-5 Cub—University of Tennessee College Training Detachment.**

In spite of the rigors of this training, enjoyable and leisurely times were also to be had. On Friday and Saturday evening there would be a party—dinner and dancing at the Cadet Club—with wonderful music provided by Glen Miller and his band. To this day, I remember those times well, while the irritating things that happened there because of being an underclassman, the heavy accent

Cadet Edward F. Logan, Jr.—primary training, Union City, Tennessee, 1943.

PT-23 Primary trainer—Union City, Tennessee, 1943.

Cadet Edward F. Logan, Jr., climbing into an Embry Riddle PT-23 primary trainer—Union City, Tennessee, 1943.

Autographed picture of original eight pilots (seven of whom went through aviation cadet flight schools and later graduated together as second lieutenants at Moody Field). Left to right, back row: Don W. May; Edward Logan; John C. Haynie; Alvin J. Gold; Marshall C. Dunn; Dick Jones. Left to right, front row: Bob Keno; Alvin W. Goodman, Primary training—1943.

on military discipline, the strict barracks inspections, the gigs, and the marching tours in full dress uniform carrying a heavy army rifle became distant memories of the hazy past.

Aviation Cadet Primary Flying School: Into the Wild Blue Yonder

Our next training assignment was the beginning of our actual "flight training" as aviation cadets—"Primary Flying School." This school was the Embry-Riddle primary flight school at Union City, Tennessee, where we learned to fly the Fairchild PT-23. The PT-23 was a marvelous airplane, and after a few flights we felt at home in it. It was a fun airplane to fly. This flight school gave us our first taste of acrobatics, formation flying and making an airplane do what we wanted it to do (such as short field landings, appropriately named "hurdle stages").

At Primary, during the months of September and October of 1943, our days were filled with a constant routine ... awake on weekdays at an early hour, then breakfast, attend ground school classes and flight training, and end the day with exercise classes. At night, particularly weeknights, we regularly "burned the midnight oil" studying diligently. Graduating from "Primary Flight School" was a happy day, but little did we realize that even more rigorous and difficult training lay ahead for us.

Aviation Cadet Basic Flight School

The next phase of training was "Basic" flight training. We would be transferred from Union City to Cochran Field, Macon, Georgia, for two months of this flight school.

During the months of November and December, we proceeded

AVIATION CADET BASIC FLYING SCHOOL - COCHRAN FIELD , MACON, GEORGIA -1943

Basic flying school cadets marching in review on Cochran Field—Macon, Georgia, 1943.

Top and bottom: BT-13 and BT-15 basic trainers lined up on Cochran Field—Macon, Georgia, 1943.

through the programs of an Aviation Cadet's next step of his flight and ground school curriculum. Again, our daily lives would be completely consumed by all these "basic school" activities. We found it to be the continuation of all the subjects, both ground school and flight training, which we had previously been subjected to in our "Pre-Flight" and "Primary" schools. In addition, all aspects of our physical conditioning would become more strenuous—running, jogging and marching in formation over long distances, singing as we went.

The airplanes which we would be taught to fly were the Vaultee BT-13 and BT-15. They were nicknamed the "Vaultee Vibrators" because from take-off to landing they were constantly vibrating. Reflecting back on these airplanes, I remember so well how large I thought the plane was the first time I walked up to it on the "flight line." Initially, I approached this flying machine with a slight sense of awe.

I remember my first night flying session in the BT as being one filled

Cadet Edward Logan (left) and Cadet John C. Haynie (right) in a BT-15 basic trainer at Cochran Field, Macon, Georgia, 1943.

with consternation. The feeling was of great apprehension and even a little terror. I remember vividly that when I looked out of the right side of the cockpit and observed that very large "ball" of red-blue flame exiting the large exhaust stack, it took me several minutes to adjust to the sight. At first glance (never having seen this exhaust flame before at night), I thought the airplane was on fire and I would have to jump from it and make use of the parachute that I had sat on so often. After a few moments, the realization hit me that the ball of flame was just the normal exhaust from its big engine—what a relief that was! If it had *not* been there, I really would have had to use my parachute.

Flying the Basic Trainers—("BT's")—gave me my first clear realization that "acrobatics"—and being anything else other than a bomber pilot—was not my forte. I really enjoyed "flying right side up" and liked the thought of the hum of more than one engine and the "safety in numbers."

However, in spite of my original assessment of the Vaultee BT's at Cochran Field, the airplane and I gradually became friends and I learned to enjoy flying it. I had become friends with that machine! But when we graduated from Basic Training at Cochran Field, we were very content to leave the BT's there.

Aviation Cadet Twin Engine Advanced Flying School

The next and final phase of the Aviation Cadet Flight School program was "Twin Engine Advanced." I, along with the others who were eager to fly bombers, had been looking forward to this portion of our flight training ever since we were at the classification center at Nashville, Tennessee.

For this training, we were stationed at Moody Field in Valdosta, Georgia, and we flew Curtiss AT-9's and Fairchild AT-10's. The ground school courses at Moody Field were continuations of the aviation- and military-oriented subjects we had been studying since our pre–Flight School days at Maxwell Field.

During January, February, and the first twelve days of March, 1944, all facets of our training were accelerated and became more complex. If we successfully completed twin engine flying school, we'd graduate from the Aviation Cadet School Program as commissioned second lieutenants in the U.S. Army Air Corps. The time I spent at Moody Field was the most interesting and rewarding of all the schools I attended, and it was also the most fun.

The Curtiss AT-9 was a very demanding airplane and not a star performer on one engine; however, on two engines it was a real speedster, and fun and exciting to fly. The Fairchild AT-10 was a delight to fly under

A twin engine advanced AT-10 trainer—Moody Field, Valdosta, Georgia, 1944.

These six cadets went through flight schools and graduated together as 2nd Lieutenants at Moody Field, Valdosta, Georgia, March 12, 1944. Standing, left to right: Dick Jones, John Haynie, Edward Logan, Marshall Dunn. Kneeling, left to right: Al Hunt, Al Goodman.

any conditions. It was a wonderful formation and acrobatic airplane. I was not at all happy to have to leave it behind. I not only became very friendly with the airplane, but also felt that it guided me to a higher level of pilot maturity.

At about the midpoint of each flight-training phase, we pilots were asked to choose which airplane we wished to fly upon completion of Aviation Cadet Flying School. I always selected the Boeing B-17—the "Flying Fortress"—and shortly before graduating from Twin Engine Advanced at Moody Field, I was informed by the commanding officer that my request would be granted. I had been assigned to the B-17 Transition School at Sebring, Florida.

After a much-needed leave of absence at home with my family in Coconut Grove, Florida, for a few weeks, I reported to Sebring Field the first of April, 1944, for my transition training in the B-17.

B-17 Transition School

During April, May, and a few days of June, I participated in the most difficult phase of my flight training thus far. The B-17, I soon learned, was a very large and very complex airplane, but it was also beautiful and graceful, and the sound of its four powerful 1200-horsepower Wright-Cyclone engines was music to my ears—it always filled me with excitement and pride. This classic four-engine bomber was all I expected it to be, and then some.

Training in the B-17 as a "pilot in command" meant learning and being proficient at every facet of the bomber's operation. The pilot in command—who was also the leader of the ten-man crew—had to be able to function capably in each of his crew members' positions on board, so his transitional training encompassed all of these functions, along with his pilot training. We soon found that learning the airplane in general, and learning to fly it, were only a part of what was expected of us.

Our ground school courses included new subjects as well as continuations of subjects we had studied previously. We were soon burning more midnight oil than we ever had before. The courses covered all of the B-17's systems in detail. An incorrect interrelation of these systems or components could seriously affect the operation of other systems and the airplane's ability to remain airborne.

As much redundancy as could be accommodated was designed into each system to make some in-flight combat fixes available to us. Learning where and how to apply these fixes would be the key to keeping our B-17 in flight and performing well during the trying days we would experience in combat.

Four systems of the B-17 were operated electrically: landing gear and tail wheel; wing flaps; bomb bay doors; and bomb release mechanism. Each of these systems could be operated manually if the electrical system was damaged. The landing gear, tail wheel, and wing flaps could be extended and retracted by means of a hand crank if these units had not themselves been damaged.

Brakes and Engine Cowl Flaps

Hydraulic pressure for the operation of brakes and engine cowl flaps was provided by an electric motor–driven pump or by an accumulator when the pump was not in operation. If the automatic pressure switch failed, system pressure could be maintained by holding the pressure switch in the "manual" position. A relief valve opened if the pressure in the system reached 900 pounds. If the system was damaged and leaks occurred, we could stop the pump (and prevent further leakage) by removing the pump fuse or disconnecting the electrical receptacle at the pressure switch. If the electric pump was damaged, a hand pump on the copilot's side wall could be used to recharge the accumulators so that the hydraulic system could be used.

Engine Turbo Superchargers

The engine superchargers were controlled by automatic hydraulic regulators that could be adjusted by a control located on the pilot's pedestal. If the electronic control system was damaged, any one of the turbo-supercharger waste gates could be closed by shorting out its circuit in the electronic circuit box.

Emergency Brake Operation

The emergency brake system operated the wheel brakes only. Pressure was applied through two hand-operated metering valves on the pilot's compartment ceiling, one for the left wheel brake and one for the right. Pressure of 650 to 800 pounds was supplied from an emergency brake accumulator. (This system was removed from later B-17s.)

Emergency Radio Unit Substitutions

The radio compass receiver could be used to power the low-frequency command radio receiver, and the liaison radio receiver could replace a damaged low-frequency command radio.

Emergency Fuel Transfer System

A hand-operated transfer pump mounted on the aft bulkhead of the bomb bay could be used to transfer fuel if the electrical transfer pump or the entire electrical system was damaged.

Flight Control Emergency Operation

Should any of the flight controls be shot away, the autopilot could be engaged to supplement or replace the flight control functions, since the autopilot tie-in control was closer to the flight controls than the control cables were.

Emergency Bomb Release and Fuel Tanks

Two emergency bomb-release handles were available in case the electrical bomb-release system was damaged.

The airplane's fuel tanks (made of thick, self-sealing rubber) were actually a bladder fuel cell, which is not the usual metal fuel tank design, meaning that if a fuel tank sustained small penetrations of shrapnel or machine gun projectiles, it was designed to self-seal those small holes to prevent fuel leaks. We studied this fuel system thoroughly and applied our knowledge during flight training by constantly operating all units of the fuel system. We learned the radio system and its uses backward and forward. We studied every emergency procedure for all the systems within the B-17—as well as the emergency procedures for the engines—until they were an integral part of our memory and could be executed smoothly, thoroughly, and automatically.

As our training progressed—both on the ground and in flight—we spent hours in the cockpit of the B-17, learning exactly where every switch, button, lever, light, gauge, and handle was located. We practiced touching, moving, and operating each of the controls and switches with our eyes closed until we knew every one by location and feel. Before soloing, we would be required to pass—with a score of 100 percent—a blindfold cockpit check.

Much of our free time, in the evening and on Saturdays, was spent continuing to learn every detail of the B-17. Some of us got together in one of the barracks rooms and practiced "flying" while sitting in two chairs placed close together (the cockpit). We simulated a mission in every respect: the preflight walk-around, the cockpit preflight, starting the engines, the taxi, and take-off. We used our cockpit checklists to check off each phase. We "flew" the "mission" and returned with our crew to the flight line from our two chairs. We performed this evening practice again and again, until it became routine. We were determined not to have any flaws in our knowledge of this airplane, and when it was our turn to solo, we were ready.

Flying our four-engine aircraft on four engines was not something we did very often during training. More often we flew on three or even two engines, and when we did, we discovered that our physical training—which we once considered strenuous but now found enjoyable—paid off. The leg strength required to operate the rudder pedal, and the arm and back strength required to operate the yoke and aileron, was tremendous when one or more engines weren't operational—and this was especially so when two engines on one side were out.

After we had flown the airplane completely under physical control for a while in any of these engine-inoperative modes, the flight instructor allowed us to "trim out" the airplane with rudder, aileron, and elevator trim tabs. After that the plane flew smoothly, even with engines inoperative, with no physical manhandling.

We were taught to fly the B-17 in a loose formation on three engines, and this soon proved to be no great feat. Our B-17s were designed to fly well under most types of adverse conditions.

Flying in formation at night by using the triangulation of blue lights embedded in the upper wing area of the airplane on whose wing you were flying at first seemed very tricky and tedious, and we didn't think it would work. However, with intensive concentration, diligence, relaxation, and, of course, practice, it became routine. When a pilot can see the correct number of blue lights, he is in proper formation with the airplane on whose wing he is flying; if he can see less than a triangle of lights, he is out of proper formation.

When our group of twenty-one-year-old young men finished our course, we were qualified as B-17 pilots in command. We had all matured as well; we had really grown up at Sebring.

The "wash-out" rate in B-17 transition training was more prevalent than at other Air Corps flight schools—about one in twenty.

Combat Crew Placement Pool

Our next assignment was at the Combat Crew Placement Pool Center at Plant Park in Tampa, Florida, where B-17 crews were formed. This was where the ten members of my B-17 combat crew—and countless others—would first come together.

Four officers—the pilot, copilot, bombardier, and navigator—and six enlisted crewmen—the engineer (top turret gunner), radio operator gunner, ball turret gunner, tail gunner, right waist armorer gunner, and left waist gunner—made up the crew. The officers were usually second lieutenants and the enlisted men were usually sergeants. The crews were chosen by a board that tried to choose crews they thought would be compatible and make a well-functioning combat team under the leadership of their pilot in command.

One afternoon, while I was still waiting for a crew to be assigned to me, I met an old and good friend by chance at the snack bar—Bob Keno. Together, Bob and I had gone through Initial Indoctrination Basic Training, Classification Center, and Cadet Preflight School at Maxwell Field, and about half of Primary Flight School at Union City.

At Union City, Bob, who had started training to be a PT-23 pilot, had switched and gone into bombardier training, and this turned out to be lucky for me. During our months of training we were frequently assigned to activities alphabetically, so Bob and I (K and L) had gotten to know each other and had become close friends. For our paths to cross again at the crew pool was nothing short of a miracle. I felt as if I had found a long lost brother.

After a long conversation, I asked Bob if he would consent to be assigned to my crew as our bombardier, and he said, "Certainly." We immediately went to see the crew pool's commanding officer. I informed him of Bob's and my history together and requested that Bob be assigned to my crew as bombardier. He was as enthusiastic about this idea as Bob and I, and said he would arrange the assignment that day. I felt certain that my crew now had one of the very best bombardiers in the Army Air Corps, and that feeling later proved to be fact as our tour of duty unfolded over the next year.

Within four days, my combat crew was complete except for the navigator's position. I was informed that he would join us in a few days at our Combat Crew Training Unit at Avon Park, Florida.

Combat Crew Training Unit

We were shipped to Avon Park, along with forty-eight other B-17 crews, for three months (June, July, and August of 1944) of combat training, and our navigator joined us a day or so after our arrival. The training at Avon Park entailed extensive simulated combat training—both on the ground and in flight—in a six-day-per-week program. Our days usually started between four and six o'clock in the morning, and the curriculum included the usual physical conditioning—calisthenics of all kinds, running for miles, obstacle courses, swimming—and weapons qualification (Colt 45 Automatic and M-1 Carbine).

The pilots in command received additional training to ensure their thorough knowledge and performance of each of the other nine crew positions. Exhaustive demonstrations of this prowess were required again and again, both on the ground and in flight.

We practiced making takeoffs one minute apart, joining up (forming in three-, six-, and seven-plane squadrons and groups [a group consists of four squadrons of heavy bombers], climbing to bombing altitude, moving to a target I.P. (initial point for a bombing run on a specified target), and finally dropping a simulated bomb on the target.

We practiced the elegant group formation breakup procedure we'd use upon our return to base after a mission. It was an enjoyable maneuver, and from the ground it looked like a ballet performance.

We practiced single-plane bombing missions during both day and night. At night we "bombed" the lighted practice range just north-northeast of Avon Park, adjacent to Lake Arbuckle and the city of Frostproof. Occasionally bombardiers mistook the streetlights of Frostproof for the ninety-degree cross of lights at the bombing range and dropped practice bombs squarely in the center of the downtown area. Although these mistakes were humorous to many people, the mayor of Frostproof took a very dim view of them, and guilty parties were reprimanded by the commanding officer. Even though we were training for war, we were not at war with the city of Frostproof, Florida.

Our gunners practiced with live ammunition on "tow targets" pulled by C-47's and other aircraft over the Gulf of Mexico while we flew single-plane operations. Our training also included flying low over a machine gun firing range set up out in the Everglades so our gunners could practice firing their fifty-caliber machine guns. This was very tricky flying, but fun.

My copilot and I were regularly required to practice operating the Norden bombsight trainer and the Link instrument trainer. We also participated in navigation classes several times a week.

The Norden bombsight bore the name of the man who invented and developed it. It automatically calculated the drop time of the bombs based on information provided by the bombardier as the target was approached. Once all the parameters—altitude, speed, course, and geometric calculations from the bombing charts—were programmed in, the bombsight took over and automatically dropped the bombs at the proper release time.

The Link trainer also bears the name of its inventor. Mr. Link developed this instrument trainer to teach a pilot how to "fly blind"—to fly solely by the use of cockpit instruments without reference to the natural horizon or other typical visual references. The Link trainer was a small, box-like, low-wing "airplane," complete with wings and tail. It had a side-opening door over the wing and box-like cover over the cockpit. The cover tilted to the right, opposite the door. When the pilot closed the cover, he found himself in a dimly lighted enclosure.

Air billows were a type of support action system that kept the trainer balanced as the pilot went through his instrument flight procedures, practicing pitch and up-and-down motions, banks, left and right turns, and left and right 360-degrees turns. The instructor communicated with the pilot via radio and monitored the trainer's automatic transcribing unit, which duplicated the pilot's exact flight patterns, both horizontal and vertical, on a printed paper "instrument exercise" that the pilot was required to fly. (I logged 357 hours on the Link trainer.) It became obsolete with the advent of the use of multi-engine aircraft and the need to test transport pilots every six months on their proficiency in dealing with the many problems they faced flying two- and four-engine airplanes, such as engine failures, fires, systems failures, etc. These drills were routinely accomplished in the airplane itself until the introduction of the "flight simulator."

Completing CTU gave us great satisfaction. We had been exposed to every "big war" combat problem or situation the instructors could imagine, and we had survived and assimilated it all. I finished training knowing that my ultimate survival during combat would depend in part on my gallant B-17 itself and in part on my profound knowledge of the plane and my proficiency in flying it and caring for it. Actual combat reinforced this knowledge: I found that the B-17 had an astonishing ability to sustain horrendous damage from enemy antiaircraft fire and still be flyable, a fact that reinforced my respect and admiration for this tremendous machine.

As commissioned officers, we were treated with respect and consideration by all of our instructors, both military and civilian. We were led, not driven, through our lessons, even though there were situations where time and expediency were drilled into us. We were frequently given words of encouragement and complimented on our diligence and progress. After all, we were very young men being trained to fight in a very serious situation—the air war over Europe.

Even with our tight schedules and tough physical workouts, we also had many happy, relaxed, and enjoyable times, including our meals. Our food, except at the Indoctrination Training facilities at Miami Beach, was wonderful. Our aviation cadet mess halls were pleasant and quiet, and the food was delicious and plentiful.

In B-17 Transition and O.T.U., the officers' mess halls were in operation twenty-four hours a day, as the pilots, bombardiers, and navigators flew day and night and often ate at odd hours. After long days and nights, we were usually starved, and an abundance of all types of food was always ready for us. Mealtime was, without exception, a joy. (The "combat food" in Italy at our bomb group was another story!)

In our last week or so of CTU training, I was informed by our Operation Officer that upon completion of training, our class of ten crews—which had been at this school for almost three months—would be transferred to the Third Air Force Combat Crew Staging Center at Hunter Field, just south of Savannah, Georgia, for further assignment.

Most of the pilots of these ten combat crews had been in training together since entering the Eastern Flying Training Commands Aviation Cadet Pilot Pre-Flight School at Maxwell Field, Montgomery, Alabama,

A B-17 Flying Fortress of the 840th Bomb Squadron (yellow crowlings and red rudders) shown as part of the 483rd Bomb Group (H) en route to strike a German oil refinery. (Picture courtesy of Boeing.)

over a year before. We had become close friends during those months of arduous training, and we valued these friendships highly.

With training behind us, we were prepared to embark on a new stage—the military flying careers we had envisioned when we enlisted in the Army Air Corps. Our "vision" was to fly a beautiful Boeing B-17 to England or Italy and add our individual efforts to bomb Hitler and his Nazi war machine to ruin. In accomplishing this, we would be destroying his oil refineries, aircraft manufacturing factories, shipyards, submarine pens, ball bearing plants, railroad marshalling yards, rail storage depots, pilot training centers, airfields and aircraft, and other facilities he possessed that manufactured war materials. Of course, we hoped to be fortunate enough to be assigned to the same bomb group and squadron so we could accomplish our strategic bombing campaign as a unit.

With the completion of CTU at Avon Park, our ten combat crews boarded a troop train in the early morning of Tuesday, August 29, and moved on to Hunter Field.

2

Our "Ferry Flight" to England and Its Preparation

I was told that at Hunter Field CCSC each crew would be assigned a B-17 and necessary flight gear in preparation for a "ferry flight" of ten airplanes to England. There we would all be assigned to the Eighth Air Force Combat Crew Replacement Pool at the Seventieth Replacement Depot.

The day after we arrived at Hunter Field, August 31, I was assigned a new B-17G with the tail number 4412436—a beautiful, shining silver craft that had recently been flown to Hunter Field from the factory where it had been produced. It was earmarked for the Eighth Air Force in England. Each of the other nine combat crew pilots was also assigned a new B-17G. We were like children with brand new toys—and this was not far from the truth.

The Base Operations Officer scheduled all ten crews to flight-check their B-17s that afternoon at 1400. At 0900, we drew our parachutes in preparation for their use on test flights and during our ferry flight to England. At 1000, the Base Operations Officer brought us up to date on exactly what would be required of us during our days at Hunter Field. Our final briefing, which would address what we'd encounter during the next five or six days, was scheduled for 1900 Thursday evening.

We were transported to the flight line at 1300, where we pre-flighted the planes and prepared for departure. Each crew had its engines running ten minutes prior to receiving orders from the control tower to commence taxi for take-off. Each plane taxied from its position in order of crew number assignment. (I was number 5.) We were cleared for takeoff at three-minute intervals, and by 1430, all ten of us were airborne and proceeding to our assigned flight test areas at our assigned altitudes.

This flight check of our new bombers entailed calibrating the three airspeed indicators as well checking the operation of the altimeters, radios, and navigational equipment, and checking the engine fuel flows and fuel consumption at various power settings and flight realms. We also checked the over-water emergency flotation equipment—such as the two ten-man life rafts and their self-contained survival stores and equipment. The two life rafts were stored in individual compartments, one on each side of the upper fuselage fairing, immediately above the bomb bay. The life rafts could be released by opening the storage compartments from either inside or outside the airplane.

Our B-17s carried two extra fuel tanks in their bomb bay compartments, which, when combined with the fuel in the airplane's wing tanks, would provide a greatly extended range should we require it. In addition, there was ample space in the bomb bay for all of our personal gear as well as spare aircraft parts.

We thoroughly flight-checked our planes for almost three hours, just as we had thoroughly ground-checked them before takeoff. All of this checking and re-checking was a necessity, as our four- or five-day ferry flight, while a test of us as crew members, was a test of our new airplanes as well.

Some of the flight legs would be long and arduous, and there was no allowance for errors. This was particularly true for the segments from Goose Bay, Labrador, across the ice cap of Greenland to Keflavik, Iceland, and from Keflavik across the North Atlantic Ocean to Valley, Wales (England).

After our flight check, orders were cut and the typical military air corps paperwork was completed. We were eager to tackle the flight to England.

Friday, September 1, was another important and busy day. The ten combat crews were scheduled to undergo final processing at 0745. The "showdown" for these crews would follow later, starting with the first three at 1100. The next three would report at 1300, and the final crews at 1400.

Showdown

Definition: A meeting of all those involved in ferry exercise to ascertain that all of their necessary paperwork (including medical requirements), clothing and equipment (both personal and issued) have been completed and are in order.

The first three crews were headed by Captain Walter L. Glass, Jr. (who became the officer in charge of our ten crews), Lieutenant William A. Haskins, and Lieutenant Gupton. The next three crews were lead by Lieutenant Galiano, Lieutenant Edward F. Logan, Jr., and Lieutenant Devereaux W. Bush. The remaining four crews were headed by Lieutenant Carmen, Lieutenant DeFrancesco, Lieutenant Henry C. Dent, and Lieutenant Marshall Clyde Dunn.

For the one hundred young men of these ten bomber crews, this was the conclusion of personal and military affairs in the United States. We were processed and prepared to depart our country, proceed to the war zone, and engage the enemy in the great air war.

The First Flight Leg

In the very early morning hours of Saturday, September 2, all one hundred of us were up and dressing for the long day that lay ahead. We packed our gear, had a good breakfast, visited Base Weather to check the conditions en route and at the destination air base, and cleared Base Operations. Then we were trucked to our ramps to load our gear onto our planes.

To start the preflight process, each crew's pilot made a walk-around check of his B-17 and then completed the cockpit "before start" and "start" checklists down to the "start engines" section. Then each copilot advised the controller—on ground control frequency—that his crew was standing by to start engines.

Upon notification from the control tower, each crew started its engines and had them idling within three or four minutes. Soon, all forty Curtiss-Wright R-1820–97 engines filled the early morning air with a soft and harmonious droning—a sound that only a B-17 can produce. The sight of these ten beautiful, sparkling new B-17s, parked side-by-side with engines idling—just as the morning was showing its first light—was as lovely and exciting as the day that was approaching.

Within a few minutes, ground control advised us to start our taxi to the approach end of the takeoff runway and hold short at a point where we'd make our engine run-up checks. We taxied in order of crew assignment number (which was the way the airplanes were parked on the ramp), so my plane followed the fourth B-17 when it taxied out of its parking spot. When cleared, I pulled out of our spot, filed in behind him on the taxiway, and taxied to the run-up pad, where we parked at an angle to the runway to complete our run-up.

The "run-up check" immediately prior to takeoff is designed to make certain that the airplane's engines and their related accessory systems are operating correctly. The engine/exercise ground test is initially conducted at 1900 to 2000 RPM to check the engine ignition system—both magnetos and both spark plugs (one plug on each side of the cylinder) are checked with the carburetor mixture controls set at the auto-rich position and the engine propeller controls set at a high RPM. A maximum RPM drop of 100 RPM is allowed for either ignition. The run-up check is also performed to exercise the propellers and check their proper function. In addition, the fuel pressure, oil pressure, oil temperature, and cylinder head temperatures are checked to make sure they're within their prescribed limits. The turbo-supercharger regulator control stop is preset at 46 inches HG manifold pressure at fuel throttle and 2500 RPM. The maximum time limit for their supercharger control check setting is one-half minute. A pre-takeoff review is made of all flight-control trim tabs, and the flight controls are exercised to ensure their full travel.

We were advised by ground control to check in when we had completed our run-up checks and were ready for takeoff. When all ten of us were ready, we were cleared to switch to the tower frequency, and once on tower frequency, we were cleared for take-off at one-minute intervals. (Normally, there are two radio frequencies used for an airport control tower because they serve two different functions—the ground control handles all aircraft movements on the ground [prior to take-off and after landing], while the tower frequency is for aircraft taking off and those landing, and airport "approach control" frequency is for approaches [instrument] to the airport.)

The plan was that each of us would climb to nine thousand feet and fly in trail formation, which would put each B-17 a little more than three miles behind the one immediately ahead of it. Each of us used the same engine power settings, which produced identical airspeeds to ensure that we stayed in formation. Within ten minutes, we were all airborne and climbing to nine thousand feet.

We were on our way—for the first time since we started our initial training program on October 7, 1942, almost two years earlier. I felt complete peace, joy, and fulfillment at successfully completing my training, reaching my goal (receiving flying credentials for this very large bomber), and being up in the air with my crew and my flying buddies.

The first leg of our trip to England—from Hunter Field to Manchester, New Hampshire—took six hours. Except for strong headwinds, this flight was uneventful—a wonderful way to experience our first pilot-in-command non-training flight.

The Second Flight Leg

The next leg of our flight, from Manchester to Goose Bay, Labrador, was scheduled to be flown the next day, Sunday, September 3, 1944. However, due to the forecast of inclement weather en route and also at our destination air base, we spent an extra day at Manchester and departed on Monday morning, September 4.

Monday saw us out of bed well before 0400, dressed and having breakfast at 0430 and reporting for the crew operations briefing at 0500. The main topic of the briefing was a change in the usual three-minute-interval takeoff procedure. Because adverse weather was forecast for this leg of our trip both en route and at Goose Bay, we would take off at five-minute intervals, placing us a little more than eleven miles apart, and we'd fly at staggered altitudes. This would provide adequate separation between planes both horizontally and vertically, and would also facilitate landing at Goose Bay, where there would be enough separation between planes to complete their initial instrument approach procedure. Just before 0600, shortly after our operational briefing, we took off for Goose Bay. We knew we were in for a long flight because of the poor weather conditions, and we encountered the predicted strong headwinds.

As forecast, the weather at Goose Bay on our arrival was atrocious—the worst flying weather that any of us had experienced. Our landing was delayed somewhat due to the low ceiling and low visibility at the air base. We spent time in holding patterns before being cleared for our instrument approaches. It was a long day.

In my thirty-eight-year civilian flying career after World War II, I flew into and out of Goose Bay many times and learned that poor flying weather was almost always to be expected there during fall and winter. The winters especially could be fierce.

The Third Flight Leg

The next morning, Tuesday, September 5, again witnessed one hundred eager young men up well before dawn—about 0300—going through our regular morning routine. This third leg—from Goose Bay to Keflavik, Iceland—would mean another long flight and another taxing day.

Our route took us from Goose Bay, out across the northern coast of Labrador, across the Labrador Sea, and across the south coast of Greenland in the vicinity of BW-1. We'd cross the southern portion of Greenland's ice cap as we followed a great circle route to Iceland, where we'd land at the military air base at Keflavik on the country's southeastern tip. We were scheduled to spend the night there and depart on the final leg of our flight the next morning.

The highest point on the Greenland ice cap, which was adjacent to our route of flight, was at 11,000 feet, and our flight plan showed an ice cap crossing altitude of 17,000 feet, which would provide us with ample clearance.

We started our takeoffs at 0600, departing at three-minute intervals. At 0630, the tenth plane was airborne and climbing to seventeen thousand feet behind his friends ahead. The weather was forecast to be good, with light winds. Crossing the ice cap was an experience I will long remember—it was a beautiful sight.

We began arriving at Keflavik in the late afternoon. By 1730, we had all landed and parked on the ramp as night rapidly approached. We were billeted in comfortable quarters and found our dinner most enjoyable. We needed a good meal, and we ate all we could hold.

After dinner, we returned to our quarters, where many of us stood outside, braving the very cold weather and wind, to watch the aurora borealis streak across the northern sky. We fell asleep early—we were tired and knew that Wednesday we'd have another early wake-up call and another full day.

The Fourth and Final Leg

As on the previous days, we were up and dressed, packed, and being taken to breakfast by 0400. We pilots and navigators checked the weather and winds aloft en route from Keflavik to our destination—Valley, Wales. The weather would be nearly perfect, with tail winds, so we expected a very pleasant flight.

During our briefing, we learned about some interesting aspects of today's flight and also about some potential hazards. First, we learned, to our delight, that several American fighter aircraft and numerous American twin-engine light bombers (Douglas A-20 Havocs, Martin B-26

Marauders, and B-25 Mitchells) would be flying along with us and using us as their navigational guides. Because of this, we would fly faster than usual so that they could be more in line with their cruise speed requirements. We had met some of the "fly-along" pilots at dinner the night before, and they were a good bunch. They were happy to have some "big company" on this long over-water flight.

The second piece of surprising information was more in keeping with what one would expect in a war zone, and was our first taste of the combat environment. The Briefing Officer cautioned us to be very certain of the validity of all radio signals we used for en route navigation. We were to make absolutely sure that the signals we used were being transmitted by American or British stations and not bogus signals being transmitted by German stations in an effort to entrap us. (These radio signals [transmissions] could be verified by the identification code voice or C.W. [constant wave] Morse code, and also by their direction of transmission.)

B-17s of the 483rd Bomb Group (H) climbing to bombing altitude on their way to strike a German railroad marshalling yard and shops. This is what we trained for. (Picture courtesy of Boeing.)

We used some radio signals for navigational track position cross-checks and speed-checks, as well as heading-homing directional checks, and we were warned to make sure all of them were verifiable. We were told that American and British intelligence had discovered German surface ships and submarines around the upper North Atlantic Ocean region which were transmitting extremely strong radio signals on the same frequencies—and at the same or greater strength—as those transmitted by allied (friendly) radio stations.

These signals were normally used by American, Canadian, and British aircraft—including American and Canadian aircraft flying the route from either Newfoundland or Iceland to England—for a portion of their navigation in this area. Some American and Canadian aircraft flying across the North Atlantic had mistakenly used bogus radio signals for navigation and had been lured way off course. Some had almost run out of fuel before realizing what a cunning subterfuge they had fallen victim to.

My crew and I were certain that we did, in fact, tune in some bogus transmissions. My copilot, George Hong, and my navigator, James R. Metz, and I found that tuning in phony German radio transmissions on our ADF receivers was easy to do. The bogus signals were very strong and sharp on some low-frequency bands, as evidenced by the way our ADF needle swung quickly in the direction of the transmission and continued to home in on it without much needle swing or movement away from the signal. (ADF is for automatic direction finding. When the low frequency radio is tuned to a radio station, there is a unit in the system which has the ability to "home in" [track this radio signal]—the needle on the set points to the direction of the signal's transmission location, while the azimuth on the perimeter of the set's face shows the bearing [heading] in degrees, from 0 degrees to 360 degrees.)

We understood the danger these false signals could represent if a pilot were to rely on one and use it for navigating, as the transmissions were emanating from areas of the North Atlantic Ocean where we knew no land mass existed, let alone a spot to land an airplane.

All ten of us were climbing away from Keflavik by 0630 on a beautiful, crystal-clear morning. We were flying through the top side and outer edge of a large high-pressure system, which made the skies clear and the sea below appear relatively calm and flat. Not more than twenty minutes out of Keflavik, the twin engine B-26's, A-20's and B-25's pulled up beside us at a comfortable distance out on our wings, where they could set up their autopilots and fly along with us easily. Within another fifteen or twenty minutes, some of the single-engine fighters had lined up well above our lead B-17, and we all settled down together for the flight to England, enjoying the beautiful weather and our last taste of good American Army Air Corps coffee and sandwiches.

I had mixed emotions about this flight. I was satisfied with our fine day's trip and happy about finally arriving in England; however, I had become accustomed to flying this beautiful new Boeing B-17 and was not pleased with the fact that once we were parked on the ramp at Valley and I walked away from this airplane, I would never see it again or know of its fate in the great war.

We had become good friends.

When we came within sight of the British Isles, our accompanying fighters and twin-engine bombers bade us farewell and proceeded on to their designated airfields. We blocked in at Valley, Wales, at 1350 after an interesting but uneventful flight. Our time, from leaving Keflavik to setting our brakes at Valley, was six plus zero five. (six hours and five minutes).

In spite of the fact that each of us had flown on his own, this had still been something of a training flight, as we gained experience in flying B-17s and in crew coordination and command. Each leg of the trip was a learning experience, and each had its own set of problems and demands. We tested our airplanes and ourselves in many areas of flight and in many types of weather. Our flying abilities and command decisions were stimulated again and again throughout the trip. I, for one, came through this experience a more seasoned pilot and officer and was more confident in my role as leader of a ten-man crew as we prepared to enter the war.After arriving at Valley, we were assigned and transported to the 8th Air Force Combat Crew Replacement Pool (70th Replacement Depot), where we were to have some much-needed rest and relaxation before being assigned to a bomber group somewhere in England.

3

Our First Taste of England

We were pleasantly surprised with our accommodations at the Combat Replacement Depot. We were billeted in heated metal Quonset huts, with nice bathroom facilities located at each end. The living quarters were clean and neat, well maintained and orderly, and they were quiet and restful. Our beds were very comfortable. The food at the officers mess was above par for a wartime military mess hall, and the mess hall itself was a very clean and bright facility. We learned from the administrative people at the depot that our accommodations were just about customary for the Eighth Air Force combat crews.

We were told that we might expect to be stationed at the crew replacement depot for as long as three to four weeks, depending on the crew replacement requirements for the Eighth Air Force bomb groups in the area that was served by the 70th replacement pool. So we settled down for our stay and began to enjoy the surrounding area, its small towns, and their eating and entertainment establishments.

The four officers in my crew soon found that we needed bicycles, and we purchased them from a bike shop on the base. They were expensive, but with them we could pedal to the small towns located a little further away (keeping in mind the necessity to ride on the correct side of the road, a topic of much humor) during the day and evening hours until curfew time.

We were often issued passes to travel to London by train, where we could spend several days or a weekend at the Duchess Officers Club there. We were required to check in with the message center at the club several times during the day in case our transfer orders had come through. The hotel was a wonderful treat for us, as the accommodations were exceptional, and very pleasurable considering that it was wartime in a large city under daily air attacks. The civilians who managed and maintained the hotel for the American military did everything possible to see that we were relaxed and happy and had some enjoyable times.

The availability of this nice hotel, the relaxed atmosphere it presented, and the possibility of meeting a young English lady and her family for lunch or dinner made the war seem somewhat distant to us. This was true even when the German rockets had us scooting into air raid shelters with hundreds of others several times while we were in London. We learned that these bombs slammed into the city quite often, but as long as we could hear the whine of the rocket, we still had a little time to reach a bomb shelter. It also soon became readily apparent that when we could not hear the rocket sound, we had better already be in the shelter, as the bomb was well on its way to hitting the earth, exploding and causing terrible destruction.

Being able to visit London was of special interest to me, as the father of a close friend back in Coconut Grove, Florida, was stationed in London with the Army Air Corps Medical Staff, in the Flight Surgeon Headquarters. Colonel Joseph M. Stewart and his son, Joe, were almost part of my family, and I part of theirs, though I had not seen Colonel Stewart for two or three years. Joe and I had grown up together, and the fact that I could visit and have lunch with his father twice while I was in London was very significant to me. Dr. Stewart was special to me, and our lunches in London made me feel as though some of the fond and memorable parts of my home atmosphere were here in England with me even though a horrendous war was raging all around us. I often asked myself, "Where will we both be a year or so from now?" My hopes and plans for survival were high.

After we had been at the 70th Combat Replacement Depot for about a week, we began to hear rumors that some B-17 combat crews were being transferred to the Fifteenth Air Force in Italy. As a matter of fact, later in the week of September 11, I realized that some of the pilots of the original ten crews that ferried airplanes from Hunter Field to England, and with whom I had palled around, were nowhere to be found. I inquired at the Pool administration office and was told that Dent, Dunn, Glass, and Haskins had been hastily reassigned and had shipped out. The office would not definitely state where these crews had been shipped to; however, reading between the lines, I felt certain that they were en route to the Fifteenth Air Force in Italy. It was possible that my crew and I would soon follow.

On Friday, September 22, our CQ told our crew that we would be leaving in the next few days. Orders were being cut, and we were to remain on the base and check the quarters bulletin board periodically for further instructions.

On Saturday, September 23, our orders for reassignment were posted. Much to our surprise, we were to be trucked to the nearby rail station to board a train on the early evening of Sunday, the 24th, and travel to a destination where we were to await further assignment. Normally, when a crew was assigned to an 8th Air Force Bomb Group, they would be trucked from the Replacement Depot to that Bomb Group. It all seemed very mysterious at that point; however, we had learned not to question, but to follow orders, and answers would follow later.

Our train was a fine English rail carrier. Once on board, we were assigned to sleeping compartments, as the journey would take all night. My compartment was very comfortable and I soon went to bed. On arrival the next morning, we found that our destination was Newquay, England, on the far southwest coast of England in Cornwall. Newquay is a summer resort with the Celtic Sea at its doorstep. It was a lovely, quiet and very peaceful place. Because of the war and because summer was waning, most of the people there were year-round local residents rather than vacationers. We were given permission to leave the base and enjoy the city, as we weren't scheduled to leave for two or three days. As usual, checking the barracks bulletin board twice daily was the order of the day.

The Transportation Officer at the Air Base had briefed me (as crew leader) on our next destination and how we would get there.

While walking along the coastal cliff in the central part of Newquay, I met an English family who lived in the city year-round. They told me that they had a very nice but modest home that had been in their family for many generations—they were very proud of their impressive heritage, and rightly so. As we continued our walk along the sea cliffs, the family invited me to their home for tea. The invitation, I supposed, was because I was a young American Air Corps pilot, dressed in my heavy trench coat and winter uniform, and appeared to be alone. They must have concluded that it would be a friendly and gracious course to invite me to their home. I knew that food was very scarce in England because of the war and long isolation the country had endured, and I told them that I hesitated to accept their invitation because of this. However, they insisted, and their two children would not take no for an answer. I finally accepted, and we had an enjoyable afternoon together over tea and pastries.

They invited me for dinner the next evening and I told them I would accept if I could obtain leave from my base and if they would allow me to bring some food from the base commissary to help out with the dinner menu. We agreed on the plan and I returned to the base. The next day I was free to leave the base, as we had just been issued orders to mobilize the next afternoon, Thursday, September 28, at 1800 to depart the base by plane at 2000. This information was not for publication outside of my crew. (As mentioned, I had been briefed on our departure and our destination, so my preparations were already made. Now that my crew was aware of our departure date and time, they could prepare also. Our destination was not stated in our departure orders and would not be revealed until we were airborne en route.)

In preparation for my dinner with the English family, I visited the commissary, which was surprisingly well-stocked. I found a small cooked canned ham, canned carrots, canned string beans, and canned yams, all of which seemed a good basis for a dinner. I found that locally baked bread was in ample supply, so I added two freshly baked loaves to my shopping basket. I picked out a bottle of white wine for the adults and found some bottles of Orange Crush for the children. Some local English cookies were also available, and I found a bag of rare American ground coffee, so we could have coffee with the cookies after dinner.

With all these goodies boxed, I hitched a ride with an officer from the base and we set out for Newquay and the lovely little home of my new British friends. I had a smile on my face and a feeling of satisfaction that I could help bring some happiness and comfort to these fine people. Dinner was very enjoyable and they were very appreciative of the things I had brought them. It was a fine evening.

I have often wondered what happened to that kind little family, both during the war years and afterwards. I am sure they also wondered what my fate was, flying on my bombing missions over Europe. They told me that I would always be in their prayers.

4

A Journey to a New Air Force

At 2000 on the clear evening of Thursday, September 28, 1944, we departed Newquay, England, aboard an ATC (Air Transport Command) C-87 (B-24 converted bomber) bound for Casablanca, Morocco. We would fly at night—out over the Atlantic Ocean—unescorted.

We landed without incident at Casablanca the next morning. Our accommodations at the air base there were very modest in comparison to our quarters in England. We were scheduled to depart Casablanca for Marrakech, French Morocco, on Saturday, September 31, in the middle of the afternoon. While we awaited departure, we were free to leave the air base during the daytime; however, we were to sign back in by 1900.

Casablanca, its people and their customs, seemed somewhat mysterious—possibly even dangerous—to us. We had come a long way since our training days, and we had a job to perform. I didn't want anything to prevent us from accomplishing our mission, so I advised my crew to be very, very cautious when they were off the base.

Our first day in Casablanca was not without some humor. During our evening meal at the officers' mess on the day of our arrival, one of the local officers told us an almost-unbelievable story of the disappearance of several hundred military mattress covers. The covers had just arrived by ship from the United States and were very much needed by several army posts in the North Africa area—particularly by the military hospitals. They were for the Army's standard single-bed mattresses and were made of typical sturdy blue-and-white striped ticking. They were scheduled to be distributed within the next few days, but they had all vanished! No one could imagine why anyone would want to misappropriate them. Of what use could hundreds of mattress covers possibly be to anyone in this country?

The answer had presented itself this very morning. It seemed that hundreds of local Casablancan Arabs had introduced a new vogue in North African desert fashion: the man about town now wore a blue-and-white ticking single-bed mattress cover! Holes for the legs and arms were cut in the bottom and sides, and a button arrangement was styled for the neck at the open (tie) end. A wide white woven sash was used at the waist to keep the garment in place, and it was worn with the usual white turban. The ensemble was certainly odd-looking to everyone—and surely overly warm for this desert climate.

Despite the amusement we took from the situation, the fact remained that these men were wearing stolen property, and the U.S. government was not amused. Someone must be held responsible for the theft. Unfortunately, my crew was leaving for Marrakech the next day, so we never heard the outcome of the story—but we did get a laugh out of it.

My copilot, navigator, bombardier, and I departed the air base in a MATS C-47 at 1500 Sunday afternoon for Marrakech, some two hundred miles to the south across the desert. After about an hour's flight, we arrived and discovered that Marrakech was even more mysterious than Casablanca. Nevertheless, we were allowed to leave the base during daytime hours to sightsee. We all wanted to explore the Casbah, a unique and very native section of Marrakech.

We were tentatively scheduled to depart Marrakech on Tuesday, October 2, the first date that a MATS airplane would have four seats available on an eastbound flight to Tunis, so we had at least one full free day to enjoy the mystique of this area. We decided to visit the Casbah on Monday, October 1, and spend the remainder of Sunday exploring other areas and relaxing on the base. One of the local young Arabs who worked at the base agreed to give us a lift to the Casbah Monday morning, and he also gave us some tips about what to do—and what not to do—while touring this section of the city (the so-called marketplace). Caution was the byword.

In 1944, Marrakech was still back in the Arabian Nights era—largely undeveloped and definitely foreign to us. We four young sightseers would definitely be different from the travelers, local merchants, desert tribesmen, professional thieves, and casual cutthroats who were part of the usual Casbah scene.

We had a few misgivings about going because of the spooky stories we had heard—it sounded like the area could be hazardous to our health. But we planned to stick together and watch out for one another. Besides, other allied military personnel were doing the same sort of sightseeing,

Original crew of "Je Reviens," October 1944. *Top row, left to right:* Pilot: 1st Lt. Edward F. Logan, Jr.; Co-Pilot: 2nd Lt. George Hong; Navigator: 2nd Lt. James R. Metz; Bombardier: 2nd Lt. Robert P. Keno. *Bottom Row, left to right:* Tail Gunner: S/Sgt. James F. Cook; Radio Operator: S/Sgt. Roger Baudier, Jr.; Engineer: S/Sgt. Leonard H. DeMeulenaere; Waist Gunner: S/Sgt. Duane F. Berthelson; Waist Gunner: S/Sgt. Ted C. Blake; Ball Turret Gunner: S/Sgt. Larue F. Wilson.

and they didn't seem overly concerned about their safety. So thinking positively, we explored the Casbah quite thoroughly and purchased a few small Arab-made gifts—there was no way to ship larger, more interesting items home.

We had one slight mishap as a result of our adventure in the Casbah, though it didn't present itself until we returned to the base in the afternoon. When we reached the gate to sign in, each of us used the guardhouse pen to sign the log—with the exception of Jim Metz, my navigator. Jim had received a splendid gold pen and pencil set from his family as a graduation gift when he completed navigator training. He had signed out with it in the morning, and he intended to use it to sign back in as well. He had carried the pen and pencil in his left shirt pocket when he left the base, but when he reached for the pen to sign in, he discovered that both implements had been stolen! The stitching on the inner side of his left shirt pocket had been very neatly cut away without damaging anything else whatsoever. Jim, of course, had not had the slightest indication that this had happened—that was the scary part of the experience.

My three officers and I were flown from Marrakech to Tunis, Tunisia, via Oran and Algiers, Algeria, on Tuesday, October 2, and we remained there overnight. We were joined by the remainder of our crew, who had also been flown in by an ATC C-47 transport plane that evening. A short novel could be written about our experiences and contacts on the trip from Casablanca to Tunis via Marrakech, French Morocco, Oran and Algiers, both on and off the airplane. It was a very interesting and unusual trip.

On Wednesday, October 3, my entire crew and I were flown by a B-24 transport plane to Bari, Italy, the headquarters of the Fifteenth Air Force, where we remained overnight. At Bari, our group assignment was made. We were now officially assigned to the Fifteenth Air Force, Fifth Wing, 483rd Bomb Group (H), 817th Bomb Squadron. The Fifth Wing was composed of B-17s. We were to be stationed in the Foggia Valley, just in from the Adriatic Sea near Lake Lesina, on the "spur" of boot-shaped Italy. We joined thousands of airmen from the bomber crews and a thousand or so B-17s and B-24s that comprised the Fifteenth Air Force heavy bomber command.

5

Our New Home
Away from Home

Of Tents and Stoves...

My crew and I arrived at Sterparone, home of the 483rd Bomb Group (H), on Wednesday, October 4, 1944, to begin adding our efforts to destroying the Nazi war machine. When my officers and I checked in with the Base Supply Officer of the 817th Bomb Squadron, we were assigned a heavy-duty-army-canvas sixteen-by-sixteen-foot tent with a dirt floor that sat in the middle of the west side of the 817th Bomb Squadron's "tent street." We were also each issued a canvas folding cot, four wool blankets (two to use as a mattress and two to cover us), and a pillow of sorts. In the spring, we were told, we'd have to return two of the blankets to Supply so they could be cleaned and made ready for next winter's issue. We were always trying to get more blankets to make our "mattresses" thicker. It was amazing what a forty-dollar bottle of Old Taylor would do in this regard.

We were also introduced to the squadron's toilet facilities. At the end of its street, each squadron had a large latrine—a twelve-seated outhouse, six seats on each side. It was a wood-framed structure with screens on the sides, a screen door, and heavy canvas flaps that could be lowered in inclement weather. The roof was also made of heavy canvas and blew off regularly during rain or snow storms. When this happened, we were cooled by Mother Nature's air conditioning until repairs could be made. Unfortunately, this type of repair wasn't high on the maintenance crew's to-do list.

Within a few months our housing improved somewhat. We made arrangements for the Italian workmen at our base to construct an open-top square brick structure with brick floors the same size as the tents. A wooden roof framework was placed on top of the walls and a sixteen-by sixteen-foot tent was attached to the framework.

Where did all of these bricks come from? The gigantic, sprawling wheat farm the 483rd Bomb Group had selected as its base was equipped with a large, modern kiln, and the Italian workers who operated the kiln for the Army Air Corps produced hundreds of bricks almost every day. The clay must have been obtained close by since there seemed to be an abundance of it.

Our new home had a magnificent Italian-style fireplace, also made of brick. It protruded from the wall and had a large, high hearth. It was stuccoed from the top to the hearth, and the stucco was painted white. It worked like a charm, and the Italian brick masons were very proud of their handiwork. (After each mission we flew, I painted a blue bomb symbol on the face of our fireplace.)

In addition to a handsome all-wood door, our new home had three small windows (no glass) with solid wooden covers that could be shut and locked in place, similar to what America's western settlers had for windows in their log houses.

Left to right: Bob Keno, bombardier; Edward Logan, pilot; Jim Metz, navigator, standing in front of their tent house, Italy—November, 1944.

Edward Logan (far left) with some of his friends, standing in front of their tent house—Italy, 1944.

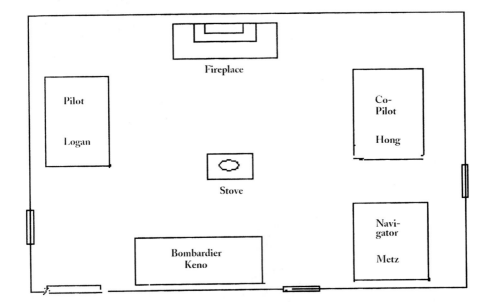

Diagram of our tent house—483rd Bomb Group, Sterparone, Italy 1944.

Some of the bomb group's crewmen making snowballs outside their tent houses—
Italy, 1944.

To keep us warm during the harsh Italian winter, we had a stove set on the floor that burned 110-octane aviation fuel, as firewood was difficult to obtain. The stove was half of a fifty-five-gallon steel drum set in a cement frame, with a fuel line (from an old B-17) coming into the house from a drum outside that was elevated on a wood frame. The fuel line came in through the brick wall by the fireplace and under the brick floor, curved up and then down into a hole in the 6.5-inch steel burner pipe, which was welded into the steel drum at a forty-five-degree angle. The fuel line was crimped to create a fine mist of fuel, and a star valve on the fuel line controlled the flow or shut off the fuel completely.

Our stove worked very well, although it required much TLC, and we had to be very careful when lighting it. A few of us were ejected out the front door when a start didn't go well. The exhaust pipe, which was also welded into the top of the steel drum, went up to the pinnacle of the wooden roof frame and extended several feet above the tent top. It had been fabricated for us in the base metal shop from fifty-caliber ammunition cans. Once we successfully started the stove and metered the fuel flow to a very small amount, the stove performed beautifully and kept us warm all night. To my recollection, no tent huts ever burned because of stoves or fireplaces overheating.

The food at our mess hall was a sore subject. Suffice it to say that none of us gained any weight while at the 483rd Bomb Group. We did not live to eat, we ate to live.

Bathing facilities were very limited when we first joined the 483rd, but after several months the construction crew built a large shower building for the flight crews. It had lines of shower heads on each side, with individual control knobs for hot and cold water, although only cold was available at first. When hot water arrived, we considered it a blessing and a real luxury.

For me, the three most important things in my life as a bomber pilot were sleeping well, being clean, and eating well—in that order. I was becoming accustomed to my cot and slept quite well, perhaps because I was so in need of sleep most of the time. When hot showers were finally available, my keeping-clean requirement was satisfied for the most part. Unfortunately, "eating well" at the base had to be put on hold—the food situation was not going to improve any time soon. Fortunately, there were occasional opportunities to have a halfway decent meal at the Red Cross Officers Club in Foggia, where we went when we could obtain leave and transportation.

Another fact of life at the 483rd Bomb Group was that our construction and maintenance personnel constantly had their hands full just keeping our 6,000-foot steel mat runway in good shape for the many takeoffs and landings of each bombing mission. This was no easy task, as winter snows and spring and summer rains of "Sunny Italy" often created serious erosion problems for the gravel "road bond"–type earth under the steel mat. The miles of taxiways and fifty-six airplane parking "hardstands" were also constantly in need of maintenance so that our big bombers could park quickly and be far enough apart to taxi freely about the air base. We knew that these mission-related tasks were the primary responsibility of our ground, maintenance, and construction personnel, so we considered ourselves fortunate that they took the time to build our shower building and add other creature comforts to our lives at Sterparone.

The antiaircraft batteries and the search light batteries on our base were manned by British army personnel—a wonderful group of men who were expert and thorough at their jobs. We Americans had to laugh at their reaction to air raids. When we were attacked by German aircraft, air raid sirens sounded all over the base. If the sirens interrupted the British during tea or a meal, their reaction was calm and deliberate. They'd take a last sip of tea or forkful of food before leaving for their stations. In fact, they always seemed a little upset with the Germans for being so inconsiderate as to interrupt their tea! Their calm belied their professionalism and skill—I'm sure our attackers always rued the days they tried to bomb our base, because these fellows always hastened them off.

A Not Too Gentle Dental Air Raid

About a month after arriving at the 483rd Bomb Group, I lost a small filling and made an appointment with the group's dentist. When I arrived at 0800, he was waiting for me. After I introduced myself to him, he showed me his working facilities, which were very primitive. The most interesting piece of equipment was his dental chair, which was identical to one in which I had spent many anxious hours—a B-17 pilot's seat, complete with head and arm rests, but minus its shoulder harness and seat belt. It was fastened to a substantial metal base that swiveled 360 degrees, and it could be tilted back to an almost horizontal position. And the dental drill was powered by a rather large electric motor and operated by a foot lever made from a B-17 pilot's rudder pedal!

I climbed into this fine chair, and the dentist went to work on my tooth. About fifteen minutes later he was almost through when the air raid sirens began to blare their shrill warnings of an enemy attack. The dental work ceased as both of us bolted out of the tent-like office to find the closest air raid slit trench. We were an odd-looking couple there in the trench. He still wore his dental gown and I had not removed my bib as we hastened to find shelter. The Germans zoomed around the base and dropped a few bombs down by the flight line, but did no real damage and were quickly frightened away by our British antiaircraft gun crews.

After the sirens ceased their wailing, the dentist and I returned to his office and he completed his work. The filling done that day was replaced when I returned to the United States after completing my combat tour, and when I related the story to my regular dentist, he thought it was hilarious. I still smile about it today.

The 483rd

The 483rd Bomb Group at Sterparone arrived at their tremendous "wheat field" in the first week of April, 1944, and became operational on April 23, 1944, when it launched its first mission—consisting of thirty-two B-17 heavy bombers striking at Wiener Neustadt, Austria. The 483rd's twenty-three ground support units (echelons) consisted of 2,000 men, including the command and administrative officers who were needed to staff the base's daily operations. The original group consisted of 646 bomber crew members. (Note: Each squadron usually consisted of twenty B-17s, each operated by a ten-man crew.) Of these original crewmen, 39.8 percent were either killed in action or missing in action. Seven-hundred-sixty crew members were shot down. Of the 760, 214 were killed in action, 315 became POWs, and 231 evaded capture and returned to duty. (Note: After World War II, statistics revealed that an air crewman fighting in the air war over Europe had less chance of survival than a Marine fighting in the South Pacific.) Replacement crews and airplanes constantly arrived at the 483rd; they filled in the gaps when crewmen and airplanes were lost on bombing missions.

The command and administrative officers' quarters were separate from the squadron bomber crews' quarters, and were located at the other end of the base in the housing complex of the original wheat field's owner/manager quarters. The air crew flying officers of the four squadrons lived on a tent street compound (one street for each squadron, with eleven to fifteen tents on each side) located farthest from the runway. The enlisted men of the four squadrons lived in a tent street compound adjacent to the officers' compound.

The 483rd Bomb Group's combat duty spanned fourteen months, from April 1944 through May 1945, during which time the Group flew 215 combat missions.

6

Our War—Flying Start

We soon became indoctrinated to life on the base, and after a flight check and an area-familiarization flight, we flew the first of our required thirty-five combat bombing missions on October 10. We bombed the railroad marshalling yards at Treviso, Italy, from a rather low altitude. We were flying so low that we could almost see the antiaircraft guns and the soldiers firing them!

The aspect of this mission that I remember most vividly is the odor of the burned black power of the eighty-eight millimeter antiaircraft pro jectiles exploding by the hundreds around my airplane. Even though I was breathing through a closely fitting oxygen mask, I took in enough outside air through my system's regulator to be able to smell the powder. Air crewmen called it the "smell of peril."

Each crew member's oxygen mask was made to fit his face exactly—for both safety and comfort. We frequently wore our oxygen masks from four to seven hours on a bombing mission, so they had to fit perfectly. We each carried two masks on each mission—the one we usually wore and a spare, just in case. A crewman without oxygen would expire in seconds above twenty thousand feet.

When a crew was breathing oxygen, a safety check-in on the airplane's inter-phone communications system was required every five minutes from each crewman to ensure that each one was all right and breathing normally. This check-in procedure saved many lives during bombing missions.

Bari, in the lower portion of the boot of Italy, is a long way from Austria, Czechoslovakia, or Germany, so the vast majority of the 15th Air Force's bombing missions involved long-range, high-altitude flights. The bomber crews breathed oxygen when they reached 10,000 feet en route to their targets, and they remained on oxygen until they were below 10,000 feet again during their return to base. Most of the missions lasted at least six and a half hours, and some—like those to bomb the Ruhland Synthetic Oil Refinery thirty miles north of Dresden—were as long as nine hours.

Flying a mission made for a long, arduous, and fear-inspiring day for the ten young men on board the four-engine bombers. There were no easy bombing missions; each had its own disquieting way of getting under one's skin, and its own set of problems and dangers.

The Foremost Consideration—My Crew

Preparing to fly a mission was an emotional time and one of mixed feelings for each crew member. Every pilot in command realized that his nine crewmen depended on him in many ways. His men expected him to use his utmost flying competence, skills, and leadership each time he flew them into harm's way, and to do his best to bring them back to their base with him, alive and in one piece. His crew was really his immediate family during a mission, and their safety and well-being were his primary concern.

Putting bombs on the mission's target was why we were here; however,

1st Lt. Edward Logan in his B-17 Bomber "Je Reviens"—Italy, 1944.

without the pilot's safely functioning and staunchly believing fellow crewmen, this would have been impossible. The pilot's concern for his crew never abated until the plane had landed and was parked on its hardstand upon the mission's completion.

We knew that our training had prepared us to excel as pilots in command of large four-engine bombers and ten-man crews. There was no doubt in our minds that we were far better than our adversaries and that we could out-perform them in every area. We were young and felt almost indestructible. We were in outstanding shape physically and mentally, and our determination, dedication to duty, and devotion to our country were supreme. We couldn't lose.

Battle Damage—A Description

My crew and I were faced with combat damage to our airplane many times during our mission history. A large hole in the fuselage was a problem in itself, but it was also usually a sign that damage had been done to other parts of the plane at the same time. Sometimes we didn't discover the other damage immediately because we weren't using the affected system at the time—such as when the hydraulic system was damaged, or there was a partial loss of the electrical system. Returning to the base after a bomb run without these systems fully operational was difficult because other components—landing gear, wheel brakes, wing flaps, etc.—relied heavily on them.

We also had to deal with engine damage. The loss of even one engine was a pesky situation at best, although we had been trained to fly with one or two engines out. The actual loss of two engines, on the other hand, was a vexing predicament in which to find oneself—particularly when the two inoperative engines were on the same wing.

If a plane loses two engines, it is very difficult to fly, but flying on two engines also means that the plane loses its place in the flying formation and its initial protection by escort planes. It's referred to as a "straggler," and stragglers were easy prey for German fighter aircraft. They could cut a limping bomber to pieces with their cannon and machine-gun fire in a matter of seconds.

The B-17's Wonderful Engines

The Wright Cyclone R-1820–97, a nine-cylinder radial engine with a B-2 General Electric turbo-supercharger, was of superior design and

Top: Our Crew Chief with "Je Reviens," our B-17, on its hardstand. *Bottom:* Our B-17 "Je Reviens" after our 6th mission to Brux. The hydraulic system is shot out. I ground-looped to stop our airplane by maneuvering the left landing gear into a drain ditch. (We were heading toward an olive grove off the end of the runway where people were harvesting olives.)

quality—and we greatly depended on it to help bring us home. This engine would continue to function and supply power for some time after being damaged. In fact, should the engine controls be shot away, four of the engine's controls automatically assumed predetermined positions: throttles went to wide-open; superchargers to 65 percent power; intercoolers to the cold position; and propellers to a minimum of 1850 RPM. In addition, the functioning of the automatic control at one unit did not affect placement of controls at other units. This allowed pilots to obtain power from a damaged engine or its control linkage for as long as the engine continued to function.

The record of *Je Reviens'* engine losses was similar to that of other B-17s that routinely flew combat bombing missions. Our record included returning from nine bombing missions with one engine inoperative. Most of these three-engine returns were accomplished with the inoperative propeller feathered, although on two occasions this was impossible and the propeller eventually flew off the engine. Fortunately, it did no damage to the airplane or crew as it did so, and it was a blessing to have it gone because the drag induced by a windmilling propeller is substantial.

When a damaged or malfunctioning engine is shut down (deliberately stopped by the pilot), he feathers its propeller by pressing the feathering button. This actuates the propeller's feathering pump, causing oil pressure to move the propeller blades to their full feathered position—front edges facing forward into the slipstream. This lessens drag, thereby eliminating windmilling.

Each time we returned to the base on three engines, we were able to remain in formation with our group. Sometimes being able to stay in formation means the difference between winning the battle—and returning home—and losing it.

Three times we returned with two engines inoperative, one on the left wing and one on the right, and on one mission both engines on one wing were out. This made flying more difficult and worrisome; however, flying on two engines with the airplane properly trimmed, and lightening the plane by discarding nonessential equipment, brought us home safely.

Returning with Two Engines Inoperative on One Wing

On our tenth mission to bomb the oil refinery at Korneuburg, our number three and four engines were damaged. Number four was shut down and feathered, but number three could not be feathered due to

An 840th Bomb Squadron B-17 after an emergency landing at Sterparone, having returned from a combat mission with landing gear damage. (Picture courtesy of Boeing.)

damage to the feathering system's oil lines. Its propeller continued to windmill even though the engine had essentially been shut down.

As the windmilling propeller began to wobble, I felt certain that it would destroy its gearing and engine shaft and probably fly off the engine, so I prepared to lose it. I could picture it flying up and over the wing and hitting the tail section, so I had all the crewmen in the rear of the plane move forward to the radio room and bomb bay just in case this worst-case scenario happened.

My past experience had shown me that it is very difficult to predict what an uncontrollable propeller will do just prior to flying off the engine and at the instant it finally does so. But I did what I could: I slowed the airplane somewhat by raising the nose slightly to decrease the propeller's speed and wobble. At the same time, I suggested to my copilot, George Hong, that he move out of his seat in case the propeller wobbled drastically enough to fly into the cockpit.

At the instant George turned to his left to get out of his seat, the propeller broke loose, and the big menacing blades momentarily swerved left toward the cockpit. A few inches of at least one blade tip sliced into the side of the cockpit exactly where George's right leg had been. The blade damaged the check-list holder, the oxygen line, and the copilot's inter-phone selector box—not much destruction considering what it might have been. The complete propeller—all three blades—then flew up and over the right wing and continued a downward departure well beyond the tail section of the plane, allowing us to continue with the task at hand—getting home.

A Mission Ends with a Traumatic Injury

On our 12th mission, we bombed the railway yards at Munich, Germany. Immediately after we dropped our bombs on the target, our top twin fifty-caliber turret was severely damaged by the explosion of an 88mm antiaircraft round, which exploded just above it. The explosion shattered the turret's Plexiglas dome and injured Len Demuelenaere, our engineer-gunner. It peppered his face and eyes with splinters of Plexiglas and shrapnel, and he also sustained numerous wounds to his chest and shoulders. He was in very bad shape and needed immediate medical attention.

I quickly contacted our squadron leader (by way of VHF radio) and told him I would leave the formation immediately and fly directly to Foggia Air Base, where one of our principal military hospitals was located. The hospital was easily accessible from the parking ramp at Foggia via a straight paved road that led directly to the hospital's emergency room. I reduced the power on the engines to slow the plane slightly, dropped our landing gear, and pulled up and out of the formation.

(In leaving [aborting] a formation, a pilot first communicates his intent to his lead airplane by VHF intra-plane radio, and the other pilots in the formation also hear this conversation. The pilot aborting formation drops his landing gear to indicate that he is executing his withdrawal maneuver and then pulls out of the formation.)

Once away from the formation, I retracted the landing gear and added maximum cruise horsepower to all four engines. As I turned toward Foggia, I set up a slight nose-down attitude to increase our airspeed in the descent from 28,000 feet.

After about a hundred miles, just south of Munich, we were attacked by two ME-110 German twin-engine fighter bombers. We probably could have shot them down, as they were not fast-flying and our firepower was much greater than theirs, but we were moving very fast, and they were able to make only one half-hearted pass at us. We were in no mood to stay and fight—we had a much more important mission to accomplish: saving our engineer-gunner's eyes. I added a few more inches of manifold pressure and left the ME-110's far behind. I'm sure to this day, the pilots of those German fighter-bombers wonder what kind of B-17 we were flying.

Approaching the airfield at Foggia well to the north from over the Adriatic Sea, we advised the control tower on the nature of Len's wounds so the hospital would be ready for him. The tower cleared us to land and said an ambulance would meet our plane.

Although Len's injury was a new experience for us, I found that it was nothing new for the hospital. Badly damaged 15th Air Force combat aircraft were parked everywhere, and ambulances scurried about off-loading wounded crewmen for a quick trip to the hospital. There were twin-engine medium bombers, many B-17s, B-24s, and even some single-engine fighters whose pilots had barely made it back to the airfield seeking medical attention for themselves.

Several of my crew and I rode in the ambulance with Len, and what a trip it was! Even though I was accustomed to speed, I had never flown this low this fast as we sped to the emergency room.

The eye surgeons soon had Len in one of the operating rooms and began trying to save his eyes by removing many small slivers of Plexiglas from them and also extracting Plexiglas and small flak fragments from his shoulders and chest. I waited outside the operating room door for over an hour before the surgeon, a lieutenant colonel, emerged to tell me his efforts had been successful. He felt that Len's eyes would recover in time, and that he would be fine. He said that our rapid journey from the target area to the hospital had made the difference—a delay would have caused more damage. Our prayers had been answered. Pleased with this good news, we obtained transportation back to our B-17 and flew to Sterparone.

I borrowed the squadron operations officer's Jeep and returned to the hospital at Foggia three days later to check on Len. Bandages still covered his eyes, but he was in good spirits and said he felt well. He was returned to the 483rd about eight days later for further recuperation and rest.

The Devastation of Memmingen

The 483rd Bomb Group took part in many sad missions during its tenure of combat in World War II. Actually, its experiences were probably

Brigadier General Charles W. Lawrence, Commanding Officer of 5th Wing 15th Air Force, presents 1st Lt. Edward F. Logan, Jr., with his first Distinguished Flying Cross for his 17th mission to strike an oil refinery at Blechhammer, Germany on December 19, 1944. (Credit for identifying Brigadier General Lawrence belongs to Yvonne Kinkaid, researcher assigned to the Air Force Historical Studies Office at Bolling Air Force Base, DC, and to John W. Leland, Deputy Command Historian for Department of the Air Force, Air Mobility Command Headquarters, Scott AFB, II.) Note: For the lead to John W. Leland, my thanks to Major General Fred J. Ascani (Ret). At the time of General Ascani's tenure with the 483rd Bomb Group (H), he was squadron commander of the 816th Bomb Squadron, holding the rank of major.

not too different from those of most bomber groups, but one's own group's experiences tend to stand out. The Memmingen bombing mission on July 18, 1944, several months before we joined the 483rd, stands out for me. I heard about it while we were assigned to the Eighth Air Force Combat Crew Replacement Pool in England.

The target of the mission was the large aerodrome at Memmingen, in south central Germany, a long way from our base at Sterparone, Italy. Twenty-six B-17 Flying Fortresses from the 483rd were dispatched against Memmingen, with the intent of putting the German air base out of com-

B-17s of the 817th Bomb Squadron (red cowlings and red rudders) on their mission to bomb a strategic German railway bridge. (Picture courtesy of Boeing.)

mission forever. Approaching the target IP at Memmingen, the 483rd was greeted by 200 German fighter aircraft, and the destruction of the group's B-17s began. Two entire squadrons—fourteen B-17s—were shot out of the sky in just a few minutes. In the ensuing fight, the gunners of the group's airplanes destroyed fifty-three of the attacking ME-109's, and probably destroyed eight others.

The Memmingen raid was a tragic day that will live forever in the memories of every one of us who flew with the 483rd Bomb Group.

Combat Mission Damage: Almost Routine

When we returned from a bombing mission and had parked on our hardstand, we made a walk-around of the plane to assess the damage it had sustained. Sometimes we counted just a few holes; other times there were nearly two hundred, some quite large.

As we flew, situations developed because of battle damage that required individual, personal response and care. We had been taught that such complicated situations were expected to arise, and each mission became a learning experience in flying B-17s. We learned that this airplane was capable of enduring almost impossible situations—even more so than expected by the Boeing engineers who had designed it.

Our Escorts

I mentioned earlier that flying back to base on two engines always translated into a long and perilous day. We initially flew alone at first—the group formation would have proceeded home without us at a much greater speed than we were capable of. But we were usually not alone for long—we'd call for a fighter escort for at least part of the way back to our base.

The 332nd Group's fighters regularly responded to our call on VHF C channel. Usually one or two P-51's, with their red spinners and tails, answered our call, and shortly thereafter they'd pull up alongside our plane with some flaps down, canopies full back, goggles on top of their leather helmets, and a big smile and a thumbs-up. When we saw them, we knew we'd make it home—guaranteed! This group of fighter pilots—also known as the Tuskegee Airmen—was there when we needed them.

7

The Tuskegee Airmen—
A Bond of Friendship

The Tuskegee Airmen of the 332nd Fighter Group were our friends and usually our aerial protectors. These pilots flew their classically beautiful P-51 Mustang Fighters and watched over our big four-engine bombers during many lengthy bombing missions.

In the air, a fraternal bond developed between us and these airmen because of their dedication to protecting us from the German fighters who continually attacked our bomber formations. Our affinity toward each was strengthened because the 332nd Fighter Group's aircraft identification markings were red propeller spinners and vertical fins, and our (the 817th Bomb Squadron's) colors were red engine cowlings and rudders. In unit identification markings, we were birds of a feather.

On the ground, our friendship grew from meeting the 332nd airmen to share cocktails, war stories, or dinner—or to play bridge on our rest days—at the Red Cross Officer's Club in Foggia. They were professional, well-trained, fearless, and astute in the air, and always fun to be with on the ground as well. They frequently committed to aerial combat with the Germans when the odds were overwhelmingly against them, but they usually came out on top.

The Tuskegee Airmen were the first black combat pilots to fly in World War II and in the immediate post-war era. These aviators were trained at Tuskegee Air Force Base, Alabama, and have always been known as the Tuskegee Airmen. In 1940, the Army Air Corps was directed by President Roosevelt to build an all-black flying unit, which was the origin of the 99th Pursuit Squadron, based at the new training base in

Alabama. By 1944, the Tuskegee Airmen from the 99th, 100th, 301st and 302nd Fighter squadrons united to form the 332nd Fighter Group.

The Tuskegee Army Air Force Base graduated 950 pilots (who became second lieutenants and wore "silver wings"), who formed four fighter squadrons and four medium bomb squadrons. Half of these men flew in combat. During World War II, they flew over 10,000 combat sorties. During 200 missions escorting B-17 and B-24 heavy bombers striking the Third Reich's strategic targets, the Tuskegee Airmen never lost a 15th Air Force bomber to an enemy fighter. They shot down more than 150 enemy aircraft in air-to-air combat and destroyed another 150 on the ground. They also sank an enemy destroyer—another unique accomplishment—and more than forty other boats and barges with machine gun fire. They destroyed hundreds of enemy locomotives, boxcars, and other transportation assets.

During the war, Colonel Benjamin O. Davis, Jr. led the Tuskegee Airmen in combat in both escort roles and ground attack missions, and he demanded a level of professionalism and discipline that earned the highest praise from the theater commander. Colonel Davis continued to lead his airmen after the war for many years and retired as a lieutenant general in the United States Air Force.

A High Speed Pass

I well remember an episode that a few of the Tuskegee Airmen's 332nd Fighter Group pilots and their P-51's took part in and still laugh about. It had to do with a dress parade and medal presentation that was to take place at our base.

We bomber crews had been advised well in advance of the date and time this ceremony would take place that all of us were to appear in full dress uniform. High-ranking officers (including a general) from the Fifth Wing of the fifteenth Air Force Headquarters would be there to give speeches and award medals. We'd also be expected, as usual, to march in review, sporting the flag of the United States, the flag of the Fifteenth Air Force, and the 483rd Bomb Group's combat streamers.

None of us relished standing at attention or parade rest for long periods of time, especially on our days free of combat flying. An hour or so of medal presentations was acceptable, since the men who received citations certainly earned them, but many parts of the long afternoon we could easily forgo. How could we get out of at least *some* of this long, boring afternoon? The weather, for a change, was forecast to be beautiful, so there was no chance of a snow storm or cloudburst.

It was to be a serious event, with a very long flatbed trailer used as a dignitary platform placed on our parade ground (wheat field). The trailer was principally used by the Air Corps to haul the fuselages of damaged (crashed) B-17s from their point of impact back to the sub-depot repair station on our base for rebuilding and/or repairs when possible.

Here's how the Tuskegee Airmen helped us out.

One evening while we were socializing with some of them at the Red Cross Club, we told them about the upcoming parade, speeches, awards ceremony and so on, and of our disdain for the length of all of these festivities. The 332nd pilots asked for the day and time of the ceremony, which we supplied. Then they asked about the schedule of events, so we laid everything out for them. We discerned a twinkle of devilishness in their eyes as they asked whether a low level fly-by ("buzzing") of the parade grounds might break up the ceremony.

We thought it was worth a try. In any event, it would be fun to watch and be a part of. It definitely would be a break from the seriousness of combat flying. A decision was made to buzz the parade grounds at about 1530, just after the citations had been presented and as the dignitaries were concluding their addresses.

Our bomb group was located on a large plateau, as high as seven hundred feet above Foggia Valley in some areas. The 332nd pilots would perform a high fly-by to make sure the awards part of the ceremony was over before making their high-speed pass. They said there would be at least three planes, and possibly as many as five. Wonderful! What a splendid show this would be!

Our plan was set. We toasted the upcoming aerial show, swore each other to secrecy, and headed home to our base, hitching a ride on a supply truck full of 1000-pound RDX bombs.

Two days later the ceremony took place. About 1515, after the citations had been presented and while the dignitaries were speaking from the flatbed trailer, those of us who knew of the fly-by plan heard what we'd been waiting for—the faint, sweet sound of Rolls Royce Merlin in-line engines.

Out to the southeast, at about 8,000 feet, we saw two P-51's flying in formation on a southerly heading. When they were about ten miles south of Sterparone, they peeled off into a rather steep dive, one behind the other, and zoomed down to the lower Foggia Valley, south of our base. We knew that within a few minutes they'd flash above us at top speed and just a few feet off the ground—and no one on our parade grounds would even know they were approaching until they whistled by. They'd be out of sight before anyone would know what or who they were.

Sure enough, in less than five minutes, the two P-51's rose from the valley floor, flattened out over our plateau about 200 feet above the ground—at full speed and with engines wide open—and headed for our parade grounds, which were less than three miles from the edge of the plateau. They flew "in trail"—staggered horizontally—as they approached. No one, with the exception of those of us who knew that they would be coming, even saw or heard them approaching.

They over-flew the parade grounds at a tremendous speed, right above the dignitaries' flatbed trailer. In an instant they were out of sight. Just a flash, some soft purring of the engines, and a smooth swish—that was it. As we had hoped, that was the end of the ceremony. The dignitaries wished us well and we were dismissed.

To my knowledge, no one ever bothered to ascertain what that noise was—surely it was an airplane or airplanes, but no one cared. After all, there was a very large war going on and this area was a combat war zone—it could have been ME-262's.

A few days later, we met up with our friends from the 332nd at the Red Cross Club and silently toasted a classic fly-by—a flawless operation.

8

A Salute to My Crew

My copilot, First Lieutenant George V. Hong, having been recognized as a superior officer and a very able pilot, was appointed to the positions of Assistant Operations Officer, Squadron Gunnery Officer, and Squadron Oxygen Officer, where he excelled. He flew his required combat missions in addition to functioning in the other three capacities.

My bombardier, First Lieutenant Robert P. Keno, one of the outstanding bombardiers of the Fifth Wing of the Fifteenth Air Force, was selected as the lead bombardier of the 483rd Bomb Group (H). I always felt confident that he would put our full load of bombs well within a 1000-foot circle from 30,000 feet—the Fifteenth Air Force's goal for our bomb pattern.

Bob was also responsible for operating the "chin turret" (a gun turret that protected the front of the airplane). After chin turrets had been added to the B-17G's, frontal attacks by German Luftwaffe fighters had lessened, indicating that these twin fifty-caliber machine guns were a deterrent to incoming fighters. Many frontal-attacking fighters were quickly destroyed by these twin fifties, which had the advantage of rapid movement and an improved sight.

During our seventh mission, Bob took center stage. He didn't have the opportunity to use the chin turret to fire at attacking planes; his luck would have been better if he had. This mission was to strike the Skoda Armament Works at Pilsen, Czechoslovakia, on October 23, 1944.

About thirty minutes before crossing the IP for our bomb run, our formation was attacked by more than fifty German fighter aircraft. The entire 483rd Bomb Group was attacked by what appeared to be a large swarm of angry, fast-flying bees—they hit us from every possible angle.

When they started their onslaught, Bob was seated at the bombardier's station, busy with his preparations for the bomb drop. Our top turret gunner first spotted the German planes and immediately announced their position and movement to the other gunners over the intercom. Because Bob was busy, the navigator manned the chin turret guns, but Bob immediately joined in, firing the left cheek gun. Wave after wave of German aircraft flew at us in wide echelons—four, six, and eight at a time, presenting very small and fast-moving targets.

When bombers are under a constant onslaught such as this, just about every gun in the formation is being fired at the attackers. Every crewman is engulfed in his job—this is a fight for survival. The intercoms are in continuous use, filled with warnings for fellow gunners, hopes, fears, and news of successes.

Bob was firing his gun so intensely that the barrel was near its melting point and had actually bent slightly, even though the air temperature was forty degrees below zero.

Fifty-caliber machine gun ammunition, which is armor-piercing and incendiary, has been known to penetrate a bent barrel and exit from its side. Bob's barrel had to be replaced—and quickly!

We always carried spare barrels for the eleven accessible machine guns in handy locations, and Bob quickly got one from the nose compartment, removed his heavy fleece-lined gloves (leaving only his heated felt gloves inside silk glove liners), and got to work. In his cramped area—and while we were still under attack by the Germans' FW-190's and ME-109's—he removed the gun from its cheek port and started to remove the damaged barrel, figuring that it had cooled enough to be handled. He was wrong. He grasped the rear case of the gun in his left hand. As he gripped the center portion of the barrel in his right hand, intense heat burned right through his gloves and burned his fingers and the palm of his hand. His burns needed immediate attention. The navigator, Jim Metz, realizing what had happed, helped Bob remove his charred gloves and then unsnapped the forward first aid kit from the compartment bulkhead, and bandaged his hand. They then attached the spare barrel and reassembled the gun, and soon they were raising havoc with the German fighters again. Despite Bob's painful injury, he continued to fight.

The Pilsen mission was a long one—the flight was eight hours and fifty minutes. It was a rough day.

My navigator, First Lieutenant James R. Metz, had a natural gift for navigation and was also very proficient with the fifty-caliber machine gun, firing from either cheek position of the nose section. The ferry flight to England was made easier for me by Jim's competence in aerial navigation.

My engineer, Staff Sergeant Leonard H. Demuelenaere, was also my upper turret gunner, and because of his many technical abilities and knowledge of the B-17, he was selected to be the Engineer Training Instructor for the 817th Bomb Squadron, helping to improve the combat-readiness of replacement engineers arriving from the United States. He could educate people about the B-17, and was an exemplary engineer/gunner under combat conditions, and a well-qualified leader.

Staff Sergeant Roger Baudier was efficient and outstanding in his position as radio operator-gunner. Sometimes I flew a B-17 known as a "Mickey Ship," which was equipped with a G Navigation Set or a radar antenna—or both. He operated them equally well. His theoretical and technical knowledge of radio, radar, and the "G Unit," coupled with his ability to operate these systems, made him an important element of our crew.

The term "Mickey" was a code name given to a B-17 which was equipped with Radar. The Radar units in the B-17 "Mickey" ships—the APS-15 type—cost upwards of $60,000 in the WWII years. They were used for both navigation and for target identification in bombing missions, with a picture of 360 degrees in a radius of about one-hundred miles. The set provided the bombardier with azimuth, bombing angle, range and absolute altitude of the target being bombed.

The electronic "G" unit was a navigation system developed in England to assist the operator in locating specific targets on the ground by the triangulation of radio signals sent from ground stations. In this case, the transmitting stations were operated by the "underground resistance fighters" and O.S.S./S.O.E. agents of the United States and England scattered around greater Europe during World War II. The "G" unit was the forerunner of LORAN and long-range aerial navigation systems that I used for many years flying all over the globe during my commercial aviation career after the war.

My armorer gunner (the right waist gunner), Staff Sergeant Duane E. Berthelson, distinguished himself by his thorough knowledge and personal attention to his duties, which required not only a detailed understanding of the fifty-caliber machine gun, its ammunition, and use, but also thorough knowledge of each type of bomb we carried. The RDX 500-pound bomb, the 1000- and 2000-pound bombs, and the incendiary bombs we carried were super-sensitive and needed special care. In addition, like my bombardier and me, Duane had been trained in the normal and emergency operation of the B-17's bomb racks and shackles.

Bomb Release

Though we had emergency backup operations, sometimes a bomb would not release with all of the other bombs—it would hang up in the rack because one of its shackles released its grip on the hanging ring while the other did not. When this happened, the bomb was still attached to the rack at one end. If, after several attempts by our bombardier to release the bomb electrically or by using the manual release lever, it still failed to release, either Bob or Duane (perhaps both of them) stood on a very narrow (less than twelve-inch-wide) catwalk in the bomb bay with both doors open, at an altitude of 20,000 to 30,000 feet (using small walk—around oxygen bottles for breathing), and dislodged the bomb with a large screwdriver—a difficult and dangerous job. (The original rigging and hanging of these bombs was done by the Ground Support Ordnance and Armament Section, which did its tiring work at night while we were sleeping.)

Duane was responsible for pre-flighting the machine guns and bombs, as well as the Vary pistol, its flares of many colors, and our smoke canisters. He also made sure that there was a spare machine gun barrel for each of the accessible machine guns (eleven of the thirteen on board—the A-16 chin turret gun barrels could be changed only by the ground ordinance people, not during a flight) and ensured that we carried spare cans of ammunition for each gun. These "tools of our trade," so to speak, were always ready to perform properly—and I flew our missions with complete confidence, knowing that the ordinance on board was getting the "tender loving care" it deserved.

My other waist gunner, Staff Sergeant Ted C. Blake, was also a multi-talented young man. Ted had served with the Army Air Corps in the South Pacific prior to his assignment as an aerial gunner in the Eastern Flying Training Command. He had been stationed with the Sixty-Fifth Materials Squadron in New Caledonia in 1942 and had learned about the supply, maintenance, handling, and use of military cameras there. Because of his proficiency in that area, he was assigned to the Airborne Photography Section of the 483rd Bomb Group. He flew on bombing missions with all four of the bomb squadrons of the group as an aerial combat photographer and waist gunner, including some with me. I often flew a B-17G that was equipped with a large vertical bomb-strike camera, and Ted usually operated it, recording our squadron's bomb strikes as well as those of squadrons flying just ahead. The purpose of the photographs was target damage assessment—if we were not successful in destroying the intended target on the first mission, we'd have to return within a few days to finish the job.

The photographs also showed our bomb pattern, which was indicative of how well we were flying—both as a squadron and as a group. The tighter our formations were, the more concentrated the bomb-strike damage was, and that concentrated damage was what we were striving for. A tight squadron and group formation, with every plane tucked in its position, also guaranteed the most prolific machine gun fire power against attacking aircraft.

Two Tight Spots: My Ball Turret and Tail Gunners

Often, when I complained to myself or to my tent companions (my copilot, navigator, or bombardier) about small nuisances—such as practice formation flying, bombing practice, operating the Norden bombsight trainer indoors, or machine gunnery practice on our firing range—I would stop and think of the real discomforts my ball turret gunner, Staff Sergeant Larue F. Wilson, and my tail-gunner, Staff Sergeant James F. Cook, endured as they performed their duties on every mission. Even on the ground, these two men lived uncomfortably in a sixteen-by-sixteen-foot tent and slept on folding cots.

Larue was a classic ball turret gunner. His turret sustained severe damage on one mission when a German eighty-eight-millimeter shell exploded just below it. The turret was bent inward, twisted and so badly damaged that it could not function. It could also not be rotated to a position where the entry/exit hatch was within the airplane, which meant that Larue could not get out, and we could not bring the turret up inside the airplane. He was trapped—there was no way to get him out while we were in the air.

As I conversed with him over the interphone, I could tell that his psychological state was deteriorating more with each passing hour on our long flight back to Sterparone. I was deeply concerned for him and devastated by the realization that I could do nothing to help him. I informed our group's lead airplane of our problem—that Larue was trapped in the ball turret and we needed to return to base rapidly, and also that we had sustained other damage, but could still fly. The group leader acknowledged our dilemma and advised me that he would increase the group's descent speed and have a ground crew standing by with the equipment necessary to quickly remove the ball turret. I requested that he also have medical personnel on hand to care for Larue immediately after landing, as well as an ambulance to transport him to the hospital.

My concern for Larue's well-being was compounded because the machine guns in the turret, because of the damage, were pointing almost straight down and slightly to the left side of the fuselage, and it was possible that they would not clear the ground when we landed. If they came in contact with the ground (our steel mat runway was anything but level), Larue could be further injured—perhaps even killed.

I was lucky. The gun barrels did not hit the runway, and Larue was removed quickly and cared for on the spot before being taken to the hospital. He had been significantly psychologically stressed by the ordeal, and the Bomb Group's doctor kept him off flight status for a few months. He recovered completely and returned to fly with us again. He was part of the crew on our thirty-fourth mission.

My tail-gunner, Sergeant James F. Cook, was another cohesive member of the crew. Although all of the members of a bomber crew are important to its function as a fighting fortress, the tail-gunner is a sitting duck for enemy fighter aircraft. He is usually first to be shot at and first to shoot at enemy fighters that attack from the rear, a favorite tactic of the Germans' single-engine and twin-engine aircraft.

In the early stages of our combat tour, we found that the ME-109 was the deadliest aircraft that attacked from the rear. With its cannon firing through the propeller shaft and nose spinner, it could approach our formation from well astern of the squadron to commence its attack. As the ME-109 pilot closed in on a formation of B-17s or B-24s, he slowed slightly to reduce his rate of closure and then commenced firing at a particular bomber from the cannon's most effective range. The ME-109's explosive projectiles could destroy a B-17 or B-24 in a matter of seconds. Our bombers then returned fire with those of their fifty-caliber machine guns that could effectively reach the quadrant where the ME-109 was flying; but in most cases, the fifty-caliber rounds fell short, as the ME-109 pilots flew just beyond the maximum range of the fifty-caliber's trajectory. An ME-109 pilot could fly like this for many seconds, firing with cannon at first and then with machine guns. When he broke away from his pass astern, he'd dive beneath the bombers, turn back to the rear of the formation, and repeat his deadly attack.

"Je Reviens" was attacked from the rear many times by three or four such fighters flying in an echelon formation. They'd sit behind us for a few moments, all firing their cannons in unison at the beginning of their pass, when they were well out of our machine gun range.

Jim Cook was always the first crewman to experience the full brunt of these well-executed rear attacks. One cannot imagine the discomfort

and contortions the ball turret gunner and the tail-
gunner endured. Even with
their heated suit, booties, and
gloves working properly, and
wearing layers of insulating
clothing, they were still bit-
terly cold. I marveled at and
was humbled by the devotion
to their tasks, the steadfast
resolve and dedication to protecting their airplane and fellow crew members that the
tail gunner and ball turret
gunner always demonstrated.

The high degree of pro-
fessionalism, fine air discipline,
and conduct of my entire crew
was considered exemplary by

The "Wonder Crew" patch.

everyone, and we were referred to as "Je Reviens and its Wonder Crew."

A New German Fighter—The Me-292—Challenges US

To make it even more difficult to survive our bombing missions, the
German Luftwaffe introduced a new airplane. This formidable new fighter
(an interceptor) could tear through our formations at the unheard-of speed
of 540 miles an hour, firing its four thirty-millimeter Mark-108 cannons
or its twenty-four R-4M rockets as it attacked us from the rear. And soon
the pilots of these planes found that they got even better results firing their
rockets at us from the side. This new flying machine was the Messerschmitt ME-262-1A-2A fighter-bomber, with twin turbojet engines. It
was called the "Swallow" by the Germans because of its trim design. Its
devastating array of explosive firepower could destroy a B-17 quickly, and
because of its high speed and small silhouette, it was hard for us to hit.

When we were first attacked by ME-262's in the late fall of 1944, we
were all awed by their sleekness, speed, and maneuverability. Our intelligence people later told us that these first planes, ME-262A-1A's 2-A's,
were those of the Jagdverband 44, which was commanded by Major General Adolph Galland, the top German ace, and they were flown by the

highest-ranking and most expert pilots of the Luftwaffe. (This fact insured that the ME-262 fighter bomber would be even more capable and destructive in its attacks on our formation.)

After a few encounters, our gunners became accustomed to being pounced on by the ME-262's and learned the tactics the German pilots used. They were then able to concentrate on their own gunnery tactics, returning accurate fire and destroying many ME-262's. The pilots of the 332nd Fighter Group (the Tuskegee Airmen) and the other P-51 fighter escort groups also quickly devised ways to shoot down the elusive "Swallows."

A particularly destructive and personally devastating battle took place during a mission on March 22, 1945—the bombing of a large synthetic oil refinery in Ruhland, Germany, seventy-five miles south of Berlin— manifesting the destructive fire-power of the ME-262. Ruhland was defended by more than 200 German fighters, and the 483rd Bomb Group lost six of its twenty-eight B-17s, four of which were part of the 817th Bomb Squadron's formation. Most of them were destroyed by the thirty-millimeter cannons of the ME-262 fighters. The others were downed by very intense and accurate antiaircraft fire from within the target area.

Left: 483rd Bombardment Group (H) Insignia. *Right:* 817th Bombardment Squadron Insignia.

During this mission, I lost a good friend and crew member, Joseph F. Pirrone, the engineer and top turret gunner who was part of my crew on March 9, 1945, when our B-17 was severely damaged by antiaircraft fire on our thirty-fourth mission—to Graz, Austria. I was informed of Joe's death at the end of March, shortly after I returned from R&R at the Air Corps rest camp on the Isle of Capri. Joe was fatally wounded by a projectile from an ME-262 while flying with his regular crew, piloted by Carroll B. Skinner. The left wing, tail section, and top turret were badly damaged by the thirty-millimeter cannon fire; however, they were able to limp back to Sterparone.

Joe and I went through a lot together on our thirty-fourth mission, and it was saddening and difficult to comprehend that this gallant fellow had been killed such a short time after the ten of us had returned to our Bomb Group from Slovenia.

Some 483rd Bomb Group (H) Statistics

The 483rd Bomb Group (H) holds the record for:

1. Destroying the most ME-262's (three) on any one mission.
2. Destroying the most ME-262's (two) by one bomber's gunners on one mission.
3. Destroying the most ME-262's (seven) by one Bomb Group during the entire war.

Each combat crew member was required to fly thirty-five combat bombing missions as his tour of duty. Each mission flown to bomb a target and return to base constituted a mission.

For the first ten combat missions or so, all of my original crew flew together. After that, George Hong, my copilot, became squadron assistant operations officer. Bob Keno, my bombardier, became group lead bombardier. My left waist gunner, Ted Blake, became part of our squadron's photographic section. George Hong flew his required missions with me. Bob Keno flew only in the lead airplane on his missions. Ted Blake flew with me each time the airplane I flew was equipped with a high altitude bomb strike camera. Other people substituted in these positions when they were vacant.

I always flew Je Reviens when it was in condition to fly (had not been damaged on the previous mission and was being repaired). I sometimes flew other B-17s when I flew a Mickey ship or a camera ship.

9

Missions

The Red Rover Missions

In addition to our required thirty-five combat missions, we also flew two "Red Rover" missions. A Red Rover mission is one flown as a "supernumerary" bomber, normally one in each squadron. The supernumerary bomber fills a position left vacant because a plane has to drop out due to mechanical difficulties or other complications before reaching the IP. The Red Rover returns to the base after flying about two-thirds of the way to the target if no plane has left the formation by that point. On his return, he jettisons his bomb load over the Adriatic Sea so he won't land with live bombs on board.

In the two Red Rover missions we flew, we didn't return at the two-thirds point; we stayed with the formation even though no planes had been compelled to leave the formation. Both times, we continued on to the target with our squadron, dropped our bombs, and returned to the base with the Bomb Group. I made the decision to remain with the group because we were almost to the target by the time we reached the dropout point—and a short time away from accomplishing what we had risen at 0400 to do. Dropping out at that point would have been a terrible waste of energy, fuel, bombs, and the preparation work of our operations, ground maintenance, and service people. We had gone through a hazardous take-off and a long flight already—why not finish what we were all prepared to do?

The normal policy is that crews don't receive credit toward their required thirty-five missions for Red Rover missions, so we did not get mission credit for these two flights, and we were credited for just half the actual flight time involved in the missions. These extra missions were a gift by my crew and me to the total war effort.

The Night Mission—A Scary Story

We volunteered for one "lone wolf" mission (planes alone—not in formation). We thought it would be of service, interesting, and different. It was interesting, to say the least, but fraught with problems. The mission was to strike the railroad marshalling yards at Linz, Austria.

We were the first airplane to take off and were to fly highest—at a bombing altitude of 29,500 feet, as high as I could get *Je Reviens* to fly at its heavy weight. Our problems began when the number one engine was damaged over the target by a 105-millimeter antiaircraft shell, and I had to feather it.

Then we were stalked by two German night fighters after leaving the target area. These two planes—a JU-88 and a JU-188—were both subsequently shot down by an American P-61 Black Widow night fighter of the 422nd Night Fighter Squadron, whose pilots alerted us on the fighter frequency to the Germans' presence; they probably saved our lives. We American pilots actually saw the two German planes explode, even though we were flying on instruments in very thick clouds. I have since been in contact with several of the pilots from the 422nd NFS about this encounter and thanked them for their courageous work. It was a narrow escape!

Shortly after the night fighter incident, while flying over northeastern Italy in the Udine area, we were caught in the triangular beams of enemy searchlights. Of course, anytime you are confronted by searchlights, you can expect immediate accompanying antiaircraft fire. Instantly, we were surrounded by large flashes from the explosions of German eighty-eight-millimeter projectiles. As we were at a rather low altitude at that point—just 17,000 feet—we were sitting ducks, and the gunners knew it.

The flak was intense, but, fortunately for us, not too accurate; however, we did sustain some light damage before I could increase our airspeed and our rate of descent and hide in a cloud bank. With some additional luck, we would soon be over the Adriatic Sea west of Trieste, Slovenia, and things would calm down, letting us concentrate on getting home (and getting some breakfast—we were always hungry).

Upon arriving at our base, we found that the ground fog was much heavier than originally forecast, and the runway was shrouded in a low,

A flight of three "Special Operations" B-17s of the 483rd Bomb Group (H) — with no armament (turrets or machine guns) — en route to their mission destination. (Picture courtesy of Boeing.)

dense fog layer. As we were flying a "Mickey ship" (a B-17 equipped with a radar scope and other electronic devices for pinpointing locations), we were able to set up our inbound descent path and approach track by using radar to line up on the runway. For our approach descent (glide slope) to the proper altitude across the end of the steel mat runway, we used our "time out" from the end to make our standard rate "tear drop" turn inbound to the runway and a time rate of descent to our landing. It worked out well. Our landing was uneventful and smooth, even on three engines.

Je Reviens was the only B-17 from the 483rd Bomb Group that returned to our base from this mission. The others ended up at various airfields in southern Italy due to the fog and low fuel supplies after seven hours' flying time. Over the years, I have been asked many times to say which of my missions was the most difficult, and it's hard to say; but this lone wolf mission was certainly one of the scariest and most mysterious.

However, my thirty-fourth mission (the next to last combat mission I was required to fly) was the most interesting — and surely the most suspenseful, trying and life-threatening — of any I flew. Number thirty-four is engraved in my mind and in the minds of all the crew members who flew with me because of its amazing outcome and the almost insurmountable obstacles we overcame to survive.

10

The Thirty-Fourth Mission

The afternoon before a mission, a squadron operations crew duty sheet was posted on each squadron's tent street bulletin board. The information on this scheduling order included the mission, date, wake-up time, briefing time, the pilot's name, the aircraft number and position in the squadron's formation, the names of the other officers on the crew and their duty assignments, the names of the six enlisted crewmen and their duty assignments, and the names of other personnel scheduled to be on board (such as a cameraman or an observer).

The information posted on our squadron's bulletin board on the afternoon of March 8, 1945, stated that our thirty-forth mission would have an early start. We would be awakened at 0500 by our squadron's CQ to start the preliminaries required for the mission. My navigator and I would be the only members of our original crew who would be flying on the mission today. Normally, the pilot, copilot, navigator and bombardier of an original crew live together in the same tent, and fly all their missions together. However, since my original copilot had become Assistant Operations Officer and my original bombardier had become Group Lead Bombardier, they would not be flying on this mission.

My thirty-fourth combat bombing mission—the story of which I tell in this book—was flown with some crew members who were not members of my original crew.

Lieutenant Leslie Anton, flying as my co-pilot on this mission, was a "first pilot" and had his own crew. He arrived at the 483rd Bomb Group on November 7, 1944, and commenced flying combat missions a few days subsequent. He was flying with me on this mission to be checked out in the second element lead position, the position in our Squadron's formation which I usually flew. This mission on March 9, 1945, was the first and only time that Les Anton and I flew together. Considering the fact that he had his "Baptism of Fire" on that day with me, and survived, he had perhaps paid his dues for further trouble-free flights, during his remaining bombing missions in the air war over Europe. However, another important consideration is that Les was lucky—perhaps as "fate would have it, or the luck of the draw"—to be flying this mission with, in our view, the very best combat crew in the 483rd Bomb Group.

Lieutenant Robert R. Mahan was actually assigned to the Carroll B. Skinner crew as their regular bombardier. He was flying on this mission with me as a replacement bombardier. He was of help to me on this mission and on the ground in Yugoslavia, not only as an accomplished bombardier, but also as a good friend. His knowledge of the French language was a plus. I was able to take advantage of his French for some communications, as a few people with whom we came into contact in Yugoslavia (Slovenia) spoke French.

Sergeant Joseph F. Pirrone, flying on this mission as my replacement engineer/gunner, was also assigned to the Skinner crew as their regular engineer/gunner and usually flew with that crew. As Joe spoke Italian, he was another asset in Yugoslavia (Slovenia). We found that a large number of people in that part of Yugoslavia were of partial Italian descent, and spoke Italian as their second language. That fact made communicating somewhat less difficult. Joe's Italian language prowess, and also Bob's French, made our relationship with the Partisans and people in the area where we were easier to establish and more friendly.

Sergeant Raymond H. Goodwin, flying as my left waist gunner on this mission, had flown with numerous other crews during his combat tour. He was flying with me on this mission as a replacement right waist gunner.

"Second Element Lead"—A Brief Outline

To explain a bit of World War II Heavy Bomber formation flying, a brief description of the "second element lead" position, relative to where it is located in the Squadron's formation, is given here, so a picture can be formed as to where in the formation we were flying. The "lead airplane" flying in the Squadron's formation has two "wingmen" on the right and left wings of his airplane. These right and left wingmen normally fly an optimum distance of about sixty to eighty feet off of, and just behind, the lead airplane's wing tip. Placing these bombers in a tight formation of an inverted "V" produces an effective "bomb strike pattern," and affords the gunners of these bombers their maximum concentrated and protective fire power for their fifty caliber machine guns.

The "second element" of these bombers in the Squadron's formation is flying in the same type of an inverted "V" as the first inverted "V" lead element. This second "V" of the Squadron's formation optimally flies some fifty to sixty feet below the flight level of the first three bombers and "in trail" of the "lead airplane" at a distance of some seventy-five feet. The

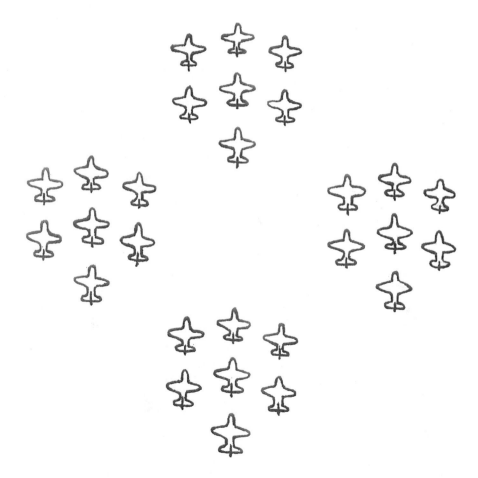

15th Air Force, 5th Wing, 483rd Bomb Group (H), 817th Bomb Squadron: 4-box group bombing formation (from above). Illustration by the author.

15th Air Force, 5th Wing, 483rd Bomb Group (H), 817th Bomb Squadron: 4-box group bombing formation (horizontal view).

seventh bomber in the Squadron's formation flies the same distance below and "in trail" of the "second element lead" airplane.

As usual for any mission, my navigator and I dressed in our full officer's uniform, including a tie, and were out of our tent before 0545 and on our way to breakfast at the officers' mess hall. From there we would proceed to our crew briefing. It was a very cold, dark morning as we walked with other members of the 817th Bomb Squadron down the squadron street between neat rows of sixteen-by-sixteen foot canvas tents and the brick/tent houses of our tent city.

The officers' mess hall at Sterparone was part of a very large barn complex previously used at the Sterparone wheat farm. It was actually part of a large, two-level milking barn. These buildings were huge, with high ceilings. They were made of field-stone and fire brick, stuccoed and painted white outside and inside. A number of the buildings were built to house farm animals, such as horses, cattle, sheep and swine. The thick walls meant that the animals could be easily housed there during the harsh winter months and fed inside.

Breakfast at the officers' mess invariably consisted of green scrambled (powdered) eggs, fried Spam, and very large, thick pieces of burned toast always accompanied by grape jelly, which was all washed down with a few cups of very strong GI coffee. After breakfast, we proceeded to the combat crew briefing hall where the briefing convened at 0700 sharp.

The Mission's Briefing Session

This briefing hall was also part of the group of barn buildings. Its domed ceiling was at least two stories high, and the building was at least sixty-five feet long and forty feet wide. The uneven floor was made of large field-stones. The acoustics in the hall left much to be desired, and we strained our ears to hear as the briefing officer and the others gave us vitally important information. Every crew member listened intently and took notes thoroughly. It was critically important to understand everything the first time.

Our seats, practical though uncomfortable, were large metal bomb fin shipping protectors made of heavy-gauge metal, and were extremely sturdy. They had four metal legs to hold and protect each bomb fin and its edges during shipping, and a strong, square, flat metal top, upon which we sat. The other square end of the unit had been unbolted and removed so the bomb fin could then be taken from its protective housing and later secured to the top end of a bomb. This large, sturdy metal fin would stabilize and guide the bomb during its long fall to the target.

The members of each crew who attended the briefing were the pilot, copilot, navigator, bombardier, radio operator, and perhaps a combat photographer attached to the crew. Each crew member played a specific role on board the B-17, and had to be able to execute his particular duty flawlessly. The briefing session was vitally important to each of them and necessary to allow the group to function as a unit. The success of the crew's mission and their survival depended on the philosophy that each of the crew's ten men must be completely "in tune" to properly carry out the tasks required of them. Each man went through the main briefings by the CO, the meteorologist and the briefing officer. After these group briefings, they paired off with their crew position counterparts for the individual briefing on their duties and functions on the crew.

At the briefing, each pilot received detailed information regarding take-off times, pilot names, and aircraft numbers in each position of the formation; which squadron would lead the 483rd Bomb Group; and the

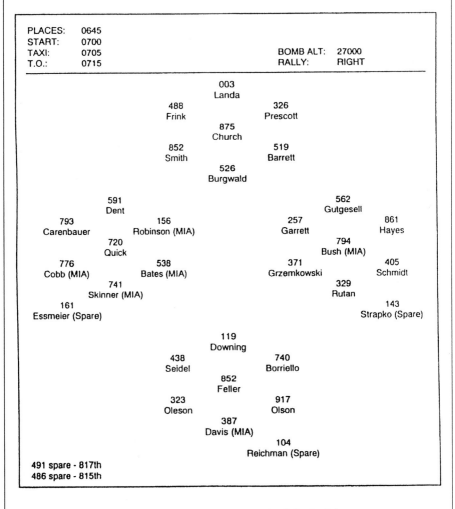

"Flimsie" for second mission to Ruhland, March 22, 1945. Three digit number indicates plane and position in formation, name indicates pilot. (MIA) refers to planes shot down.

PLACES:	0645		
START:	0700		
TAXI:	0705	BOMB ALT:	27000
T.O.:	0715	RALLY:	RIGHT

003
Landa

488   326
Frink   Prescott

875
Church

852   519
Smith   Barrett

526
Burgwald

591   562
Dent   Gutgesell

793   156   257   861
Carenbauer   Robinson (MIA)   Garrett   Hayes

720   794
Quick   Bush (MIA)

776   538   371   405
Cobb (MIA)   Bates (MIA)   Grzemkowski   Schmidt

741   329
Skinner (MIA)   Rutan

161   143
Essmeier (Spare)   Strapko (Spare)

119
Downing

438   740
Seidel   Borriello

852
Feller

323   917
Oleson   Olson

387
Davis (MIA)

104
Reichman (Spare)

491 spare - 817th
486 spare - 815th

Bomber Call:	Schoolroom	Russian Call:	Starfish
Escort Call:	Burglar	Russ. Rec. Signal	
Recall:	Skipper		1. Rock left wing
Weather Ship:	Front-room		2. Fire green flare

15th Air Force, 5th Wing, 483rd Bomb Group, 817th Bomb Squadron, Italy, 1944–1945: Typical Example of a "Flimsie" for second mission to Ruhlan–March 22, 1945.

time we were scheduled to start engines and taxi. All this information and the various call signs would be listed on a flimsy. Such information would include: the fighter escort, the Russian call sign and Russian recognition signal, the bomber call, the weather aircraft and the mission recall signal.

On the main wall at the end of the grand briefing hall was a very large color wall map of Europe shrouded by a drawn curtain that initially concealed the route and target information about the mission to be flown. Below the map was a stage used by the briefing officers. The first portion of a session was always a chilling description of our task for the day. As the briefing officer opened the curtain, there would come a sigh from the men, as they quickly studied the map. It was always a sobering revelation.

The first thing everyone noticed was the target itself circled in red, then the wide red and blue tape lines, and finally the irregular, somewhat circular patterns outlined in red that were all over the map. The wide red tape lines from Sterparone to the target indicated the flight path of the "first wave," or "red force," including the primary target's initial point (IP) and the bomb run flight path to the target itself. The red tape lines continued beyond the target to indicate the direction of the "rally turn" after the bomb release and our flight path away from the target area, as well as our intended route of flight back to our base. The wide blue tape lines depicted the same information about the second wave, the "blue force." Usually, the blue force bombed a different target from the red force, although sometimes they bombed the same target from a different IP and bomb run track at a later time, and at a different altitude.

We were told today that the 483rd Bomb Group would launch forty-two bombers—twenty-one in the first wave and twenty-one in the second wave. This type of operation was called "maximum force" or "maximum effort."

The irregular red circular patterns on the map marked known locations of German antiaircraft batteries—so-called "flak" locations. This vital "flak battery" location information was gathered from very reliable sources. They could have been photographed, located by allied agents living underground in the area, or pinpointed by triangulation of a "Mickey ship" or an Allied bomber or fighter that had been fired upon by one of the batteries (with the pilot, navigator, or bombardier then plotting the location on a map to be revealed at a later debriefing session). The flak battery outlines on the map contained large numbers denoting the estimated number of antiaircraft guns and their caliber. Each could have as few as fifteen or twenty medium and heavy caliber guns, or as many as eight hundred heavy millimeter guns at the site or in other batteries circling the target. The route of flight to and from a target was based upon avoiding, as much as possible, flying over these known antiaircraft gun emplacements.

The guns at and immediately surrounding a target, of course, were a danger we couldn't avoid.

The crews intently scrutinized the locations of the flak batteries and hoped that their flight paths would skirt them all. They continued studying the map, visually tracing the plotted lines to the target and back again. They cross-checked the data with their mission flimsies, and reviewed the various "call signs" to be used during the day.

I'm sure each crew member was saying to himself: "Will we make it though this day? It really looks like a tough one." We all entertained the same thought—getting home. These young men knew only too well that a combat bombing mission into any part of the heart of the German Third Reich was not just another day's work.

Once the crew members had studied the maps, the lengthy mission briefing commenced. First our CO gave his usual pep talk. He told us he'd be waiting for us on our return, and wished us good luck. Next, the briefing officer outlined our route of flight in detail, and gave us the estimated flight time to the target and back to base. He described the IP (initial point)—the place at which our formation would turn to the selected navigational heading (track) for its bomb run to the target—and discussed the squadron's "in trail" run to the target. He reviewed the reason for the selected heading to the target (either upwind or downwind) and the projected length of time for the bomb run. The estimated duration of the bomb run was always of deep concern to the crews because during this period they were the most defenseless.

Today was to be somewhat of a "cross tail wind"—a bomb run almost downwind—which made us happy. Winds at high altitude (for example, at twenty-six thousand feet) can be very strong, perhaps a hundred miles an hour or more. In such conditions, a normal downwind ground speed of over three hundred miles an hour is reduced to two hundred miles an hour or less when flying into such a strong head wind. Because flying upwind on a bomb run makes the time from the IP to the bomb release point much longer than flying downwind, our officers had to sell us on upwind missions (since using the "into the wind" approach to a target means that the flak gunners will have more time to target the bombers on their bomb run). Of course, upwind bomb runs do have advantages as well as disadvantages. An advantage is that the bombardiers have more time to synchronize their Norden bomb sights to the target drop point, assuring a more accurate bomb strike pattern and resulting in more destruction.

The briefing officer explained in detail our turn away from the target after the bombs were released and the route back to our base. This turn is a very important flight maneuver and must be done correctly to ensure everyone's safety and to keep the group formation close together.

The bombing altitude over the target today was to be twenty-six thousand feet. The Bruck Main Station would be bombed by visual reference only.

The Bomb Run

On a bomb run, the pilot concentrates on keeping the airplane on a stable course with no variations of any sort—no change in altitude, heading, speed, or yaw is allowed, whether a pilot or the auto-pilot/bombsight is flying the airplane. One reason for this precision is that the bombardier must be able to program his Norden bombsight from a stable platform so that at "bombs away," all of the flight parameters will have been constant and the bomb load will hit the target as programmed.

Of course, the German antiaircraft gunners on the ground know full well that bombers will not move from their intended flight paths. They know that pilots will not take evasive action to avoid being hit by flak. This means that German gunners could track a squadron or an individual airplane and continually correct fire to the bomber's heading, altitude, and speed until they were right on target.

During a bomb run, German fighters intercepting our planes will not attack us at that time, as they too could be knocked down by the heavily concentrated and accurate barrage of ground fire. They did, however, attack us while we were en route to our IP and after we had dropped our bombs and started the steep descending turn away from the target area, known as the "rally." The rally turn was made to a pre-determined heading, which in most cases was the first of several homeward-bound headings for the group. During this turn away from the target, the entire group was vulnerable to heavy damage from cannon and machine gun fire from attacking German fighters. Since the rally required an immediate and rather steep high-speed descending turn, some bombers might be out of their usual tight formation. Besides making individual planes easier to hit, a loose formation also reduced the overall concentration of firepower from the B-17's thirteen fifty caliber machine guns.

The briefing officer told us that the usual policy for releasing the bomb loads would not be followed on this mission. The bombers normally release their bomb loads at the same instant the lead airplane in each squadron releases its bomb load. Today, we learned, the "waves in trail" (squadrons in trail) formation would be flown from the IP to the target rather than the usual four-squadron box formation.

When flying a four-squadron box formation, to assure the precise timing of the simultaneous bomb release, an electronic system of light signal transmissions was often employed. The light signal would emanate from the lead bombardier's bomb-sight mechanism and would be transmitted instantaneously to all of the other airplanes in the squadron's formation. An amber light on each bombardier's radio panel in the nose compartment would glow, informing the bombardiers that the squadron's lead airplane was releasing its bomb load. This transmission also illuminated an amber light on each pilot's instrument panel to inform him that the lead airplane had released its bombs, and that his bomb load should be on its way, so that he would be prepared to turn away from the target immediately. Even though this light signal system was used, each bombardier programmed his individual bomb-sight to release his bomb load as he normally would on any bomb run. This was a safeguard in case there was a failure of the light signal system.

As our briefing continued, we were told the number and caliber of antiaircraft guns in the area we would be flying over, and the approximate number and types of enemy fighter aircraft which could be expected to attack our formation, both en route to the target and in the target area. In addition, the briefing officer gave us the rendezvous time with our escort fighters and the approximate location and altitude at which we should expect them to join us. We were also given the number of escort fighters, the group and squadron they were from, their identifying markings, and their "call sign." Each bomber group had escort fighters assigned to it to provide protection against enemy aircraft during the mission. A call sign was designated for the "top cover" fighter umbrella to identify the bombers they would escort. When a bomber was damaged and forced to drop out of the formation (becoming a straggler), it could request help by radio from an escort fighter using the call sign to identify itself. The call sign was usually one word, such as lobo, linebacker, lofty, shadow, racer, etc.

We were shown slides of emergency landing areas available for our use in southwestern Yugoslavia. These emergency landing strips sometimes consisted simply of a plowed field or landing areas in Slovenia and Croatia that had been used before the war. These landing strips were all in German-occupied territory. However, because the Yugoslav Partisan Army

(Tito's people) had substantial strength in some of these areas, the chances for rescue by friendly forces made them acceptable for use. We studied the location and views of these emergency landing areas thoroughly. If one of the B-17s in our group was not able to continue its return flight across the Adriatic Sea to Italy, it might need to make an emergency landing on one of these fields or one of the many airfields in eastern Italy's coastal areas that were available for emergency landings.

Pilots considered carefully what they would do if their plane was damaged too heavily to return to base. An emergency landing, rather than bailing out, was required if any crew members were wounded. However, emergency landings and bailouts were a last resort. Flight crews of damaged bombers used every method available to them to keep the planes in the air. On many combat missions pilots flew on only two engines, the other two having been rendered inoperative because of severe damage from enemy fire.

Bomber pilots learned to keep their planes in the air despite devastating damage—hundreds of holes torn in the fuselage; vertical fins and rudders shot away; horizontal stabilizers so severely damaged that the airplane was nearly unusable. I have observed B-17s in our group still flying with a section of the nose blown away. Some had holes in the fuselage large enough to drive a jeep through, and they, too, continued to fly. When, despite all efforts, a plane is too damaged to fly or even to crash land, the pilot must know how to get his crew to bail out safely.

Addressing another item, the briefing officer would advise the "Red Rover" crews of their "drop out time" and the geographical point at which they would begin to return to base. "Red Rovers" were one or two extra bombers that flew with the squadron on a mission. They remained with the group up to a given time. If none of the group had had to abort the formation up to that point, the Red Rovers would return to base.

We were told the size and type of bombs we would be dropping. The bomb load varied from mission to mission. It could be five-hundred-pound bombs, or one-thousand-pound bombs, or two-thousand-pound bombs. On some missions, they would be all incendiary bombs.

The fuses in the large bombs could also vary. There were direct impact, delayed action, and booby-trap fuses. The booby-trap fuse caused the bomb to explode if someone attempted to disarm it by extracting the nose fuse. Turning it as little as one quarter of a turn would cause it to explode.

On this mission, each plane would carry twelve five-hundred-pound bombs.

The briefing officer reviewed fuel loads, fuel consumption (estimated amount to be consumed en route to our target), and the expected fuel remaining for the return flight to the base.

Meterology

Now it is time to talk about the weather. The chief meteorologist briefed the crews on the weather expected en route to the mission, over and in the target area, and at our base when we returned.

Each day in the late evening or very early hours of the morning, a group's B-17 weather ship flew to the target area for that day, flying the same route we would later use in order to compile a report of the exact weather our mission would encounter. The weather gathering B-17s would normally take off on their mission around midnight, fly to the target, and return with their report in time for the regular mission's briefing session. They were fully crewed, fully armed and ready to fight if attacked—and often they were. Because they carried no bomb load, they were very fast-flying airplanes, posing a dilemma for German night fighters.

Icing conditions en route to the target were always discussed in detail, as severe icing problems for the engines, wings and tail surfaces could create an additional hazard for the pilots to deal with. We were constantly on the alert for any signs of icing while flying missions.

Assembling

The next part of our briefing addressed assembling and routing the hundreds of bombers of the Fifth Wing and the many other four-engine bomber groups of the 15th Air Force flying this day. Each group was assigned a time for its take-off and a time and altitude at which to cross the radio assembly beacon at Lake Lesina before proceeding to the mission's target. Crossing the assembly beacon at exactly the right time and altitude was key to safely getting these hundreds of large airplanes where they should be. Each group had to fit into the total formation of B-17s or B-24s in its correct place in the scheme of the battle plan. Each had to be exactly in position behind the bomb group scheduled to cross the beacon immediately ahead of them.

Each group's formation climbed toward its target on a different flight track and at a different altitude so that each succeeding group flew through stable air—undisturbed, it was hoped, by the formation flying directly in front of it (because a pilot flying a heavy bomber in close formation can experience acute control problems if the air is unstable or turbulent).

Vapor trails (contrails) can also produce difficult flight conditions for heavy bombers. They are often created by escort fighters flying in front of the bomber formation and crossing their paths at high altitude—this is particularly true in the case of a P-38, which leaves two contrails, or "double bumps." Flying into one of these contrails at a very high altitude is somewhat like flying into the instability of clear air turbulence.

As the hundreds of B-17 and B-24 bombers of the 15th Air Force climbed en route to their targets, the sky was filled with airplanes, as far as the eye could see. It was a beautiful, awesome sight to behold. At times, as their altitudes became higher, climbing in the thin, crisp, cold air of a clear day, one could literally see over a thousand vapor trails (contrails) being generated at different altitudes by the engine exhausts of these magnificent big bombers.

Our commanding officer was a stickler for perfect formation flying. He often flew as an observer on our bombing missions, watched every airplane's formation flying during the entire flight, and critiqued the pilots on their formation flying both during the mission and on their return. To further hone the capabilities of his "Flying Circus" (as we were affectionately known in the 5th Wing), our C.O. often parked his Jeep off the side of the *approach end* of our runway to observe our formation breakup (maneuvers) and landing techniques at the end of the mission. His Jeep was equipped with tower/aircraft radio communications so that he could converse with each pilot if necessary.

During landings on return to base, three B-17s were on the runway at one time: one touching down, one rolling out in the middle, and the third preparing to turn off at the end of runway, as it completed its landing roll. Every airplane in the formation except those that were falling apart because of combat damage participated in this formation breakup and landing exercise—even those with one engine inoperative. Our landing procedures were truly a beautiful sight to behold—a very graceful and moving ritual of flight. We were proud of our bomb group.

To further enhance our formation flying and bombing technique, we practiced high-altitude bombing on a small, rocky, uninhabited island well off the Italian coast in the Adriatic Sea. At times we thought that this practice formation bombing was entirely unnecessary—a waste of time and money in a war zone. However, maybe it kept all of us young tigers on our toes and out of mischief. It kept our minds off the rainwater in our tents, the periodic visit of snakes and other critters, the lack of hot water for bathing, the green powdered eggs and Spam for breakfast, and even the mud or snow up to our knees.

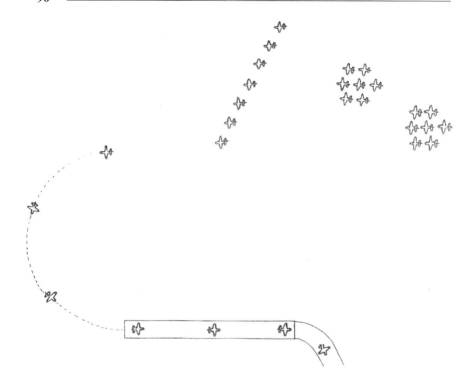

The Cities of Bruck and Graz

Both Bruck and Graz, Austria, are located on the Mur River. The Mur flows southeastward from its origin high in the Salzburg Alps near Wald, Austria, to the large valley of the eastern Austrian Alps that runs from Bruck to Graz. Upon reaching Bruck de Mur, as the city is officially called, the Mur turns in a more southerly direction and continues down through the valley past Graz, flowing southward close to Maribor, Slovenia, and then through eastern Croatia. The valleys of the Mur form a linkage between most of the major cities in Austria's rugged eastern region, such as Vienna, Wiener-Neustadt, Salzburg, Loben, Bruck, Graz, Klagenfurt and Villach. The valleys also contain primary railroad lines and major roadways.

The rail yards at Bruck were a very important link in the far-reaching logistical support system of railroads and highways between the German homeland production facilities and their military occupation operations to the east, southeast, and south. Graz, Bruck's sister city a few miles to the south, was considered even more important than Bruck.

The German Armed Forces occupied many of the countries in this area of southeastern Europe—such as Hungary, Romania, Bulgaria, Yugoslavia, Albania, and Greece—and supply of these forces was dependent upon the rail and truck routes through Austria from Germany. Germany required

Opposite top: Overhead view, Lead Squadron, No. 2 Squadron, No. 3 Squadron, No. 4 Squadron. Four squadron combat box formation breakup upon returning to base—breakup and landing procedures. The lead squadron is first to break up, echelon and land. During these landing maneuvers there will always be three B-17s on the runway at the same time—one B-17 just completing its landing roll and proceeding to turn-off at the end of the runway, one B-17 on its landing roll in the center of the runway, and one B-17 just touching down at the approached end of the runway. The remaining three B-17s of this squadron are flying on their descending left turn in their approach landing pattern. The second squadron has formed its staggered echelon, in preparation to commence its peel-off into its landing maneuver. The other two squadrons will circle the base in a left hand flight pattern at 2,000 feet and will move into a squadrons-in-trail pattern as they arrive on their downwind leg. For their landings, they will execute their landing maneuvers in the same manner as the previous squadrons have done. The total time for the 4 box formation to fully complete its landing procedure is about twenty minutes. World War II, Italy, European Theater, 1944–1945. 15th Air Force, 5th Wing, 483rd Bomb Group (H): 817th Squadron, 8116th Squadron, 815th Squadron, 840th Squadron. Drawing not to scale. *Bottom:* B-17s of the 840th Bomb Squadron—yellow cowlings and red rudders—(in echelon formation) preparing to "peel off" for landing at Sterparone after returning from a bombing mission. (Picture courtesy of Boeing.)

large volumes of every conceivable type of petroleum product to supply its forces. Crude oil, of course, was the basis for these products, but Germany itself could not begin to supply all the crude oil or refined products the forces needed. It depended on the crude oil of nations with oil fields and refineries for its petroleum products.

Hitler invaded, conquered, and occupied nations that possessed raw materials needed to further his plans for military conquest. Two such nations were Romania and Hungary, which had large amounts of crude oil and refineries for producing the petroleum products Hitler desperately needed. In Romania, the Polesti oil fields and a large oil refinery located just a few miles north of the capital city of Bucharest became the apple of Hitler's eye. Romania was soon occupied by the Third Reich, and Polesti oil was shipped by rail to refineries in Germany and German-occupied countries of central and western Europe.

The constant flow of these petroleum products to the many German military distribution centers was of critical importance to the Third Reich. Even a few days' delay could spell disaster for the German military's warfighting capabilities. The railroad lines, storage depots, main stations, marshalling yards, and shops of Graz, Bruck, Linz, and Vienna, Austria, were all of critical importance in conveying oil to the distribution centers, and therefore they were prime targets for the 15th Air Force's "saturation bombing" campaign. We wanted these facilities put out of business.

The 483rd Bomb Group attacked the Graz rail yards five times, the Bruck rail facilities several times, and the Linz marshalling yards thirteen times; but by far our largest efforts were aimed at the enormous marshalling yards in Vienna, one of the most heavily and fiercely defended targets in all of Europe during World War II. Vienna's facilities possessed the capability of routing war materials in all directions, and, in particular, to Germany itself. The next most important rail target was Linz, which also had broad rail routing capabilities and was able to ship directly to Germany.

Graz, Linz, and Vienna were "choke points" on this route. In addition to attacking these transportation facilities in the southern part of Austria, the 483rd Bomb Group bombed the large oil refinery at Polesti, Romania, seven times. We also attacked other petroleum-related facilities in Romania—such as marshalling yards, warehouses, goods depots, and vital railroad bridges. We attacked the same types of targets in Hungary, in addition to the refineries in the Budapest area, for a total of sixteen missions.

The bomb strikes carried out in Romania and Hungary were intended to destroy the Germans' ability to obtain petroleum at its source, well before they reached the Graz, Bruck, Linz, or Vienna rail terminals. Every other heavy bomber group—B-17s and B-24s—of the 15th Air Force struck these same targets over and over again, and the entire 15th Air Force also attacked scores of other targets in Europe, some of them as far north as Berlin. For example, the 483rd Bomb Group bombed the heavy tank works on the outskirts of Berlin on March 24, 1945, with devastating damage to the factory.

11

Dressing for the Occasion

When the briefing sessions concluded, we were transported to our supply building, where we checked out our A-12 bag and other equipment needed for the mission. The A-12 bag was a large, long, heavy-duty olive drab canvas bag with a sturdy metal zipper across the top and two strap type handles at the top—ideal for carrying all our vital combat gear. Each crewman stored his bag in a location on board that was readily accessible to his crew station.

When initially arriving at the 483rd Bomb Group, each of us was issued two oxygen masks custom-fitted to our face so that they fit perfectly and comfortably under all combat conditions. At high altitudes, a poorly fitting mask could leak, causing anoxia and quite possibly death in a very short time. These precious masks were thoroughly cleaned, checked and serviced by supply personnel after each combat or training mission and then stored safely so they'd be ready for the crew member's next flight.

Our A-12 bag also contained three pairs of gloves. One pair was made of sturdy gray felt and was electrically heated. These gloves were worn next to the skin and were attached by a wrist plug, connected to the central wiring system of the heated suit we wore. The second pair of gloves was made of tightly knit silk. They were worn over the felt gloves to help retain the heat they generated. The third pair was made of fleece-lined leather and was worn over the other two sets.

The two-piece heavy flannel heated suit and heated booties were also essential parts of our flight clothing, as the temperatures at very high altitudes could range from thirty to sixty degrees below zero, and without the warmth of the heated suit, we would soon freeze to death. Each battle-station control panel had an electrical outlet cord to which we connected our main heated suit cord.

As we boarded the airplane prior to the pre-engine start alert time we donned the heated suit over our long johns, then redressed in our regular uniform and gabardine jump suit for starters. Next came a heavy fleece-lined leather jacket. Over that we were required to wear a bright yellow Mae West life vest from take-off until after crossing the Adriatic Sea, outbound, and then again when crossing the Adriatic on return to base in case we were attacked by German fighters based in Northern Italy or Yugoslavia. Such an attack could result in having to "ditch" the airplane in the Adriatic.

Each of us also wore a flak suit made of sections of hardened steel plate sewn between two pieces of canvas. It clipped together at the shoulder, and hung down in front and back—the forerunner of today's bullet-proof vest. We donned our flak suits and helmets just prior to reaching the IP, and removed them when well out of the target area, heading home.

Each man was also issued two parachutes. One was a slim backpack type with a twenty-six-foot canopy; it was part of the regular parachute harness. It was a back-up in case the main chute was damaged or failed to open. The main parachute was a snap-on chest pack type. It had a twenty-eight-foot canopy and was kept close to a crewman's battle station. At the signal to bail out, we could easily clip it to the large rings on the front of our chute harness, and out of the airplane we'd go.

We also wore large, heavy, hardened steel flak helmets during fighter attacks and while in target areas. The flak helmets had a curved extension at the back of the head that protected the neck and had large metal ear flaps that covered the ears and the sides of the head.

On our feet we wore heavy wool knit socks over our other socks and our heated booties, and then fleece-lined leather high-top flying boots with rubber soles and rubber lower sections. They zipped up the front for a secure fit. These boots, for the most part, kept our feet warm; but we were warned that if we had to bail out they could fall off when our parachute opened, meaning we would have nothing on our feet when we landed. The proposed procedure to remedy walking barefoot through a foreign country, for who knows how long, was to make certain, just prior to jumping, that you tied your GI high top shoes together, and that they were clipped to one of the lower rings of our parachute harness for safe-keeping.

Finally, each man other than the pilot, co-pilot, navigator and bombardier was issued a coverall-type fleece-lined leather pantsuit. The legs were long enough to come down over the tops of the flying boots, and the top was high enough so that the chest was well covered.

Each crew member wore a fleece-lined leather flight helmet that contained earphones for radio communication. The helmet was equipped with goggles, almost like a face mask for scuba diving, that were worn mostly by the gunners for protection from the cold temperatures and wind, as well as for eye and face protection from smoke or fire on board the airplane resulting from enemy fire.

You may wonder how we were able to move about and perform our duties while wearing all of this heavy and cumbersome clothing and gear. In fact, it was very difficult. But we realized that it was vitally necessary to our survival.

Each of us also carried two escape kits in our jumpsuit's pant-leg pocket. The kits were packed in pliable plastic boxes about the size of a thick five by eight paperback book. The top cover of this container came down a third of the way over the bottom portion, and the two halves were sealed with waterproof clear tape. The top portion was large enough to be used as a drinking cup, if needed, while on the ground. These unique escape kits contained a marvelous array of items we could use while escaping from or evading the enemy: Silk maps of the countries we would be flying over; a small compass; fifty-five dollars in American gold seal currency; sulfa powder and other medications; morphine syringes; bandages; adhesive tape; photographs of the individual in a suit and tie for use in making identifications cards or a passport; matches sealed in a waterproof container; hard candy; water purification pills; and a few other items personally chosen by each man. (The kit's small compass, housed in a brass case about the size of a man's thumbnail, had luminous compass points and a red-tipped needle. It was designed to be swallowed if necessary and retrieved at a later time. The kit's detailed thirty-by-thirty inch silk maps were printed in color on both sides. The silk was so fine that each map could easily be folded to about four inches to fit in a uniform shirt pocket. Hundreds of combat air crew members used them to evade and escape after being shot down in enemy territory.)

Each crewman wore a Colt military 45 caliber automatic sidearm in a chest holster, with two extra clips of ammunition in addition to a full clip in the weapon. We also carried a trench knife in a scabbard attached to our webbed belt, chocolate candy bars, chewing gum, cigarettes, a lighter and matches (if we smoked), and two partial rolls of toilet paper.

Now dressed, briefed and armed, we were ready to fly.

12

Armed and Ready for the Day Ahead

After we checked out our gear from the squadron supply building, we were driven to our airplane to begin our final preparations for the mission. I named our plane, a lustrous silver B-17G, "Je Reviens" ("I Shall Return")—after a perfume my mother wore. The plane's official number was 44–6437.

Our crew chief was a wonderful fellow and a terrific mechanic. He cared for our B-17 like a mother would care for her child. Whether it needed an engine, a wheel and main gear strut, hydraulics, electronics, radio, fuselage repairs because of bullet and flak holes, or a new turbo-supercharger, he and his men did the work and had the airplane ready for our next mission. I know that at times he worked all night and slept near the airplane (or even in it) as it sat on its hardstand—a large key-shaped area of hard-packed gravel topped by steel matting located off the main taxi strip, where planes parked, ready for their next mission. The mechanics were one of the secrets of our success in surviving thirty-seven missions over enemy territory.

Well before we arrived at the airplane, this maintenance crew would have methodically checked out the airplane's engines, turbo-superchargers, propellers, hydraulics, oxygen system, and radios, and pre-flighted the engines. Having the engines warm and ready for a moment's start was a necessity in cold weather, and pre-flighting them meant that the engine oil was warm and fluid so that they could easily be started again with expediency, relieving the flight crew of the time-consuming procedure of diluting the cold engine oil with fuel prior to starting. Our mechanics were jewels.

97

Our procedure for starting each mission was the same: When we arrived at the airplane, I gathered my crew and gave them my personal briefing. I then asked each man about his readiness and whether he had encountered any difficulties or needed anything before we boarded. Once on board, each crewman pre-flighted his station, stowed his gear, and prepared for the engine start, taxi, and take-off. Meanwhile, I conducted a walk-around check of the exterior of the airplane and discussed the log-book and maintenance work with our crew chief. Then I climbed on board, stowed my gear, and assisted the copilot in pre-flighting the cockpit. We completed the cockpit checklist and the before-engines-start check list down to the "start engines" line. Once all of these things were accomplished, we sat in the cockpit and waited for our assigned engine start time to be confirmed by a green flare from the control tower. As soon as our engines were running, we completed the check list and prepared to taxi to the runway.

On this, our thirty-fourth mission, Je Reviens would follow the number three B-17 in our squadron, whose tail number and formation position were indicated on the mission's flimsy. We would be the fourth to line up in position on the runway.

Flares from the Control Tower

Signal flares were fired—or light signals shown—from the base air traffic control tower to tell us when to start our engines, when to taxi, and when to take off. Although our flimsies contained the same information, the flares allowed everyone to see when each plane had been signaled to take off, and were the official signal to go in case the information on the flimsies had been updated. The flares were used in place of radio communications for obvious security reasons—Italy was an active combat zone in every aspect.

The first green flare fired was the start-engines notice. The second green flare told us to commence taxiing for take-off. Another green light, flashed after all of a group's airplanes were on the taxi strips with their engines running and in their proper departure sequence, would indicate to the squadron in position on the runway that they were cleared to commence take-offs at thirty-second intervals. An amber or yellow flare told pilots to immediately hold their airplanes wherever they were, no mater what they were doing. Finally, a red flare announced that the mission had been scrubbed and that pilots should return their planes to their hard stands and shut down the engines. In other words, it's all over for the day.

The Germans Were Aware of Our Presence

On some missions, while we awaited the start-engines flare, we tuned in our low-frequency radio to the German *Axis Sally* broadcast. She would tell us that the Germans knew that we, the 15th Air Force's big bombers, were coming to bomb one of their installations today, that their very efficient German antiaircraft gunners and fighter pilots would be waiting for us, and that they would certainly destroy us in the air. Sometimes she named the 483rd Bomb Group specifically, or even correctly named the target for the day's mission. When this happened, we would "stand down" the mission—cancel it altogether. How the Germans obtained this information is anyone's guess.

13

The First Wave
(Red Force)

The 815th Bomb Squadron will be the lead squadron in the group's formation. Because they will "lead" the 483rd Bomb Group on this mission, they will be the first airplanes to taxi to and line up on the runway in preparation for take-off.

The 817th Bomb Squadron will be the second Squadron to take off. Hence, we will be on the taxi strip close to the end of the runway, to move into position for take off immediately after the 815th's last B-17 is rolling down the runway.

The 815th Squadron and each successive Squadron will line up in position on the runway in a series of inverted "V" formations. The first airplane of the "V" formation of three B-17s will taxi down the center line of the runway just far enough so that the remaining airplanes in the squadron's formation will have space to "form up" beside and behind him. The number "two" airplane (the lead airplane's right wing man) in the formation will taxi up on the right side of the lead airplane, so that his left wing is positioned just slightly behind the lead airplane's right wing. The wings of the two airplanes will actually be paralleling each other. The third B-17 in the first "V" (the lead airplane's left wing man) will place himself in the same position to the left side of the lead airplane as the right wing man had positioned himself on its right side. The fourth B-17 of the 815th Squadron would follow the first three airplanes onto the runway, lining up directly behind the lead airplane—and so close to the lead airplane that the nose of his airplane is just a few feet behind its tail. The other two, or three, B-17s would place themselves in the same

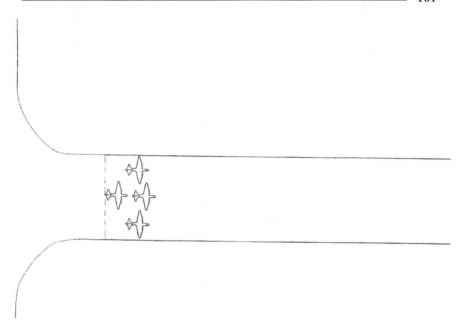

Squadron runway lineup prior to takeoff (four B-17 Flying Fortresses). The takeoff interval between airplanes is thirty seconds. Drawing not to scale.

positions as the first three had—if the Squadron were to have six or seven airplanes in it instead of just four.

As there would only be four B-17s in the 815th Bomb Squadron flying in this "first wave" of today's operation, these four airplanes in position on the runway would not take up much of the total runway in their close formation. As one can easily visualize, the reason for this very tight fit of an entire Squadron on the runway at one time is to preserve as much runway in front of them as is possible for their take-off run.

As the scheduled take-off time for the 815th Squadron approaches, all four of these B-17s will set their throttles for "take off power" to be prepared for immediate brake release at the control tower's signal to commence take-off. When these airplanes are cleared to go, they will each execute their take-offs at thirty second intervals.

There is the green light signal from the control tower—the 815th is cleared to go. The four B-17s of the 815th Squadron are now on their way down our six-thousand-foot runway at just a minute or so before 0700, to execute their take-off join up procedure and circle the base, awaiting the other three squadrons of the group to join them. At that same time, our six B-17s of the 817th Squadron are taxiing into position on the runway immediately behind them. Within five or six minutes, we are all in position on the runway and ready for take-off. We are now just waiting for the green light from the tower to clear us to go.

This day of March 9, 1945, our thirty-fourth combat bombing mission, was about to get underway. In a very few seconds, there were twenty-four Wright R-1820–97, 1200 horsepower engines of the 817th Squadron's six B-17s roaring at full take-off power, at just seven minutes or so after 0700.

14

The Takeoff

Every takeoff for a bombing mission is difficult, demanding, and precarious—there are no exceptions—and early morning humid air makes taking off especially difficult. Takeoff difficulties are not caused by any design deficiency of the B-17, but by insufficient wind, so that prop wash— unstable air generated by the propellers of other airplanes—is not dissipated and remains over the runway for some time. As more B-17s—each with four engines roaring—travel down the runway, this unstable air problem becomes worse and worse. As I sat in the cockpit waiting to take off, I witnessed the difficulties experienced by the pilots just ahead of me and knew that conditions would be even worse when my turn came.

It was no fun to watch as each airplane lumbered down the uneven steel mat runway through turbulent air while trying to increase its speed and eventually take off. At times I even held my breath, fearful of the outcome of some of the pilots' efforts. And even after takeoff, a pilot was not home free—the flight could be momentary, and the airplane might, in its unstable condition, settle back down to the runway in a graceless and dangerous fashion. As each airplane accelerates down the runway, pilots try to maintain their original position relative to the side and center line of the runway in order to expose the airplane to less prop wash created by the airplanes taking off ahead of them.

The Valley, A Welcome Setting

Our bomb group's base was located on a plateau just above the lower portion of the Foggia Valley, which stretched to the southeast. This plateau

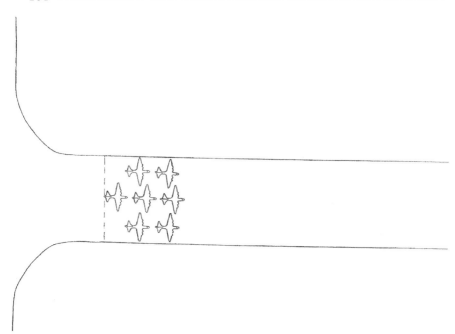

Squadron runway lineup prior to takeoff (seven B-17 Flying Fortresses). The takeoff interval between airplanes is thirty seconds. Drawing not to scale.

was five to seven hundred feet above the valley floor, and the southeast edge of the runway was very close to the edge of the cliff that fell to the valley below. This geography created something of a safety net; if an airplane was just barely flying as it crossed the end of the runway, the drop of a few hundred feet toward the valley floor was just enough to allow the pilot to stabilize his flight, increase his airspeed, and commence climbing. Still, it was alarming to see airplanes suddenly disappear from sight, sinking below the level of the runway's end. Each time it happened, our hearts sank as we feared the possible explosion of a fully combat-loaded B-17. Happily, as I recall, that tragedy never happened.

Other Takeoff Topics

The takeoff part of a mission was only the first in a long list of heart-in-your-mouth experiences we pilots encountered each day. Even though we knew our B-17s inside and out and most of us by now had become well-seasoned combat pilots (if such a thing is possible). We had to be aware of our conditions and be ready to make decisions instantaneously.

At takeoff, for example, we were very much aware that we carried more weight than the B-17 was designed for because we packed a few extra items we considered necessary:

Extra Fuel

Every pilot wanted to be certain that he had more than enough fuel to fly to the target and back to the base, and most missions were of such extended duration that the fuel tanks were always filled to maximum capacity at takeoff. This way the pilot was covered in case of longer than normal climbs or having to fly with one or more engines inoperative, which meant drawing more power (and therefore more fuel) from the good engines to keep the airplane in the air. Taking off with full fuel tanks also provided a buffer in case fuel was lost from tanks damaged by enemy fire, or fuel transfers could not take place.

Extra Machine-Gun Barrels

Extra fifty-caliber machine-gun barrels—usually extra barrels for eleven of the thirteen fifty-caliber guns.

Flak Protection

Small pieces of steel runway matting were placed under the radio operator's and waist gunners' feet to protect them from flak coming up through the floor, and one-quarter to one-half-inch pieces of steel armor plate were inserted under each seat cushion. (It was always with a great sense of relief that we noted how many pieces of flak these seat plates had stopped—indicated by deep dents on their undersides, and not ours.)

Food

Our engineer always brought along a lunch, prepared by our mess hall, for all of us—peanut butter and grape jelly sandwiches on giant slices of Italian bread and GI coffee in large thermos bottles. The idea was that we'd eat after we had descended to an altitude where we could take off our oxygen masks, but usually by that time the food was frozen rock solid and didn't thaw out before we landed back at Sterparone!

All of these additional weight items delayed our lift-off ever so slightly and necessitated the use of only a few additional feet of runway, so considering their usefulness and desirability, they were well worth the effort.

For the 817th, It's Time To Go

The green light flashes from the control tower, and the lead airplane of the 817th releases his brakes and starts down the runway. He moves slowly at first, and then accelerates. The thirty-second time interval between departures expires almost before the next pilot in sequence can release his brakes to start his takeoff roll.

The next two airplanes start their takeoff runs. A minute and a half has elapsed since the lead airplane started down the runway. Now it's my turn. Having previously set my throttles at takeoff power, I release my brakes and start our takeoff. The mission we've been preparing for since 0500 has begun.

Our squadron's lead B-17 is in the air about three miles off the end of the runway on the runway heading. He's accelerating, endeavoring to climb about five hundred feet per minute. He'll continue to fly straight ahead, climbing for about four minutes from the time he crossed the takeoff end of the runway until he levels off at 2000 feet. (His time off the end of the runway may vary due to weather, winds, and the number of airplanes taking off behind him.)

At the end of the four minutes he will start a 180-degree standard rate left turn. As he turns, he'll initially be at right angles to the runway but will end up parallel to it and about two miles to the right of it, flying at a somewhat reduced airspeed to facilitate the joining up of the other airplanes taking off behind him.

The lead airplane's right wingman is now about four miles off the end of the runway at about 1000 feet, climbing straight ahead, following the lead airplane, and steadily increasing airspeed. He will increase his speed to about twenty miles per hour faster than that of the lead airplane's and will continue to fly the runway heading for about three and one-half minutes. At the end of this time, he will start his joining turn to the left, to intercept the lead airplane, which he can now see flying toward him and a few hundred feet above him.

During his left climbing turn he will cross beneath the lead airplane and come up on its right wing, slightly above and a short distance from it. As he approaches the lead airplane, he will gradually reduce his airspeed so that when he is stabilized in his formation position, his airplane

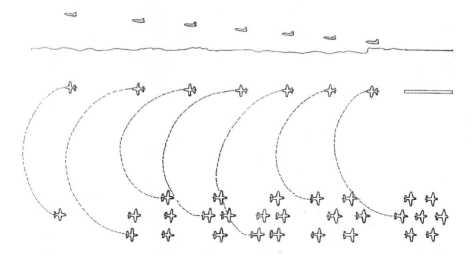

Illustration of standard squadron takeoff and join-up procedure. The takeoff interval between airplanes is thirty seconds. Drawing not to scale.

and the lead airplane will be flying at the same airspeed in a close formation.

The third B-17 of the first "V" is now about three to four miles off the end of the runway at about fifteen hundred feet, climbing and also slowly increasing his airspeed. He has just commenced his left turn to join the first two airplanes, which he can see, ahead and to his left, approaching him and flying level at 2000 feet on a course parallel to the runway. He will complete his 180-degree left turn, reducing his airspeed, and join the other two airplanes in a position as the left wingman of the lead airplane, and slightly above and behind the lead airplane's wing in close formation.

This completes the first "V" of the 817th Bomb Squadron's formation.

My airplane is number four in the squadron's formation (the "second element lead airplane"). I am about three miles off the end of the runway at about eighteen hundred feet, climbing as I increase my airspeed. As I start my 180-degree turn, I can see the other three airplanes to my left, approaching me at 2000 feet. I will gauge my rate of turn, angle of bank, and airspeed so that I will complete my turn and join the formation in a position slightly below and in trail of the lead airplane, matching the squadron's airspeed. The remaining two airplanes (numbers five and six) of the second "V" will join the first four in the same manner as the first three joined the lead airplane, and number seven will join the squadron in the same manner as I joined the first three.

While the airplanes in the 817th have been taking off, the 815th airplanes have climbed to 4000 feet and have been circling the base in a racetrack pattern to the left. The turn legs are planned so that the 817th squadron, when it is fully formed, can easily continue its climb to 4500 feet to join the lead squadron in the number two position of the group's four-squadron formation.

These two squadrons will continue to circle the air base in large elongated circles until the remaining two squadrons have taken off, formed, and joined them. When the group's "box formation" is complete, they will circle the base in climbing turns, planning the turns so that the group crosses the assembly beacon at the assigned time and altitude. After crossing the beacon, the group will turn to the heading for its target, and will be immediately behind the group it is scheduled to follow.

The Takeoff—My Personal Experience

It seemed that on many takeoffs, just when everything was falling into place, my B-17 would suddenly lose speed (due to erratic airflow over its wings) and settle back toward the runway. But then, within a few precious seconds, I'd get it to regain flight—with the landing gear just two or three feet off the runway—and quickly call "Gear up" to the copilot. Soon we'd be six to eight feet off the runway, then fifteen feet as the tremendous drag created by the landing gear was eliminated. Finally my heart would return to its proper place, I'd give a slight sigh of relief, and I'd enjoy a momentary bit of relaxation—we were off and away.

Unfortunately, on this takeoff my feeling of relief was very brief; in an instant my left wing stalled out due to very unstable air just above the surface of the runway—the left wing was no longer flying—and dropped toward the steel mat. My airplane did not want to continue flying. It was sliding sideways to the left, and the left wingtip and the propeller of the number one engine were just a few feet above the runway. *Je Reviens* was a sad sight, sailing through the air in a very unnatural manner.

The left wing must, somehow, be made to fly again, and instantly! If I could not right this situation, here is what could take place: The left wingtip will strike the steel mat runway, and then the propeller of the number one engine and the left wing will disintegrate as they are torn from the fuselage. The plane will cartwheel to the left, nose first, throwing itself to the ground at the left side of the runway. These events will take place rapidly—within seconds. The other results of the crash—the fire, the series of explosions as fuel is ignited and thousands of rounds of ammunition cook off, the detonation of the super-sensitive five-hundred-pound bombs—are terrible, unthinkable, but definitely possible.

So I *must* level this airplane and get it flying again, and there is little time to do so—a few seconds at the most. To level the left wing and stabilize its flight, I needed a boost of instantaneous power—immediate additional thrust from all four engines—regardless of the cost. This surge of power would bring up the left wing and increase its lift because of the increased airflow over it. The only source of such power was the engine's turbo superchargers. The electronically controlled waste gates on the superchargers had to be instantly and completely closed. I reached for the control knob, moved the red over-boost guard lever aside, and turned the knob to the number ten setting, completely closing all four of the superchargers' waste gates. (With the guard lever in its normal position, the pilot is limited to a setting of seven or eight—about three-quarters of the waste gates' maximum closed positions.)

Thankfully, this action worked: I heard the four engines softly answer with magnificent support. I felt a surge of newly found power as the left wing came up and my B-17 leveled out and started to climb. Once again the B-17 lived up to its reputation and capabilities. As we gained speed and climbed away from the runway, I mused that perhaps we might have awakened a late sleeper or two in the valley with that short rumble of additional power; however, it was a small price to pay to avoid waking everyone for miles around with the boom of an exploding B-17.

Once our climb airspeed was established, I returned the waste gate control knob to its normal setting and re-engaged the guard lever. The electronic control unit operated perfectly, bringing a satisfying smile to my face and a newfound peace of mind. After those disconcerting few minutes during takeoff, I joined the first three airplanes of our squadron and left that unpleasant memory behind.

In its final turn over our air base at Sterparone, the 483rd Bomb Group (H) was its usual classic sight to see: a tightly knit formation of B-17s, proudly outward bound in an early morning clear blue sky, on the way to join the other bomb groups of the 15th Air Force for another day's mission against the German war machine.

Our group reached the assembly beacon at Lake Lesina right on the minute, and we turned on course to our target. Now came a long, steady climb to our bombing altitude and flight to the initial point (IP), and then the bomb run to hit the marshalling yard main station at Bruck, Austria. Looking ahead, I could see numerous groups of B-17s and B-24s that had taken off before us climbing to their assigned bombing altitudes. Airplanes filled the sky as far as my eye could see—an impressive sight.

As our climb continued and we crossed through 10,000 feet, I advised our crew to don their oxygen masks and make sure their flow regulators were functioning properly. I also reminded them of the hard-and-fast procedure of checking in on the intercom every five minutes while breathing oxygen. The entire crew was required to do this until advised to stop using oxygen during our descent on the return flight to our base.

Shortly before we crossed the Adriatic seacoast of Yugoslavia, in the area northwest of Split (on the Dalmatian coast), the gunners of each B-17 in the group's formation charged and test-fired their fifty-caliber machine guns and continued to maintain a thorough watch for enemy fighters, as we were now flying over very hostile enemy territory. From this point to our target and back, we could expect to be attacked by formations of German fighters at any time.

As we crossed the Yugoslavian coastline, our formation was indeed fired upon by German 88 mm flak guns, and in no time the all-too-familiar hourglass-shaped puffs of black smoke (from exploding shells) filled the crystal-clear sky well to the east of our formation.

The German antiaircraft gunners at Split, Yugoslavia, were noted for their tenaciousness and always fired at anything flying near them, even though at this point in the war no one dropped bombs there on regularly scheduled missions. We often joked about the Split gunners; we surmised that the reason they always shot at us, no matter how far our flight path was from them, was that perhaps there was an antiaircraft gunners school there and they had their students practice on us.

Undeterred by this explosive welcome to Yugoslavia, we continued gradually increasing our climb toward Bruck while maintaining our optimum climb airspeed of 135 miles per hour. At 20,000 feet, our fighter escort of P-51 Mustangs from the 332nd Fighter Group, 100th Fighter Squadron, appeared just above us, right on time, which gave us a feeling of satisfaction and security. They were unconditionally there when we needed them, and we were well aware of their splendid reputation—they had never lost a bomber to enemy fighter aircraft. These escort fighters would remain with us from here to the target area, and for a portion of the return flight to our base. If a B-17 were damaged over the target and could not maintain formation with his squadron, one or two P-51's would fly on his wing most of the way home. That's what I call protection!

The group reached 26,000 feet well prior to reaching the IP, and all the B-17s settled into a tightly knit "four box" formation for their flight to the target. Bruck, here we come!

On the Way to Bruck de Mur

While flying on our track toward the IP for Bruck, cruising at our optimum speed at 26,000 feet, we encountered the headwind that had been forecast by our meteorologist. Our route to the target takes us just to the east of Ljubljana, Slovenia, then almost directly over Bielburg, west of Graz, and then north-northwest to a point just a few miles northwest of Bruck itself. As we approach the border between Slovenia and Austria, the day is cloudless and bright—it seems as if we can see forever. The very high and heavily snow-covered mountain ranges of the Austrian Alps rise majestically before us, and if we look to the west-northwest we can also enjoy the splendor of the sunlit mountain ranges of the Swiss Alps—what a picture! Though the beauty of this area never fails to impress us as we pass this way, we never forget that a gigantic war is all around us, and realize that we could be attacked at any moment by German fighters, putting an abrupt end to our tranquility.

Our formation (the Red Force) is the first part of a strategic bombing effort today by the 483rd Bomb Group. We are the initial wave—twenty-one four-engine heavy bombers carrying over sixty-three tons of devastating high-explosive bombs, which we will drop on the railroad marshalling yards in Bruck in a short period of time. Less than five minutes after we strike Bruck's yards, the second wave—the Blue Force of the 483rd Bomb Group, with its twenty-one B-17s—will attack the marshalling yards at Graz, Austria, just thirty miles or so south of Bruck.

Even with a nine-tenths cloud cover at 14,000 feet in the area of Bruck, we intend to saturate our target with 252 of these lethal 500-pound bombs. The damage to the railroad yards and their related facilities will be tremendous. A *single* 500-pound bomb is a most formidable instrument of destruction. When it explodes, it shakes the ground for hundreds of yards around its point of impact. The sound of the explosion deadens the ears of anyone close to the detonation. Just imagine what it sounds like when *252* of these bombs explode almost simultaneously in close proximity to one another!

In a short while, we will cross the mountains well west of Graz, Austria, giving that city a wide berth. Then we will fly about twenty-five miles west-northwest of Leoben and will continue northward toward the high mountain peaks of the area just northeast of Eisenerz, where we will turn south and from there commence our bomb run on the rail yards of Bruck de Mur. Although we're somewhat relaxed as we enjoy the beauty of the surrounding panorama, we never forget the seriousness and danger of our situation, and we take great satisfaction that high above us we can see the contrails of our top cover—the twenty P-51 Mustangs from the 332nd Fighter Group.

15

The Bomb Run

We Approach Bruck

As we made our turn inbound to our target, we crossed the IP at 1358 and settled down on the bomb run track to our release point. We were beginning to see the black hourglass-shaped puffs of smoke created by exploding 88- and 105-mm antiaircraft rounds fired at us from around Bruck. Having sighted our formations both visually (our contrails were a stunning giveaway) and on their radar, Bruck's flak-gunners were preparing for our attack, but at this point the barrage of exploding shells was well in front of our group's formations. Fortunately for us, our bomb run would be downwind, so within just a few minutes we would drop our bombs and rally away from the target area, leaving these guns well behind us.

Just prior to establishing our attack on Bruck's marshalling yards, our group quickly set up a "squadrons-in-trail" formation (one squadron behind the other in a line), and we thought we were ready for anything. However, at this point our situation threatened to take a turn for the worse. Our lead airplane's pilot, Captain Walt Glass, announced to all of the pilots in the formation (via the inter-aircraft VHF channel) that he was considering the possibility of first making a dry run on the target to ascertain the feasibility of bombing it by visual reference instead of using our radar-directed bombing technique.

I found this to be a disconcerting and frightening idea, and soon it appeared, as the other pilots voiced their opinions over the radio, that everyone else in the formation felt the same way. No one considered this plan either brilliant or safe, because it would give the German antiaircraft

113

gunners two chances to shoot us down. If we made a dry run just to see if we could bomb it visually and found that a visual bombing could indeed be accomplished, we would then have to turn away from the target, return to the IP, and commence a second run, using the same track, same altitude, and same speed as before. In less than a minute, our leader decided not to attempt the dry run due to what he could now see of the target area ahead.

The cloud cover in the target area was still about nine-tenths stratocumulus clouds at 14,000 feet. Another restriction to visibility was smoke the Germans generated at ground level to obscure the marshalling yards, shops, and storage facilities from our view. They hoped, of course, that if we could not see the target area, we would not try to bomb it. They knew that in our efforts to hit their strategic military facilities, we were always aware of possible collateral damage, and that we would not want to destroy the city itself—or even damage it.

Collateral damage was a real possibility in Bruck. I have described the narrow valley we were in—it lay between high mountains on either side of the Mur River. Railroad tracks and a highway paralleled the river. The city of Bruck almost completely surrounded these two critical transportation lines, and bombs dropped anywhere other than directly on the railroad yards and their related support structures would inflict heavy damage on a very old and charming little city. Walt Glass, considering this, decided to bypass Bruck and hit our secondary target in Graz, Austria.

On to Graz

Graz now lay directly ahead of our formation, and as we were using a squadrons- in-trail formation (flying at slightly staggered altitudes) rather than our usual spread out 4-squadron formation, it would be easy to bomb Graz's marshalling yards. Graz was less than thirty miles south of us, also in the Mur River valley, so our flight to the bombs-release point would take only a matter of minutes (actually, less than four minutes, considering the good tail wind we were experiencing). At "bombs away," we would execute our rally turn to the right, away from the target area, and fly over the Austrian Alps to the west of Graz.

At no point on our flight above the long, narrow valley between Bruck and Graz was there any letup in antiaircraft fire from the Germans. The flak guns around Bruck were fired at us until our high altitude and speed rendered them ineffective. At that point, however, we came into range of the guns around Graz—a real double whammy. Even though our intelligence people called this barrage of antiaircraft fire "moderate," it seemed very intense to me. In fact, the Germans seemed to be trying to shoot down our squadron in particular as we proceeded on our bomb run.

Our squadron would be the second to drop its bombs. Because I was flying lower than our squadron leader, I had a clear view of the lead airplane and the other airplanes of the first squadron that were directly in front of us and a few hundred feet above our altitude less than one-eighth of a mile ahead. I would be able to see their bombs release and gauge when our bombs would drop. I was anticipating our bombs-release moment and then our rally turn immediately afterward.

As I monitored the operation of the autopilot, letting our bombardier and the bombsight fly the airplane, I thought to myself how intense the flak bursts were becoming and how close they were to our squadron and my airplane specifically. I could hear pieces of shrapnel hitting our frontal area and wings, coming from all directions and causing the airplane to bounce a little, and I thought, "These gunners just about have my airplane bracketed."

As the lead squadron's bombs fell and the squadron commenced a steep turn to the right, I saw the bombs-release light flash on my instrument panel. I felt the airplane lighten and lift upward ever so slightly—a sensation I had experienced many times previously. At the same instant, our bombardier, Bob Mahan, called "Bombs away" on the airplane's intercom.

We're Hit!

The usual next step after the bombs dropped was for me to disconnect the autopilot and then smoothly hand-fly the airplane in formation with our squadron's lead airplane as it made its turn. But this time the usual didn't happen—instead, our airplane was jolted by numerous antiaircraft projectiles exploding at the same instant and heavily damaging *Je Reviens*. Fierce explosions tore into our right side and left wing, causing severe damage to the number one and number two engines and the left wing itself.

These flak bursts set in motion a rapid series of events. Because the left wing had completely lost lift, we started rolling from right to left. The airplane flipped over on its back and instantaneously curled into a tight, diving, left-hand spin. I immediately executed a spin recovery, the procedure which had been drilled into me by flight instructors in primary, basic, and advanced flying school. I had practiced the procedure over and over and knew it well. Although our B-17 *Pilot's Flight Manual* stated—and we were emphatically told on our very first flight in the airplane—that we must never spin, roll, dive, stall, loop, or attempt an inverted flight with the B-17, I had just done all of these maneuvers in less than a minute! We made almost four complete revolutions before I could stop the rotation. When I did recover, we were in a steep dive almost straight down.

With the help of Les Anton, my co-pilot, we were able to pull the airplane out of its dive and I then managed to get us flying again, albeit somewhat awkwardly. At this point, I was feeling very lucky just to be able to keep the airplane in the air. I had a split second to think about my crew members and hoped they were holding onto something and not tumbling around. Were they all right? Had any of them been killed or wounded? I almost didn't want to inquire; however, I asked my engineer to check on them for me.

Then I quickly assessed the damage to our B-17—what was left of it—to determine how to keep us in the air long enough to get to a safer place where we could crash-land the plane or parachute from it. We had lost about 3000 feet immediately after we were hit and another 1000 feet during the recovery process. The damage to our trustworthy bomber was substantial and very disheartening.

The terrible force of the explosions had torn away part of the windshield, damaged part of my left window, shattered part of my instrument panel, and destroyed a section of my copilot's instrument panel. Our oxygen system had been knocked out and our intercom system, radios, electrical system, and hydraulic system had been destroyed.

There were two elongated holes in the left wing just aft of where the number one and number two engine mounts joined it. The holes were smoking profusely, but I could see no flames. The right wing had been damaged by shell fragments, but not extensively. I later learned from my crew that the fuselage, the vertical fin, and the horizontal stabilizer had been perforated by shell fragments.

The distinctive red cowling around the number four engine had been ripped away and a few of that engine's top cylinders had been damaged, but it continued to function and was contributing to our efforts to remain airborne. (Its turbo supercharger waste gate was fully closed.)

When the airplane rolled over on its back and started its downward spiral, it seemed to me that a giant hand had clutched us in its fist and was angrily thrusting the airplane downward toward the high, snow-covered mountains below, as if determined to destroy us.

Many times since this incident I have wondered how, as all of this was taking place, and given the adverse conditions, a pilot could instantly react to correctly unscramble such a potentially disastrous situation. Of course, the answer is training—and lots of it! Training in Aviation Cadet Schools, in the B-17 Transition School, and in the Overseas Combat Unit. We had been trained to act instinctively, decisively, and without hesitation, and because of what we were taught and our respect for the airplane, we reacted and performed correctly. Unfortunately, we were not taught the fine art of aerial acrobatics, and the tenderness required to recover a B-17 from a spin, in B-17 Transition School. In my later aviation career, as I flew all over the globe for thirty-eight years after my Army Air Corps duty had ended, the importance of thorough flight training always proved true. I found it to be the case with every airplane I was taught to fly, both reciprocating-engine and turbine-engine craft, one of which was another fine Boeing—the 727.

I continued to use the number four engine, even with its damaged top cylinders, at reduced power, while guarding its manifold pressure, RPM, oil pressure, and oil temperature with much tender, loving care, as having it continue to function would enable us to cover more ground and lose less altitude. The number three engine was intact—why, I could not imagine, unless it was part of a divinely conceived plan for our survival. Its turbo supercharger's waste gate was also fully closed and its throttle at full forward. It was delivering fifty-three inches of manifold pressure (seven inches more than normally allowable) and 3300 RPM (far more than the "maximum allowable" 2600 RPM). This Wright R-1820–97 power plant was, thankfully, not at all mindful of what its power charts recommended.

The destruction of our electrical system meant that we had lost electrical supervision of some of the engine controls; everything had to be done manually. In an effort to stabilize our remaining two engines I first tried to reduce the high manifold pressure and RPM on the number three engine by retarding the throttle and then the propeller control lever, but this did not work. I was concerned that the engine would destroy itself— literally blow apart. I needed the power it was delivering, as without it our day would be over. It was as though someone other than I had control of it, however, and its power settings were meant to stay just as they were.

Another worry I had about this engine—and the number four

engine—was that at these uncontrolled power settings its propeller could "run away," destroying the planetary gearing in the nose section of the engine and shearing the shaft so that the propeller would fly off the engine and probably create all sorts of damage. Losing the propeller of either of these engines would spell disaster for us. The airplane, having lost its source of power and lift, would crash into the mountains.

Altitude was our most precious commodity. Losing it jeopardized our ability to clear some of the mountains that lay between us and the area where I felt my crew could safely leave the airplane, and we *were* losing it. Because I was enticing the airplane to stay in the air at an airspeed just slightly above its present weight's stall speed, I was compelled to accept a slight descent rate to prevent a full stall. The only way to slow our loss of altitude was to lighten the airplane; we must discard every item that was not essential for flight or operation. And it must be done immediately! It was amazing that the number four engine was still functioning at all, and it wouldn't be long before its oil supply would be exhausted and it would cease to function. I asked our engineer/gunner, Tech Sergeant Joseph F. Pirrone, to supervise this procedure. Not many of the war-fighting capabilities of our wonderful B-17 would remain when he completed his job.

Where to Jump?

The terribly high, deeply snow-covered mountains presented a formidable barrier between our position, just a little southeast of Graz, and a safer area in south central Slovenia, the location I would try to reach. If we were able to reach it, my crew could parachute into an area that would afford them the maximum degree of security for both their jump and their escape once on the ground.

I planned a course that would take us from just southeast of Graz to the east of Klagenfort and southeast of Bielburg, Austria, which is on the Austria-Slovenia (Yugoslavia) border. Then we would continue southwest into lower central Slovenia to a point south of the Sava River. The Karawanken Mountains, southeast of Bielburg, rise to about 8000 feet, and I felt that we would need an altitude of at least 10,000 feet to safely cross them.

The next highest mountains on our irregular route would be the eastern edge of the deeply snow-covered Savinjske Alps, which lie almost east-to-west in Northern Slovenia, just south of the border of Austria. These peaks vary in height from 3000 to 7000 feet, so I would need to keep the airplane at a minimum of 9000 feet there.

My hope was to be able to continue to fly our crippled B-17 to an area of Slovenia well southeast of Ljubljana and fifteen or twenty miles south of the Sava River, an area that has fewer high mountains and is far less rugged than the area north of the Sava River. The region I had in mind was much more open and somewhat more level in places, possibly allowing me to crash-land the airplane after I had all of my crew bail out.

The Bailout Planning

It was of paramount importance to me to have my crew leave the airplane in a safe and orderly manner. I wanted them to bail out at the right time and into an area where they could land safely and, with any luck, walk away uninjured. The first phase of my plan was to have all the enlisted crewmen (sergeants) jump at an altitude of at least 3500 feet. I wanted to allow them enough altitude and time so that they would not have to scramble just to survive. The second phase was to have the three officers (copilot, navigator, and bombardier) jump at 2500 feet, also as safely as possible—no panic jumps.

Using this plan, the nine crewmen would land fairly close to each other, so that they could regroup and immediately start seeking safe shelter rather than staying in the area to search for missing crew members, which could lead to the capture of the entire group by the Germans. If the men were able to bail out over the area I had chosen, their chances of being located by Yugoslavian Partisans rather than Germans would be increased. Partisan forces were reported to be concentrated in several sections of this region.

When we were hit, I had worried about my crew having to bail out in the target area, near Graz, or perhaps along the border between Austria and Yugoslavia. This would have been a disaster. Because of the heavy concentration of German military forces in Austria and northeastern Yugoslavia (as had been impressed upon us repeatedly during briefing sessions), I realized that my crew would have a much better chance of evading capture if they could parachute into central or southern Yugoslavia (Slovenia) rather than anywhere in Austria.

We had also been briefed about the topography of Austria and Northern Yugoslavia, over which we flew on many of our bombing missions. We were aware of where we'd have the best chance of making a successful jump—if we were afforded the luxury of a choice in the matter. And we knew of the nature and existence of a well-organized underground movement in Yugoslavia, as well as two friendly Partisan army organizations, and where their forces were likely to be strongest. We were cautioned to avoid capture by a paramilitary group of Yugoslavian people called the Domobranci—the so-called "Homeguard"—who were closely aligned with the German military forces. We were told that they would either execute captured American airmen or turn them over to the German forces.

Fulfilling my plan would certainly stretch the capabilities of my airplane in its present condition—and probably my own. I surveyed the damage to the airplane once more. The left side of my windshield had been damaged by shrapnel—why it hadn't hit me, I can't begin to imagine. The holes were large, the air coming through them was frigid, and most of the instruments in my left instrument panel were unusable. My left sliding window had been hit in several places; however, it had no actual holes.

The two holes in the left wing had evidently been caused by large pieces of antiaircraft shells coming up through the wing from below. The metal skin around these holes in the top of the wing was bent up and outward from the ferocious force. One large hole, the one closest to me, in the center section of the "wing's cord"—midway between the leading edge and the trailing edge of the wing—was ten or twelve feet out from where the wing joins the fuselage. Could it be that a 105 millimeter projectile came completely through the wing from below and did not detonate? This hole was at least a foot and a half in diameter, and black smoke was pouring out of it. Fortunately, there was no fire. I could see many other holes—from an inch to over two inches in diameter—in the top of the left wing. With all this damage, it was difficult for me to imagine how the wing was staying attached.

All the fuel in the left wing tanks had drained out, making what was left of the wing very light. This was actually a good thing: we didn't need the fuel, as we would not be going very far, and empty wing tanks meant a lighter—and therefore more easily flown—airplane. Without the weight of the fuel and some of the weight of the two engines, we needed less power to stay in the air, and we had very little engine power remaining.

Since the entire electrical system and radios had been rendered useless, we could not tell any of the other airplanes in our group or squadron about the seriousness of our situation. They were not aware of our condition or my plans. We also had no heat for our heated suits, and functioning in the intense cold was very difficult and tedious.

Even though the hydraulic system had been destroyed, this presented no immediate difficulty since we would not have to use the wheel brakes, and the cowl flaps on our good engine were preset. We didn't need the hydraulic regulators for the superchargers either, as the waste gates for these units had fortunately been completely closed when we were hit.

Since the oxygen system had been destroyed, no oxygen was available other than our standby high-pressure walk-around bottles, and the crewmen used these briefly. Because we were descending (out of necessity), oxygen was not a critical requirement, although it would have made things much easier.

Because the vacuum selector valve had been on engine number three when we were hit, and that engine continued to function, we had vacuum pressure, which meant that vacuum-operated instruments—such as the flight indicator, and turn and bank indicator—still worked, which was a help to me.

This difficult situation did have its bright spots: we still had the horsepower to keep our B-17 in the air, we were all alive, and no one had been wounded.

Trimming the airplane to fly with the engine power available was my first order of business and required the use of almost full right travel of the rudder trim tab control to counteract the lack of engine power on the left side. To keep the dead left wing anywhere near level required the use of over two thirds of the aileron trim tab control's "right wing down" setting. Actually, it was not so much the weight of the wing that necessitated trimming it up as it was the torque created by the thrust produced on the right wing. Also, the loss of lift on the left wing caused it to be almost a non-contributor to flight; it would, of course, not fly or stay level on its own. The elevator trim tabs also came into play in this exercise, as without sufficient engine power lift and speed to keep the nose up, I had to use them to help with the total trim condition and establish a nearly balanced attitude. We were fortunate that no damage had been done to the trim systems.

From experience on an earlier combat mission, I knew what this airplane could do on just two engines. This time, we had only one and a half engines with which to fly away from the target area and across the high mountains to the northeast of Slovenia, so the flight would be a real challenge.

Since the airplane would perform more efficiently if we discarded everything we did not need, I had set that plan in motion as our immediate priority. Our engineer/gunner, Joe Pirrone, was supervising this process. All of the fifty-caliber machine guns and their spare barrels and ammunition were thrown overboard, with the exception of Jim Cook's two tail guns and a few hundred extra rounds of ammunition for them in case we were attacked from the rear by roving German fighters. The protective pieces of steel matting were tossed out, as well as all of the built-in protective armor that it was possible to remove. The ball turret and all radios and radio equipment went, along with the crew seats that weren't needed. The Norden bombsight was destroyed by shooting it several times with a forty-five automatic and dropped into the snow-covered mountains. The flak helmets, flak suits, and all personal clothing and A-12 bags containing non-required items were discarded. But we kept our warm clothes, jackets and other items we'd need on the ground, hopefully walking through Slovenia.

Throughout this process, there wasn't time to worry. We were going to get there, for certain!

Unflinching Devotion to Duty

That day, March 9, 1945, was a day of compounding hardships for Jim Cook, our tail gunner, and he went above and beyond the call of duty. Because I had asked that the two tail guns and a supply of ammunition be retained on board, Cook felt that he should constantly be at his position in the tail manning his guns. He wanted to be at his station to protect us all if necessary.

This was not my intention. Actually, I had relayed word back to Jim to be available in the waist area or the radio room, and that it was not necessary to station himself in the tail gunner's compartment continually, but only to be ready to be there if we were attacked. My logic for this was that if we were attacked as a straggler—which is what we were—before bailout time, he could easily scamper from the waist/radio room area to the tail guns and return fire. I also realized that the heating components in his clothing would not be operative and that he would be subjected to extreme cold if he stayed back in his tail gun compartment.

Despite all of this, and unbeknownst to me, that is where he was from the time we pulled out of our spin until the time all the enlisted crew were told to leave the airplane. During this time, Jim sustained frostbite to his toes, feet, and hands. For his unselfish devotion, dedication, and courage under extreme duress, Jim was awarded the Distinguished Flying Cross. It was a well-deserved citation.

Joe and the rest of the crew worked rapidly, and as the weight of the airplane diminished, I was able to use less nose-up elevator trim tab, which substantially reduced our descent rate and still retained a good airspeed, slightly above stall speed for our weight. This very much improved our prospects. My innermost feelings about surviving were improving, and I was ready to accept the challenge of accomplishing what lay ahead.

When we were hit, I had a fleeting thought of trying to make it to Switzerland, but that was too far for this damaged airplane to fly. At that time, I had asked our navigator for a heading to southern central Slovenia. Jim responded quickly with a south- southwest course, and we were on our way to a safer place over which to bail out. I continued formulating my plan. I expected to lose the number four engine at any moment, so the rest of the flight would have to be planned and executed with only one engine—number three. I roughly calculated that I could stretch our powered glide, at its present altitude of about 22,000 feet, about seventy-five or eighty miles, perhaps even farther. With some additional luck and answered prayers, I might possibly keep *Je Reviens* in the air long enough to fly considerably farther south of the Sava River and have my crew bail out in an even more suitable location.

To summarize our situation so far: We had been hit by antiaircraft fire at the instant of our "bombs away" time—1403. When I had fully recovered from the spin and regained control of the airplane, we staggered away from Graz, licking our wounds and gathering our thoughts. (Although we were concerned about our own situation, of course, we were also hoping that our complete load of bombs had hit the center of the marshalling yards at Graz, thus completing the main requisite of our mission.) Our roll after being struck by antiaircraft fire and our downward spin and recovery had taken us to the left of our original bomb run track and we were now about eighteen miles southeast of Graz. It was from this point that we commenced our flight to Slovenia.

As we commenced our flight away from Graz to the southeast, it was 1415. We had lost less than 4000 feet after being hit and had consumed only about twelve minutes. We were a hundred feet or so below 22,000 feet and established on our heading to the south-southwest, with a good descending airspeed of about 125 miles an hour, which I felt I could increase as we became established in our powered glide. I hoped we would experience a good ground speed, as our meteorologist had told us that winds aloft and at medium altitudes would be from the north.

Along with the safe bail-out of my crewmen, my plan included trying to keep the plane in the air until I could find a halfway decent piece of land on which I could belly-land in sort of a controlled crash. I had a fleeting humorous thought of what an odd picture we must make for anyone who saw us struggling along. How strange this wonderful big bomber must look as it made every effort to continue to fly. There it was, almost mushing along—its left wing high, with fragments of two former engines protruding from it, and the right wing low, with one engine and another partial one urgently trying to keep the airplane aloft.

But I soon returned to the situation at hand and started planning for that rapidly approaching time when I would no longer have control over our flight and the airplane would become an unstable jumping platform. There was a delicate balance between wanting the right time and altitude for the jump and not waiting too long, and I had to be unflappable as I continuously evaluated our options. The altitude and the type of terrain beneath us must be absolutely correct at the jump point. I had to make certain that there would be sufficient altitude remaining between our airplane and the ever-changing terrain below to give my crewmen's parachutes time to properly deploy.

Now that my plan for the safe exit of my crew members was complete, what would be in store for me? Would my envisioned belly landing become a reality?

The Jump Plan Finalized

The number four engine ceased to function about 1429, losing its propeller in a gentlemanly fashion as the engine froze. At this point, we were crossing the highest terrain of northeast Slovenia, about eighteen miles south of the border between Slovenia and Austria, well beyond the Drava River and to the southwest of it. Losing the propeller intensified the powered glide matter, and I concentrated my efforts on reaching out for as much distance as possible while flying on just one engine.

As we continued to make our way southwest, my copilot, navigator, bombardier, and I constantly monitored our progress on our maps so we could be as sure as possible of our actual position over Slovenia. Dead reckoning navigation was made rather difficult because we were flying through the unstable air of stratocumulus, and large cumulus clouds and large snowflakes were flying around us, some even entering the cockpit through the holes in the windshield. I was actually flying on instruments much of the time, although we were able to use breaks in the cloud mass to try to pick up landmarks such as villages, rivers, highways, bridges, and railroads to keep track of our progress.

To make matters more complicated, our speed fluctuated because of the type of flight I was attempting—flying in turbulent air on one engine very near stall speed and having to trust some of the battered instruments on my panel for the flight data I needed. None of my crew realized that at times my heart was not where it should have been, and I often felt it was in my throat during various points of this almost Herculean task I had set for myself. Despite all this, we were proceeding better than I had expected.

Our true airspeed (and, therefore, ground speed) was decreasing as we continued south-southwest in Slovenia. This was because of cloud conditions and the fact that I was striving to reduce our descent rate in an effort to stretch our powered glide as far as it could go. At this point, we were about sixty-nine miles southwest of Graz, a mile or so east of the town of Trbovlje, and almost exactly over the Sava River at an altitude of 8500 feet, descending at a faster rate than I was happy with. It was 1439, and the time was rapidly approaching for me to execute my evacuation plan for my nine crew members.

From what we could see through the breaks in the clouds, some of the mountaintops in this area were about 3000 feet below us. The higher ones appeared to be lessening in number and also decreasing in height, and more valleys and somewhat open areas were now appearing below us.

16

Day Number 1—Friday, March 9, 1945

Jump Time—An Actuality

I reasoned that I had about eight or nine minutes to get all nine of my crewmen out of the airplane. Even though the mountains and hills and the ground around them were covered with a blanket of beautiful white snow, this seemed to be the area into which they should parachute. I wanted them to prepare to jump now—as quickly as possible—because I wanted their bail-out to be unhurried; despite our circumstances, it had to be accomplished correctly, and planned with some caution and deliberation.

Because of our increased descent rate, I knew that the distance we could travel would be shorter than I had planned, and the bail-out procedure would have to start sooner than I originally had in mind. The airspeed and altitude indicators became my primary focus points—thank goodness that these instruments had not been damaged by flak. The all-important altitude of 3500 feet was fast approaching, and 2500 feet would follow very quickly. The safety and well-being of my crew depended on their jumping at these altitudes.

In the picture now unfolding in my mind I saw all of my crew members leaving the airplane almost immediately and jumping into an area which I estimated would be fifteen or so miles south-southwest of the Sava River and about twenty-eight miles southeast of Ljubljana. There was no other choice—our great airplane, in its severely damaged condition, trying to fly on one engine, was nearing the end of its far-reaching capabilities. It had more than outperformed itself: it had taken us away from the frozen peaks of the Austrian Alps. We would surely have perished if we had had to leave the airplane in that region. I wanted as many of my crewmen as possible to exit from the starboard rear entry door, the easiest and safest opening from which to bail out. All six sergeants were now assembled in and around the radio compartment, and as we crossed 4000 feet, they were told to start their jumps.

They bailed out in perfect order. I believe Duane Berthelson, our armorer gunner, was the first to jump. The other five followed him out the rear entry door. In-depth research about the actual recorded events of that day suggests that Duane Berthelson jumped from the airplane first—a short time before the other five—and he landed some distance north of the area where the others came down. Duane hid in the brush, snow, and trees to prevent being captured by soldiers—who he thought were Germans—searching for him. He was found early on the morning of March 10 by Slovenian Partisans who had seen his parachute float down the previous day. They had been actively endeavoring to locate him before the Germans in the area did.

The other five sergeants landed in an area a little southwest of the villages of Mirna and Mokronog, one or two miles northeast of where my navigator, bombardier, and copilot later landed. (Duane had come down a mile or so northeast of there.) All of the men except Duane were promptly rescued by the Slovenian Partisans and local farm people (civilians) of the area and very quickly routed southward to TV-15 at Kocevske Poljane. The area where all nine men landed was some twenty-five miles northeast of the village of Gradenc, located along the valley close to where my B-17 made its own belly landing on the upslope of the mountain, and where I landed in my parachute (actually between Gradenc and the tiny village of Lopata).

At the same time that my six crewmen were bailing out, I called to my navigator and bombardier, who were in the nose compartment, to prepare to make their jumps. They quickly came to the cockpit, clipped on their chest parachutes, and were preparing to leave the airplane—I thought.

I can visualize these two men and my copilot at this very moment, as though all of this took place yesterday afternoon, and I smile every time I think about it. Les Anton, my copilot, was in his seat in the cockpit. My navigator, Jim Metz, was standing in the catwalk between Les and me, and Bob Mahan, my bombardier, was standing just in back of Jim, toward where the upper twin fifty-caliber machine guns used to be. Jim and Bob both had their chest packs clipped to their parachute harnesses, but Les had not yet clipped his on because maneuvering out of his seat wearing a fat chest pack was difficult.

As I looked at these three wonderful fellows, I could sense in a matter of seconds that something out of the ordinary was going on—it showed on their faces and I could feel the thought transmissions between us. I got the idea that they did not want to leave me alone in this scrappy B-17— they did not want to bail out!

We were descending through 3000 feet, and I suggested that they get ready to jump and to maneuver to the exit as fast as possible, since I wanted them all out of the airplane at 2500 feet. They all looked at one another and then at me. Bob said, "We're not leaving! We're going to stay with you and the airplane, so we'll all be together when you belly it in."

I explained to them that it would be easier and safer for them if I crash-landed the airplane alone, and that I could easily accomplish this maneuver by myself. But they replied, "We will not leave. We're not leaving you alone in this predicament."

Time and altitude were running out while this worthy but time-consuming conversation was taking place. All three of them knew only too well that their safety and perhaps even their lives hinged on all of them getting out of the airplane quickly.

I appreciated their sympathetic words, but I could not let them lose their chance to jump safely. I grasped the control yoke more firmly in my left hand and rapidly pulled my Colt 45 automatic from my chest holster with my right hand. I pointed it at the overhead of the cockpit and said to them in a firm voice: "If you three don't jump from this airplane immediately, I will shoot all three of you! *Jump, damn it, jump!!!*"

And Then There Was One

The expressions on my officers' faces when I threatened to shoot them were of surprise and concern. After a very quiet but friendly moment, Bob Mahan said, "He means what he says—let's get out of here." They all knew I always meant what I said—I suppose that's one of the reasons that, soon after our combat crew relationship began, they gave me the nickname "Iron Pants Logan."

A moment later they had left the cockpit and quickly jumped from the airplane. I believe that one jumped through the open bomb bay and the other two jumped from the starboard main entry door opening. I had suggested earlier that they not plan to jump from the small crew escape hatch beneath my seat because doing so could be extremely dangerous—the left bomb bay door was sticking straight down just aft of this little hatch.

After they jumped, the quiet of the cockpit seemed very unhopeful and I was heavy-hearted. Even the loud roar of the number three engine seemed tamed by the solitude of the cockpit. I had never felt more lonely.

Of course, I would never have shot my crewmen! My gun was not charged, there was no cartridge in the chamber, and the safety was on, to boot. Nevertheless, threatening to shoot was the most expeditious method to make them jump and thus ensure their survival. These three men—as well as all my other crew members—are classic people. They were very much like brothers to me by then, and brothers they will be forever. I wanted them safe and felt certain they would be. I hoped that they were now walking around Slovenia with the six crew members who had bailed out a minute or so earlier. I certainly did not want them slamming into the side of a mountain with me and this courageous B-17, or sliding or crashing along the snowy ground of Slovenia in it somewhere down the way.

I now had two thousand or so feet that I hoped would give me time to find a more or less suitable place to put this plane on the ground. After my officers bailed out, at times the airplane seemed to become more difficult to keep in the air. It gave me indications that it just did not want to continue to fly, and it appeared to me that it was resisting my efforts to make it do so. I guess that it was as tired as I. Perhaps this fine airplane was asserting itself and trying to tell me that it was worn out and wanted to call it a day. It may even have been trying to communicate to me the fact that this was the appropriate time and place for me to make my exit, if there was to be one!

The flight controls were becoming more sluggish, but still functioning, aiding me in keeping the airplane airborne with the remaining power available. The number three engine was still providing me with all of its power, and then some. It should have torn itself apart long before this.

In spite of the rapidly changing conditions, all sorts of observations galloped through my weary mind. The flak holes in my main windshield were allowing snowflakes as big as silver dollars to blow into the cockpit with a wintry blast. The instrument panel was a sad sight. The damaged instruments created an eerie atmosphere, as some were half there, some with their indicating needles gone, some bent and some completely still, with their glass covers shattered. I continually searched for the information I needed to help me keep the plane in the air. The whistle of the wind through the cockpit was a constant reminder that the dynamic forces of nature—wind, snow, and cold—were ever-present and waiting to take over should I falter. The intense cold and wind were beginning to take their toll on my fingers and feet, making operating the controls more taxing.

I heard the door from the cockpit to the bomb bay banging open and closed again and again. It was a spooky sound and I wondered just what kind of message it was sending me. Was it telling me that my time to leave all this desolation was at hand, and I'd better hurry?

Despite all this devastation and adversity, I paradoxically found that I was stimulated by it. It aroused a stubborn determination and an awareness that I would never give up—I shall return. Joining all my other crew members on the ground somewhere in Slovenia, so we could all get home together, was now my prime objective.

I knew that the belly landing I planned to execute would actually be a controlled crash; I didn't have the means to do otherwise. I felt that the bomb bay doors would be a problem, as they had been damaged and were frozen in the down position, with no way to retract them. They would create a frightening and terrible noise when they contacted the ground on touchdown, and I didn't want to think about it.

But being the optimist that I am, I imagined that I would break out of the clouds I was currently in the midst of and fly the airplane visually. Then I'd select a likely piece of land on which to make my belly landing, put the plane on it, and when it came to rest, climb out, hurry away in case of an explosion, and then hide from the German patrols who would surely be hunting for me. A nifty plan, to say the least!

I refused to consider at any length other difficulties I might encounter upon contact with the ground: uncontrollable direction because of the terrain on which I would crash land; the number three engine's propeller blades digging into the ground and cart wheeling the plane; the distinct possibility of combustion or explosion of the remaining fuel in the wings; and several other unpleasant things that could occur while the plane slid across the ground. In spite of all these potential occurrences, my main considerations were still to find a suitable piece of land, try to control the plane as well as possible, belly-land it, pray a lot, and hope for the best.

As it turned out, the belly-landing plan was like my B-17—shot full of holes.

I didn't break out of the clouds as planned. Instead, the clouds parted briefly—sort of a final curtain call—and ahead, instead of seeing the ground, I was staring straight into the side of a mountain! I knew immediately that the belly landing was not possible, and that I could survive only if I got out of the airplane *now* and hope that I still had sufficient altitude remaining so that my parachute could open completely before I came into contact with the mountain.

Even though I had the airplane well trimmed, it could still roll after I released the controls and before I could scramble to the escape hatch beneath my seat, get into the proper position, and push myself out far enough to miss the bomb bay door, which would be sticking straight down to my left. Joe Pirrone, in his quest to rid the plane of extra weight, had pulled the hinge pins of this small door and jettisoned the door itself, so I'd be able to quickly exit when I got down to that area.

I hurriedly got out of my seat and stood in the walkway between the seats (which runs from the nose compartment to the bomb bay door) while maintaining back elevator pressure and right aileron down pressure on the yoke with my left hand to keep the plane from rolling or going into a nose-down attitude. With my right hand, I retrieved my chest pack from under my seat and clipped it to my parachute harness. Realizing that my trip to the escape hatch had to be a very speedy one, I released my grip on the yoke and quickly dropped down to the area in front of the open hatch. I rechecked my chest pack parachute to make sure that its fastenings were secure and made sure that my GI shoes were properly attached to a parachute harness clip. At the same moment, I placed my left hand at the top of the hatch with my fingers on the outside of the opening. With the heels of my flight boots hooked over the bottom side of the hatch, toes pointing outward, I squatted down, spread the straps of my parachute harness outward from the crotch area, clutched the rip cord ring in my right hand, pushed firmly outward with my heels and soles of my feet, and exited the airplane into the very cold slipstream air.

As I pushed myself out of the little hatch, I saw the left bomb bay door flash by—it had missed hitting my head by inches. My survival depended on doing everything rapidly and correctly. Even a few seconds were very important, and knowing this, I pulled the rip cord ring at the same time as I pushed myself out of the little escape hatch—and at the same moment, I saw the bomb bay door dash past my head.

As I hit the slipstream air, I went through half a tumble, and then my parachute opened with a pop and a very firm jerk upward. At the same moment, I came into contact with some very large trees. A split second before hitting them, I realized that I would collide with them at a terrific force and instinctively wrapped my arms around my face and head for protection. This effort paid off.

Before I jumped, I had carefully secured my GI boots by clipping them to my parachute harness, but when the parachute popped open, they snapped away from me, one going in one direction and the other going in the opposite direction, to be lost forever in the deep mountain snow below me. Each crewman always kept his high-top GI boots close in case of an emergency such as this. I always kept mine beneath my seat in the cockpit, tied together by their heavy laces, so that I could snap them onto my parachute harness quickly—and, I thought, securely.

Obviously, this plan had failed, but there was a sunny side to the saga: My big fleece-lined leather flying boots stayed on my feet throughout the parachute jump. I considered this almost a miracle, as we had been told in our training that flying boots always came off your feet when your chute popped open, so be sure to have your GI boots securely attached to you. Walking around in enemy territory in bare feet would be very difficult, especially in the snow. And it turned out that my flying boots were much more suitable for the walking I would be doing for the next few days.

The large trees into which I had fallen had saved me. They had softened my impact with the side of that mountain. I realized that I had jumped just in the nick of time—only a few hundred feet separated me from the mountainside. The clump of trees into which I had landed grew on land that sloped rather steeply down and outward into a long, wide valley—just the sort of place to make a belly landing if you happened to have the engine power, the speed, the time, and altitude to turn and maneuver for a landing approach.

As I hung in the trees in my parachute harness about forty feet above ground, thinking about how fortunate I was just to be there in one piece, I was also taking stock of my physical condition. I was amazed that I had not been hurt—it did not seem possible that crashing into these trees with such tremendous force had not injured me! After convincing myself that I was all right, I began to wonder just how I would get down from my dangling position in the trees, and started formulating a plan for extricating myself—but soon I had a more urgent concern.

At the moment I had crashed into the trees, I had heard my B-17 roaring away from me, but still close. As I looked up and out in front of me, I could see *Je Reviens* gliding away from me. It was in a very slow descending left turn, and was actually on its way to executing a complete 180-degree left turn, aiming itself directly back toward me! What a frightening sight!

After the catastrophic events of the day so far, here I was thinking I was safe in the trees only to see my wonderful B-17, its one engine still going strong, flying directly at me. It appeared that this airplane, which I loved so dearly, would slam right into me as I hung there, defenseless. I can close my eyes and still see that picture today. It was unbelievable!

But as I continued to watch, I realized that because of its descending path and the up-slope of the hillside, it would come into contact with the ground before it could reach me in the trees—and this is what happened. It flew into the ground about 250 yards from me at a very slight nose-up angle, as though someone were in the cockpit flying it, and skidded up the sloping terrain directly at me. It did not turn to one side or the other. It slid straight ahead—up the slope at me—as if it were asking me for help. The engine stopped as the plane clanged, banged, and scraped across the ground. The propeller blades chewed into the soil and bent into weird, contorted shapes. The fully extended bomb bay doors did not seem to have much effect on the path of the airplane as it slid across the slope. It finally came to rest about a hundred yards down the slope from me.

I had mixed feelings at that point—feelings about being alive and uninjured; feelings about my illustrious B-17 being in such terrible condition, never to fly again; and, for the second time this day, the feeling of being all alone.

As the plane stopped sliding, grinding, and bumping over the ground, its right wing caught fire in the area of the engine, evidently from a ruptured fuel line as the propeller had dug into the ground. The entire forward part of the airplane, from the nose section to aft of the right wing, became engulfed in flames and burned profusely. Since we had lost all the fuel in the left wing, there was no fuel on that side to burn. Our lionhearted B-17 had arrived at its supreme day and its inevitable last hour.

I was thankful that the slope of the hill increased as quickly as it did. If it had not, the airplane might have reached me in its ending flight and I would have come face-to-face with, and become involved in the untimely end of, our big bomber—and perhaps even myself!

As I watched from my hanging perch, the fuel and oil continued to burn. There was little or no wind in the long valley, and the fire sent a large column of black smoke hundreds of feet straight up into the air. This was a disconcerting sight, as it was a dead giveaway to any German soldiers in the area. They had probably heard the airplane, and earlier and farther northeast, some of them may have seen some of my crew members parachuting.

Besides the smoke from the burning gas and oil, smoke bombs and

Vary Pistol flares of red, yellow and green (evidently missed when we jet-tisoned all our unnecessary equipment) were creating a classic Fourth-of-July display. The flares were igniting and rocketing skyward in every direction, just like large Roman candles, and the smoke containers were exploding from the intense heat, some being propelled high into the air and smoking heavily as they traveled upward.

The most frightening and deadly serious part of this spectacle hap-pened when some of the fifty-caliber, armor-piercing, incendiary ammu-nition (which we had saved for Jim Cook's two tail guns) began to cook off. About 300 of them had been stored in the radio room. These deadly projectiles flew everywhere. Some zinged through the trees where I was suspended, cutting through limbs and slamming into the hillside, hitting large granite rocks and ricocheting off them at all angles. If I had not known differently, I would have thought someone was shooting at me. I was lucky that the thick snow cover prevented the incendiary shells from causing a fire in the area where I hung.

I needed to get myself out of the trees and down on the ground—and fast—so that I could hide and make some plans to evade the German soldiers I knew would soon be searching for me. I looked down and saw some rather large rocks protruding from the snow beneath me, exactly where I would drop when I cut my parachute harness risers. It seemed that the most logical way to avoid landing on top of the rocks—and pos-sibly breaking a leg or something else—was to try to slant my fall so that I landed in the soft, deep snow beside the rocks instead of on top of them. I reasoned that if I cut the left riser completely and then cut through about two thirds of the right riser, the remaining portion would support my weight until I severed it completely. I'd swing from side to side as far as I could, and when my swing reached far enough to the right, I'd cut the remaining portion of the right riser and throw my trench knife to a spot where I was sure I could retrieve it when I dropped.

Did my plan work out as intended? Yes, except for one minor difficulty. When I landed in the snow, I missed the big rocks, but my right foot slammed down between two other rocks that were buried under the snow, hurting the arch of my right foot. I found out later that I had bro-ken some of the small bones at the top of my foot. They could not be set, but could be wrapped and would heal on their own if I could take it easy and favor them. Almost everything else worked well; my only other phys-ical hurt was a few frosty toes and fingers.

I found my knife and returned it to its sheath, and unclipped my parachute harness and buried it in the deep snow. Looking for a place to collect my wits, I walked out from the trees to an open area—which almost seemed to be a pathway with less snow on it—and up the side of the mountain to a very small knoll. This somewhat flat area was about 200 yards up the hillside and seemed a fine place to take a few minutes to rest. I sat down on a large round rock protruding from the snow, got out one of my escape kits, removed the small compass, and found west-southwest, the direction in which I intended to walk. Then I checked my forty-five-caliber automatic and charged it to be certain that it had a shell in the chamber and that the safety was engaged, so that I would be ready to defend myself if need be. Next, I took my cigarettes from the inside pocket of my jacket and lit one. Lucky Strikes were my choice at that time, and I sometimes smoked a pipe. (At that time, the Lucky Strike Green had gone to war! The cigarette package was never the same.)

I began to feel the effects of our long day's work—the fast-moving events of the past five or six hours were starting to slow me down. As I sat looking down into the valley, I could see our stalwart B-17 continuing to burn, and again I felt extremely sad. *Je Reviens* had saved my life, as well as the lives of all my crew members, but now its life was ending. I was full of remorse.

Pilots who have not flown the B-17 day after day in a theater of fierce combat—and have not witnessed firsthand the severe damage it could take and still continue to fly—cannot possibly understand how those of us who have done so feel about that airplane. Time and time again, even though very badly damaged, B-17s stayed in the air and created a survival machine for their crews. It always seemed to me that the B-17 Flying Fortress sheltered and took care of its crew members while it had them within its care, and those of us whose lives it saved *are* forever grateful to it. Many times I spoke to this marvelous flying machine, and it always answered and constantly reassured me. It brought us through just about the very worst that the air war would subject us to.

The Partisan Captain

Realizing that I had no more time to waste and that I must quickly get away from the area of my burning airplane, I buried my cigarette in the snow, put my little compass in my pocket, and turned to see if anyone was on the mountainside above me. As I moved slowly away from my big rock seat, someone said something to me from down the hill behind me in a loud and commanding voice. It sounded like "Stop!" I could not

Map A

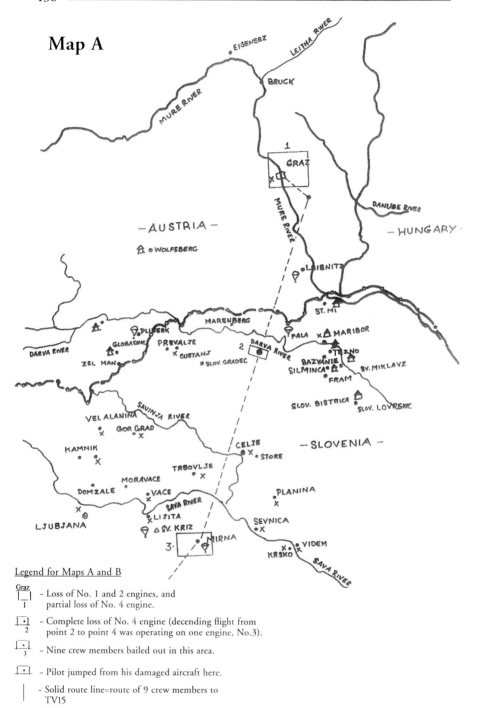

Legend for Maps A and B

$\frac{Graz}{1}$ [diagram] – Loss of No. 1 and 2 engines, and
partial loss of No. 4 engine.

$\frac{[\cdot]}{2}$ [diagram] – Complete loss of No. 4 engine (decending flight from
point 2 to point 4 was operating on one engine, No.3).

$\frac{[\cdot]}{3}$ [diagram] – Nine crew members bailed out in this area.

[diagram] – Pilot jumped from his damaged aircraft here.

| [diagram] – Solid route line=route of 9 crew members to
TV15

Map B

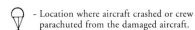

Legend for Maps A and B

- Dotted route line = route of pilot to TV15 with partisan captain.

- Solid long arrow = route of crew to cervisce.

+ - Grass landing strip by Kolpa River at Krasinec, Solvenia, and adjoining countries (1945).

--•-- - Yugoslav state boundary.

X - Location over which an aircraft was hit by antiaircraft fire, or was actually shot down.

- Location where aircraft crashed or crew parachuted from the damaged aircraft.

+ - Airfields.

+ - A central partisan hospital.

- Prisoner of war facility.

Opposite, Map A: Route flown after our airplane was initally hit over our target—Graz, Austria—and the route of our descending flight after number one and number two engines were lost, and ultimately the loss of number four engine. *Above*, Map B: Region where my crew and I parachuted into Slovenia, and the rescue of my nine crew members by the partisans (and my rescue by the partisan captain) and our trek with them. South to the Croatian Border and Safety. Maps not to scale.

recognize the language, but I was sure from the tone of voice that it was telling me to halt.

Instinctively, I reached inside my flight jacket, pulled my forty-five out of its holster, and disengaged the safety. I spun around and pointed it at whoever was behind me. There, about thirty yards down the slope of the mountain from me, standing in almost knee-deep snow, was a very large—about six-foot-three—soldier. He wore a brownish tan heavy wool uniform and held an automatic weapon that looked like a cannon. He was obviously not a German soldier in outward appearance, although he *could* still be a "bad guy," and, of course, that concerned me. He held the weapon waist-high with both hands and pointed it directly at me. I could see that it was a Bren gun, and I knew that its shells would pack a wallop like a cannon, particularly at such close range. Besides the Bren gun, on his belt he wore a pistol in a full leather clipped holster, and he had many extra ammo clips for both the sidearm and the Bren gun in leather clip holders.

As he started up the slope toward me, I had my gun pointed at him. I wasn't as heavily armed as he was, but my big forty-five was no toy. However, there was another difference between his firepower and mine: my right hand was shaking. I was quite unsteady, not from fright, but from cold fingers and the wear and tear of the day's trials. And I had not had one bite of food since my breakfast of green powdered scrambled eggs, fried Spam, burned toast, and coffee (in which a spoon would stand up) before 0600. Hunger had left me a little weak.

Within a few seconds, I realized that not only was I outgunned, but because of my unsteady hand, I also wouldn't be able to hit the broad side of a barn. If this confrontation became a shoot-out, it wouldn't be a fair fight; I would instantly lose. So I returned my forty-five to its holster and extended my right hand to the man as he trudged up to me.

When he was within a few feet of me, the small red star on his wool cap became visible and I realized with relief that he was a Slovenian, one of Tito's Partisan soldiers. When he reached me, he held the Bren gun in his left hand, put his right arm around my neck, and embraced me. I thought how nice a big bear hug could be and how happy I was that I had decided to put my gun away. He then pointed to the red star on his wool cap to reassure me that he was a friend.

Many people reading this story are probably more familiar with the British Army's Bren gun than I am. However, for those who are not, let me supply some statistical data that I acquired on this marvelous weapon. It was originally designed and manufactured by the Czechoslovakians at the Brno Arms Works. It was modified by the British Army in 1937 when they changed it to a .303 caliber machine gun and made other alterations. The British gave the reworked machine gun a new name—the Bren gun—from the first two letters of BRno and the first two letters of ENdfield, where the Royal Small Arms Factory was located in England.

The Bren gun this Partisan soldier was carrying was (I discovered when making a closer inspection of it later) a Mark II gun. The Mark II has a twenty-five-inch barrel and weighs 23.8 pounds unloaded. It has a muzzle velocity of 2400 feet per second, and its rate of fire is 540 rounds per minute. The cartridge magazine normally holds thirty rounds of ammunition. As one can see from these numbers, this is a very large and impressive weapon. I often reflect back on my impromptu meeting with this Partisan captain and his Bren gun, and I am very happy that the two of us became friends and that there was no shoot-out.

The epaulet insignia on this big fellow's shoulder indicated that he was an officer in the Partisan army of resistance. The dull gold braid with several small stars in the insignia field indicated his rank, I believed, although I didn't know exactly what it was—captain, I guessed. I have since learned that this fine gentleman was, in fact, a captain in the Partisan army and also the Vice Commander of the 4th SNOUB Matija, Gubec Brigade, XV Division, VII Corps. He was Captain Milan Vujinovic, a genteel, caring man of courage and dedication—a real soldier. He wrote his name, rank, and military unit on a small piece of paper that I had kept in my wallet for a while. Interestingly, the piece of paper happened to be an Army Air Corps application for war bonds!

Captain Vujinovic spoke to me very rapidly and motioned with his right hand toward the downward slope of the mountain and my still-burning B-17. Of course, I could not understand a word he was saying, and he realized that conversation wasn't the answer, so he took my left hand and beckoned to me to come with him back down the mountain. We walked down the slope through snow that was almost knee-deep in places, and when we arrived at the spot where my parachute and I had hung in the trees, there were three older women, bundled up in heavy winter clothes, standing in the snow beneath the trees. One was holding my parachute harness. She had dug it out of the snow, so I guessed that I had not done a very good job of burying it—or perhaps someone had been watching me when I hid it under the snow, or maybe even from the time my parachute popped open. I presumed that I would never know.

In later experiences with the Slovenian people, particularly the Partisans, I found that sometimes when you thought you were totally alone

Top: Captain Vujinovic's note to me (it is written on a section of a War Bond Application that I had in my wallet at the time). *Bottom:* Captain Vujinovic's military organization (written by the Captain).

and hidden, they were almost beside you. I quickly learned that they are very clever, intelligent, and patriotic people, and because of the terrible period of the German occupation of their country, they had learned many ways to elude and conceal themselves from the invaders.

Over the course of time, I have learned some interesting information concerning the last few minutes of the life of my B-17 on that day. The research was done on my behalf by the curator of the Slovenian Museum of Modern History in Ljubljana, who conducted the research at the Slovenian National Archives, also in Ljubljana. The facts reveal that my airplane had been observed by many Slovenian people in the area while I was trying to keep it in the air on one engine during the last ten minutes or so of its last flight. German military forces were also watching.

The Slovenian Partisan forces realized, because the airplane was operating on only one engine and because it was very low, that it would soon crash, so they endeavored to position themselves to be close by when it did. The records state that the parachutes of all nine of my crewmen were seen floating down as the plane flew over an area well to the northeast of Zuzemberk, close to the villages of Mirna and Mokronog. Our airplane was also seen flying to the southwest, passing almost directly over Zuzemberk, by the German forces garrisoned at their large headquarters there.

The Slovenian farm people in the area where our bomber made its own belly landing—in addition to the Partisan soldiers in this locale—saw the airplane make a descending left turn just prior to its contact with the mountainside. These same farm people had witnessed my jump from the bomber, but they did not realize that I was the last crewman in the airplane. They had presumed that there were eleven men on board, not just ten. (The B-24 carried eleven crewmen.)

The records also show that people were watching as I got myself out of the tree and buried my parachute harness in the deep snow. They saw me walk up the slope to sit on the large stone, where I lit up the Lucky Strike and sat to rest for a while. Reading this report, it was intriguing and also rather spooky to recall that all during this period, although I felt alone, I still had a distinct sense that someone was observing my every move—and it was true!

The Blister Boot Patch.

This research further revealed that the mountainous area in which I had landed was a mile or so west of the very small hamlet of Malo. The airplane had made its turn back toward me, over the small village of Gradenc, in the open valley close by. These two villages are west of a line almost an equal distance between the large towns of Zuzemberk and Smuka. All of the mountains to the south and southwest of Zuzemberk and in the Smuka region are about the same height. They are from 1500 feet to just over 2800 feet high, and some of them are shaped almost conically at their peak. Considering the rough terrain, the spot where I had to abandon my airplane was obviously chosen by someone with a higher authority than mine.

My newly acquired Partisan friend stopped to speak to the women and, motioning toward me, told them that I was an American—*Amerikanski*. They repeated the word and smiled. As we stood there for a few moments while he conversed with these women, I could hear other voices coming from high in the trees. Looking up, I saw several young children high on the branches trying to remove my parachute from where it had been entangled when I slammed into the forest. There must have been six or eight of them up there, talking rapidly to one another and moving quickly and confidently about the treetops.

My Partisan rescuer took my arm and motioned for me to follow him down the slope. He waved to the women as we plodded away from them through the snow. As we neared the airplane, he told me in sign language—and in hundreds of words in his native tongue—that a German patrol was close by and moving quickly to find the airplane, and it hoped to capture any of the crew who were close by. It was evident to me that he wanted us to move out of the area as quickly as possible, and I agreed.

As we neared the bottom of the steepest part of the slope, seventy or eighty yards from where I had landed in the trees, I saw a fine-looking saddle horse tethered to a tree. When we reached it, Vujinovic motioned to the horse and then pointed to me, and again to the horse—telling me that I should get into the saddle. He moved his fingers in a walking manner and pointed to himself, indicating that he would walk and lead the way.

He helped me into the saddle, which was quite an exercise, as my big fleece-lined boots would, of course, not fit into the stirrups. I must have been a funny sight, sitting on a really big horse, dressed in my flying gear, with cords and plugs hanging out everywhere and wearing my leather, fleece-lined helmet—which contained headset radio earphones—with its cord and plug hanging down the left side of my head. I'm certain I looked like someone from outer space, and evidently created much humor for my traveling companion. However, riding really beat walking in that deep snow.

We started our journey through the lower mountain valley—also covered by almost knee-deep snow—with Vujinovic trudging out in front, carrying his heavy Bren gun, and I on his horse following close behind. As we passed about fifty yards from the still-burning B-17, he turned and looked back at me and gave the airplane a soft salute. I will never forget the tragic sight of our airplane and the emotion that welled up within me as we walked past and then away from it. To this day, remembering that sad picture still brings a lump to my throat.

We soon left that lamentable image behind and traveled into the forest. Vujinovic made every effort to let me know where he was taking me; however, I was not sure just what he was telling me. He seemed to be indicating that we were traveling to some type of headquarters. I finally realized that I would just have to wait out the journey to find out our actual destination.

We climbed up some fairly large hills, thickly forested with very tall trees, and down the other sides into small valleys, but we always seemed to stay very close to the tree line, if not actually within the trees. I purposely did not consult my little escape-kit compass, as I did not want anyone to know I had it.

As we continued our trek, it seemed that the very high mountains were now behind us to the northeast, and the terrain was becoming somewhat flatter—a rolling, hilly countryside. During portions of the first two-hour period, the traveling was very tough. The snow was quite deep in some places, most likely drifted by the wind, and even though my traveling companion was a large fellow, I could easily see that walking through the snow, up and down the hills, carrying his heavy automatic weapon, was becoming a difficult task for him. So about every twenty minutes I called to him and suggested through sign language that he ride his horse for a while and I would walk.

He always refused.

Finally, to try to even things out, I tried to get him to let me carry the Bren gun. I attempted to convey to him that I was not at all comfortable with having him walk, carrying the big gun, while I rode his horse in luxury. He finally looked at me, smiled, and handed me that big machine gun. It was very heavy and difficult to carry, even on the horse, but I placed it across the saddle and we proceeded on our journey.

As we continued traveling, the depth of the snow decreased to less than a foot, and in the warm afternoon, the sun was beginning to melt some of it in the small valleys. It was a very pretty picture, this country-side of Slovenia.

At about five-thirty in the afternoon we emerged from the forest onto a narrow, dirt wagon road. There was very little snow on it, and our travel was considerably easier. For me riding this fine horse, it was actually relax-ing. After a few minutes, we came upon a small farm in a very picturesque setting. Large trees lined the small road that passed the farm—some sort of evergreen, apparently, as they were almost full of green foliage, giving the setting a sense of tranquility even though we were in a hostile area occupied by Germans.

The main farmhouse was small but neat, and well cared for—of typ-ical Slovenian rural architecture (a low one-story house made of stone, cement and wood, with a thatched roof). A large barn sat to the right of and behind the house, and several smaller buildings were clustered around the area behind the main house. This was a prosperous-looking farm-stead.

As we approached the big open main gate, my companion called out to people who were evidently watching us from inside the house, and when he did, several people came out on a run. It appeared to me that they were well aware that we would be arriving.

Three women, a teenage girl, and an elderly gentleman came run-ning up to us as we stood out in the middle of the small road. My rescuer greeted them, and they all conversed and pointed at the funny-looking fellow on the horse. *Amerikanski* was the only word I understood. I could tell from Vujinovic's gestures that he was explaining to them about my airplane crashing, the parachute floating down, and our journey through the snow. Shortly, two of the women hurried back into the farm-house and returned within a few minutes carrying a big green bottle of red wine, a small metal container of very sour milk, some mold-covered cheese, and about three-quarters of a loaf of rather hard white bread.

My Partisan companion took the big machine gun from me and I climbed down from the horse with some difficulty. I realized that these gracious people were offering me food they probably needed for their own sustenance. Though it looked very unappetizing, I accepted it with grat-itude, for I knew it would give me much-needed nourishment. I also drank a few swallows of the wine from a tin cup we all shared.

The older gentleman had brought a large bucket of grain from the barn, and he placed it on the ground so the horse could feed before we continued our journey. Everyone seemed happy about feeding us well.

Vujinovic thanked them, hugged them all, and I'm sure told them several times that we must hurry, as daylight was quickly running out. He said something about the Germans and pointed back to the direction from which we had come, perhaps telling them that the Germans could come here, as they were surely following us. We had been there just inside half an hour enjoying our meal and rest. I somehow managed to climb back up on the big horse, Vujinovic handed me his machine gun, and off we went down the small road, waving good-bye to our kind friends. In my mind, I still have priceless pictures of my climbing on that huge horse again and how funny I must have looked.

As we proceeded south-southwest, the land gradually rose in front of us and the snow became somewhat deeper. We left the small wagon road on which we had been traveling and again moved into the forest. We crossed several small streams that ran between some of the rolling hills we were climbing. It was very picturesque country, and I questioned why it had to be marred by the war the Germans had brought.

My traveling companion assured me often that we would arrive at our destination soon and that we had not far to go. Of course, he was the one with the really difficult task—my part was a snap.

Luck had been with us so far on our trek. Darkness was close, but that didn't seem to concern my friend. He knew this country well, so on through the thick forest and snow we proceeded. Shortly after seven-thirty we emerged into a small field with very tall trees edging it on all sides, creating sort of an arena, and we stopped abruptly right in the middle of it. I had an eerie feeling that we were being watched very closely by someone. We stood motionless for a minute or so in a foot of snow. What were we waiting for? I knew, because the starlit night was clear and visibility perfect, that we were silhouetted there in the white snow as though spotlighted on a large stage.

Finally Captain Vujinovic turned to me and motioned with his outstretched arm to the forest directly ahead of us. Two soldiers carrying sizeable guns emerged from the trees and walked silently toward us. My companion waved to them and they waved back. What a relief to see that they were friends.

When I thought about this scene later, I realized that had these men not been friends—had they been German or other enemy soldiers—there would have been a firefight and both of us would probably have been killed. I also realized that this meeting must have been planned and timed almost to the minute. I wondered how they accomplished the planning. What means of communication did they use?

It was not until years later, in research done at the Slovenian Museum, that I learned that the Slovene Partisans established a unique system of inter-brigade and inter-unit communications. Via this network of courier posts linked by courier routes, the Partisans always knew where we were, where we were going, and what we were doing while we were traveling with them during our time in Slovenia. This critical communication network greatly facilitated the liberation and pacification of large portions of their country.

One hundred fifty-two courier posts functioned throughout Slovenia during the war. They were placed in strategic locations around the country and were hidden from the enemy forces. They employed 1800 couriers, who operated twenty-four hours a day over the "courier lines," delivering communications between posts to keep the Partisan military forces' command and control functioning smoothly. The couriers were aware only of the locations of the posts they served, the paths between them, and the units who manned them, and were not aware of the locations of the other posts. They functioned on a "need to know" basis for obvious reasons. Security surrounding this communications system and the posts linked by it was extremely strict and staunchly maintained, and this made it very successful.

When the soldiers reached my companion, they all hugged one another (as, I was finding out, the Slovenian fighting people, both men and women, usually do). However, they were very quiet in their greetings. It was evident that most of their conversation was about me, our airplane, the rest of the crew, and, of course, the Germans in the area. I sensed that the two new Partisans wondered why their friend had let me carry his machine gun, although the reason should have been very obvious to them. There was a lot of gesturing and finger-pointing, as had been the case with the first group of friends at the farm.

It was abundantly clear that they were all very happy to see one another and to be together. This meeting made me aware that my traveling companion was of considerable rank in their organization, and highly respected. The entire encounter in the middle of this small field lasted less than five minutes, although it seemed much longer. After all the salutations, the three Partisans proceeded into the forest from which the two had originally come, and I followed close behind on the big horse.

As we traveled through the forest, the trees became more numerous and the snow deeper. The elevation seemed to be increasing, and the land was dotted by rocks, some very large and rising five or six feet out of the snow. As I rode behind these men, I marveled at their constant pace. They walked with swiftness, not speed, and made no wasted motions.

After about fifteen minutes we were met by another Partisan soldier who seemed to have just been standing by a large rock, waiting for us to arrive. Again there were hugs, greetings, and friendly conversation. In another five minutes we came upon the small command post my companion had tried to tell me about earlier in the day. The unimpressive rectangular wooden building, in its secluded landscape, was surrounded by the stillness of the forest. With the clear air, a clear sky (some of which was visible through the trees), and the cover of snow on the ground, the time seemed more like twilight than just past seven-thirty. Even in the dark, the scene was picturesque—almost a storybook setting—like a ski cabin in the Vermont woods.

The command post was set atop very heavy logs sunk vertically into the ground. It sat among numerous large boulders, some twelve or fifteen feet high, and the ground sloped sharply upward at the rear of the building. The shake roof was partially covered with snow, and steps lead to a railed porch with a rather large single door. There were two big windows on the side facing us, and there appeared to be some living quarters in the end of the building that backed up to the hillside. A small stone chimney in the center of the structure emitted a scant amount of smoke. Very little light was reflected from within. It was a tranquil setting, not at all the sort of place one would expect to encounter in a land occupied by a cruel and belligerent enemy.

By this time my rescuer and I had been traveling cross-country for about four hours. We had departed the burning B-17 at 1535, stopped a few times en route so he could rest a little and let his horse drink from one of the clear, cold streams we had crossed, and paused again at the farmhouse. But for most of those four hours, we had been moving toward our destination—this small Partisan command post (which I have since learned was Partisan Command Post TV-14 in the village of Stari Log). I was very tired of riding the horse and could appreciate how worn-out my companion must be. Watching him tenaciously endure our long journey without any sign of fatigue made me realize the really supreme dedication and perseverance of this man, and what a superior person he was. My admiration of him grew with each hour of our travels, even though I had known him for little more than four hours. By the time we reached the little command post, I felt as though I had known him for years.

More Partisan soldiers came out of the command post to greet us with more hugging, slaps on the back, and conversation. I gathered that we had come through some very dangerous territory. Captain Vujinovic relieved me of his machine gun and helped me down from his horse. As

I started to walk toward the command post steps, I wobbled a little, as my legs were somewhat numb from spending all that time in the saddle. One of the Partisans quickly put his arm under mine and steadied me for a moment, and then we all climbed the steps and walked inside.

One of the Partisans, a sergeant who was fluent in English, introduced me to the others, and then we all sat around a long rectangular table. There were six of them, including Vujinovic. Two of the men were dressed differently from the others. Each wore a soft gray uniform and did not have the small red star on their cap. They even seemed to have different builds than their Slovenian counterparts, and different mannerisms. I was immediately suspicious of them and wondered what military organization they belonged to.

During the time I had been flying with the 483rd Bomb Group, we were frequently warned by our intelligence officer about the various political and military factions in Yugoslavia, and how they interrelated with the Germans occupying their country, with one another, and with us—American air crew members who might have to crash-land or parachute into Yugoslavia. Our intelligence people characterized some of these groups as being very hostile and cruel to Americans—they would treat us in a barbaric manner if they captured or found us and they would eventually turn us, over to the Germans. The advice of our briefing officers was to be very cautious and try to link up with the "right" Partisan group if we ended up in Yugoslavia—to find a group that was not aligned with an outside faction and did not have dual motives.

With this advice in my mind, I was quite uneasy about these two "different" soldiers. I was not quite sure of anything that was transpiring, and I became concerned about my safety. After surviving my earlier ordeals, I was not ready to lose any points here. I seated myself, took off my helmet, unzipped my flight jacket, and tried to act nonchalant, despite my concerns. I believed that I had to quickly find a way let these men know that I was not entirely sure of their allegiances or their reasons for bringing me here. I decided to imprint in the minds of my table companions the fact that I was not sure I could trust everyone in the group—other than perhaps my rescuer. I had to know! The atmosphere in this room was one of mystery and trepidation.

Before anyone noticed, I reached inside my jacket, pulled my forty-five from its holster, removed the safety, and quickly put the weapon on the table in front of me. This got everyone's attention. They all looked at that big gun, at one another, and then at me. They must have wondered what this crazy American was planning.

There was a very brief moment of absolute quiet. During that silence, I looked at each of them as if to say, "Now tell me who you are and what this meeting is about." They looked at one another again. At that moment the Partisan soldier seated to my left reached out and placed his right hand on the 45, attempting to pick it up. Seeing his motion, I placed my left hand over his and removed his hand from the gun. I picked up the 45 and ejected the ammo clip and caught it in my left hand and placed it on the table. Grasping the 45 in my left hand I charged it to eject the round which was still in the chamber. It flipped over my right arm and fell to the floor behind me.

I picked up the clip, inserted it back in the handle, engaged the safety and handed it, handle first, to the Partisan who had originally attempted to pick up the gun. He accepted it and smiled. When the ammo round was ejected from the gun, there was a low, hushed "oh" from the group as they realized the once-very-dangerous weapon had now been rendered safe for handling and examining. They could see that by proceeding as I had, someone's life at the table may have been saved, as the weapon could have easily been fired by simply pressing the trigger without the safety engaged. At that point, there was much discussion among these men, and the English-speaking Partisan thanked me for what I had just done. They passed the 45 around the table, each inspecting it and commenting about its size and weight. This episode released my tensions and the doubts I had felt.

The Partisan sitting at the head of the table, who was evidently the officer in command of this post, said something to the Partisan who had been interpreting as the others listened intently. After their brief conversation, the sergeant turned to me and said that their leader had asked him to explain that he realized I could have some apprehension about the events that might lie ahead, and also concerns about my personal safety. He said, because of the rather mysterious and fast-moving events I had experienced over the past few hours, he could understand my reluctance to trust everyone I met in this German-occupied country. He wished to assure me that I was in good hands—that all of the men at this table were my friends, and that they would help to protect me from unfriendly forces by whatever means necessary.

I felt a sense of profound relief. His characterization of the circumstances was well-put and poignant. After that, our relationship became almost one of old friends fighting a war together, and now the atmosphere in this little post was like another one of those Slovenian family reunions. I realized that the two soldiers in the different uniforms were friendly, too.

Someone boiled some very bad coffee and we ate some very dark bread with it. I got out my Lucky Strikes and offered each of them a cigarette. We all lit up and they began asking me all sorts of questions. They told me that the patrol of German soldiers—which my rescuer had previously mentioned—would surely be looking everywhere for us. The Germans had located our crashed B-17 and had searched around it thoroughly.

A piece of interesting information has since been presented to me involving Jim Cook's two tail guns on our B-17. The records of that day show that a group of Partisans were the first to reach the smoldering airplane. They reached it before the Germans could get there, removed the two tail guns and the usable ammunition still remaining, and whisked these items away into the forest. Evidently, the heat of the burning airplane had not destroyed these items—only the forward section near the number three engine had burned.

I wondered how the Partisans knew about the Germans. Did they have a means of communication other than a courier? Several other Partisans had come into the command post while we were having coffee and bread, and conversed with the leader. I supposed that they could have delivered the news.

We talked about many things: the Germans and how the Partisans abhorred them; Tito, Roosevelt, and Stalin. I noticed that there was a small picture of each of these three men on the far rear wall of the room. We discussed the Americans' almost daily missions to bomb Hitler's Germany. The Partisans said that they watched the hundreds of bombers flying northeastward each day and watched them returning near the end of the day—and they observed that many of the planes they saw in the morning did not return in the afternoon. They told me again and again how wonderful all the American airmen were, what a tremendous job we were doing, and how they appreciated our heroic efforts. They spoke of their families; of the harsh, cold, snowy winters; and of the lack of sufficient food and supplies for both their families and themselves.

We discussed their rescue of many downed American airmen, and they expressed their desire to help save and repatriate every one of them that they could hide from the Germans. I showed them my silk escape maps and my little compass. They were impressed with the marvelous detail of the silk maps, particularly because they were in color and each side of the panel had a map on it. When I explained that the little compass could be swallowed and then at a later time retrieved to be used again, they all grinned.

As we were conversing, a rather frail man in his sixties or seventies arrived and spoke to the Partisan in command. The others listened with great interest. After this conversation, the older man was given hot coffee, bread, and a little wine. Upon finishing his meal, it was evidently suggested that he lie down and rest for a while, as they showed him a small cot in the corner of the room adjacent to the fireplace. He seemed eager to stretch out and was soon sound asleep. They explained to me that he was a courier and guide who had been sent here to guide me to the divisional headquarters, which he would do after he had rested. I was thrilled to hear that he had brought information about my crew members. Eight of them had been rescued and were being gathered together and taken to another command post for safety.

The courier also brought word that another group of Partisans to the northeast had seen my airplane flying past, operating on one engine and trailing smoke, and believed it would soon crash. They had counted nine parachutes coming down from the bomber. They had scoured the countryside where they had seen the first of the six parachutes land, as it was some distance from the other five, which all seemed to be close together. However, they had not yet located that one lone crewman who they believed was the first to bail out, and were continuing an impassioned search, as they knew there were many German soldiers in the area who had undoubtedly also seen the plane and the parachutes. They wanted to locate this missing crew member before the German patrols did, but with darkness rapidly approaching, they would probably have to wait until the next morning to continue their search for him.

The English-speaking Partisan explained to me that the courier guide and I would face a long trek over rather difficult terrain to reach the divisional headquarters building, and it would take us about three hours. Once we arrived, I would be fed and have time to rest, and the eight other members of my crew who had so far been located would be reunited with me. Then we would all be guided to the southern part of Slovenia by Partisan soldiers, who would protect us on our journey. This journey would take from one to three days, depending on the amount of German resistance we encountered en route and how fast we could walk. We would rest in barns or houses at night and then continue our journey each morning.

He mentioned that some of my crewmen had been slightly injured during their parachute landings and were not able to walk. A hay wagon pulled by two horses and driven by two Partisan soldiers would be used to transport them. The other crew members would walk behind the wagon with additional Partisan guards. Once at our destination, we would be flown back to Italy by a Douglas C-47 of the Balkan Air Force Supply Mission.

It was now nine-twenty. My elderly Partisan guide had been awakened and was drinking something hot, and I sensed that we would be departing very soon. The commander explained through the interpreter that my guide was ready to depart whenever I was. He explained that the guide knew the route over which we would travel very well, as he traveled it almost daily, and in spite of the fact that it was nighttime, we would have no difficulty—few German patrols moved about in the area at night.

We all exchanged hugs and farewells and assured one another that we would defeat Hitler's armies in the very near future. I thanked them all for the help and care they had given me, particularly the Partisan officer who had rescued me and led me through the forest on his fine horse while he walked in front for the entire journey. I will never forget that courageous gentleman!

A Rugged Partisan Guide

For an hour or so, I followed close behind my new Partisan guide. We moved at a very steady—but not too fast—pace. Every so often he turned slightly to look back at me and see how I was holding up at the speed we were walking.

At first our route took us through snow about a foot deep, making travel somewhat difficult, and because the terrain began to slope upward as we progressed, the trek became a little harder for us both. However, the snow-covered ground turned the would-be-dark night into almost twilight, making our footing less dangerous. My flying boots, even though snug and warm, were a little burdensome for walking. I was beginning to feel some discomfort in the top of my injured foot, and my slightly frost-bitten toes were letting me know they were there.

We soon moved out of the forest and onto more upward-sloping terrain, to some extent steeper than the previous woodland over which we had progressed. The snow was now only about six inches deep, but still posed some difficulty for us. Our walk was beginning to tire me, and I was becoming concerned about how my much older companion was holding up. I increased my pace and caught up with him. I walked up beside him, and he looked at me as I reached out and put my gloved hand on his right arm and slowly brought him to a stop. He had no idea, of course, why I had stopped him, and I could see confusion in his eyes.

I had not looked at him closely prior to this face-to-face observation and had not formulated an impression of him. I saw that my previous guess at his age was probably correct. From what I could see on this somewhat dark evening, he was between sixty-five and seventy years old. However, his physical condition made him seem much older. His face was drawn and heavily lined. His eyes were sad, with no sparkle at all; they revealed many years of hardship. He was very thin and appeared to be very frail. I was saddened when I looked at him and was almost angry with myself for creating additional stress and hardship for him. He did not seem strong enough for a long, strenuous trip such as this.

A large stone with a fairly flat top provided a perfect place to sit down and rest. As we had been walking for about two hours and still had another hour or more remaining on our journey, this was a good time to take a rest. Holding my guide by the arm, I led him over to the stone, seated him, and motioned for him not to get up. It was a shame that I could not converse with him, as he was not sure what I had in mind, but he remained seated.

He wore a very old and tattered three-quarter-length wool coat, evidently from a previous war. His boots seemed old and too large, and I'm certain that his socks were tattered and old as well. It was a very cold night, probably zero or less, so he really should not have been out there with me at all. I motioned for him to unbutton his coat to allow me to check his heart. Over his thin shirt and undershirt, I placed my hand against his chest. His poor old heart was pounding like an air hammer. I had never witnessed one beating so heavily. He could surely see the amazed look on my face. He smiled and I realized that he was both surprised and pleased that my interest in his well-being ran so deep. My greatest concern was that he was in such bad condition that he might expire right there.

I sat down beside him and we rested for about fifteen minutes. I wished there were something in one of my flight suit pockets that I could give him to eat, but I had nothing, which made me very sad. All we could do was rest and then slow our pace somewhat during the remainder of the trip.

Knowing that we must keep moving to keep our blood circulating and our body temperature normal, we started walking again. At first, I thought, we would walk at a very leisurely rate. Then, after a while, we could possibly increase our speed if he was handling things well. The terrain began to flatten, making our effort much easier, and as we progressed we found ourselves in a more closely forested area, with trees well over one hundred feet tall. The countryside was full of nature's beauty, even at night.

There was no way for me to tell how much higher in elevation we now were compared to the level where we had started. I knew that our elevation had increased quite a bit, and the altitude was affecting my breathing. Our strides were somewhat slower than they had been previously, although we kept a regular pace and my guide appeared to be holding up well.

We had been walking for approximately three hours, so if the time estimated by the Partisans was correct, we should be within a half hour or so of our destination. I suggested that we stop again to rest for just a few minutes, and my friend seemed to agree, so we found another stone and sat down. (I thought it would be a good idea to arrive at the divisional headquarters in good shape—not with my companion ready to drop.) During the ten minutes or so that we rested, I tried to find out how much farther we had to go. Pointing to my watch, he indicated that we should arrive there in less than thirty minutes. With that time frame in mind, we departed that cold hard stone and continued on our trip.

After about twenty minutes, the terrain again began to slope slightly upward and the forest became much denser. I felt that this heavily wooded area would be an ideal place in which to conceal a headquarters building, and that we were perhaps even now under observation. Within a few minutes, my companion tapped my arm and pointed to the forest ahead of us. As we covered another quarter mile through the tall trees, I discerned a somewhat clear area in the trees ahead, and my guide again took the lead. We soon walked out of the forest into a large semi-cleared area. Numerous Partisan soldiers, each wearing a rifle or small automatic weapon, tried to warm themselves around small fires built in holes in the ground that were surrounded by large stones. They must have been aware that we were coming—forewarned I'm sure by the eyes I had felt watching us half an hour ago. And they all knew my escort and came over to say hello and wish us both well.

In front of us, among the tall trees at the far end of the open area, were several wooden buildings, their roofs covered with a thick layer of snow. One was quite large; I thought it must the divisional headquarters building itself. It was a wide one-story structure with large eaves and perhaps some offices or living quarters on the sides. Several stone chimneys protruded from the roof, and the slight plumes of smoke that arose from them drifted lazily up into the tall trees.

I wondered whether the Partisans were concerned about the smoke being seen from above, possibly by German observation aircraft—I had seen some earlier in the day. However, I supposed the smoke was almost completely dissipated as it filtered through the high tree branches. My first thought when seeing the smoke was, "Where there's smoke, there's fire," and a fire meant that I could finally get warm. It had been a long, cold, tiring day.

My guide led me to the large front doors of the building, where two heavily armed guards stood on duty. One of them opened a door for us and my guide escorted me inside. We entered a small foyer, and to my surprise, he stood a few paces in front of me, came to attention, and saluted me. To look again at this dear fellow and reflect on what he had endured to bring me here brought tears to my eyes. He was a fine man and a dedicated soldier. He would have expired before he'd have given up. He had accomplished his assignment and had done it exceedingly well. I had great admiration for him, and our journey together had been enjoyable. I returned his salute, walked over to him, put my arm around his shoulders, gave him a big hug, and then shook his hand and bade him good-bye.

The Reunion

As I walked into the large hall before me, I had a sense of security once again. As I recall, the time was around 0015. We had been en route for a little less than three and one-half hours from the time we left the small command post. I learned that this Partisan military building was the brigade headquarters of the 15th Division of the 7th Corps Slovenian Militia, or Slovenian Partisan Courier Command Post TV-15, adjacent to the village of Kocevske Poljane.

I thought at first that I was alone in this very long and dimly lit room, which was odd, because this had to be an important headquarters. But when I looked more closely, I saw that many soldiers were seated at tables on either side of the room, and several more sat at a long table on a slightly raised platform at the far end of the room. There was a large stone fireplace in the center of each long side wall of the room, the one on the left side considerably larger than the one on the right. Soldiers stood about these sources of warmth chatting with one another. Smoke filled the room and made visibility very poor, but it was nice and warm.

Looking again down the long hall, I saw that one of the soldiers who had been seated at the far end was now standing and beckoning to me. I started walking down the center of the hall toward the man, who was presumably the officer in charge. As I walked past the fireplace on the left, one of the men standing by it called out "Ed" and rushed over to give me a big hug. It was my bombardier, Bob Mahan, and I realized that the men standing around this large fireplace were all members of my crew. The rest of them came over to where Bob and I stood chatting. The four who had been injured in their parachute landing took a little longer, but everyone was there except Duane Berthelson, who had not yet been accounted for. This meeting with my crew members was a truly American-style old-home-week reunion, with bear hugs for all, tears, quivering lips, handshakes, and pats on the back. The Partisan soldiers in this hall had probably never witnessed such joyful American soldiers.

My crewmen were delighted to see me walking around, as they were not sure whether I had been able to belly-land the airplane as I had said I would try to do, and whether I had had time to bail out before the plane hit the mountainside. The Partisans had told them the airplane had crashed and burned, but at that time they didn't know of my fate.

During this joyous meeting a soldier came up to the group and asked me to come with him. He took me to the end of the room and introduced me to the officer in charge and the other officers in command of this garrison. The officer in charge spoke perfect English. He related to me the story he had been told by one of his couriers of my recent tribulations.

It was his Partisans who were in the area where all of my crewmen had landed in their parachutes and who had rescued them and brought them to this post earlier in the evening. The same courier had told him about hearing our airplane and sighting it through the clouds as it made its way toward the southwest, and said that they believed it would not stay in the air much longer. This was evidently just after my crewmen had jumped from it.

He mentioned also that some civilians (farm people) living in the area had told the Partisan soldiers they knew our airplane had crashed on the slope of a hill some miles to the south-southwest. They had observed our B-17 passing by them a few minutes prior to its crash, and they told the soldiers they did not know whether anyone had been on board when it crashed. They had not inspected the wreckage since it was still burning and its ammunition was still exploding. They were aware of German soldiers in the area.

He said that he and his people were surprised and elated when word came to them that I had been found and quickly shepherded away from the area of the crashed bomber. He and his men originally thought that I must not have survived the crash, as they had sighted no other parachutes. He knew of the Partisan officer who took me to his outpost and arranged for me to be guided to this headquarters.

At the end of our conversation, the commander arranged for me to have some bread and hot soup while he filled me in on where we would go when we left this site, guided by Partisan soldiers. He told me they would provide a small hay cart drawn by two horses to transport my injured crewmen. The cart would be driven by two guards, and the rest of us would walk behind it with additional Partisan soldiers. He hoped that Duane Berthelson, our tenth crew member, would be reunited with us as soon as possible. He assured me that our route and procedures had been fully arranged. Six Partisan guards would travel with us at all times, and their express duty was to protect us and to make certain that my crewmen and I were safely and expeditiously taken to a more secure area of Slovenia to the south-southwest. He explained that we would depart this building as soon as I had finished eating, as it was safer to travel at night than during the day. It was almost 0100. He wanted us to make good use of the night time remaining to clear this location. We would stop after about two hours in a hamlet or farm and sleep for a few hours. Then we'd proceed with our journey.

17

Day Number 2—Saturday, March 10, 1945

Away from the Farm and Over the Bridge

Anyone seeing us leaving the command post would have thought we were a group of relatives leaving a reunion rather than the almost-strangers some of us were to one another. Our rescue was heart-warming and showed how much these wonderful and noble Slovenian people cared for the many men they saved, befriended, hid, and repatriated during World War II, even, in some cases, at the cost of their own lives.

As we left, there were handshakes, hugs, and some teary eyes as our rather curious-looking group of tattered and tired warriors ventured out into the snowy forest in the darkness of the cold early-morning hours of March 10, 1945. As we walked away from that warm, secure headquarters building, I reflected on the upcoming journey and wondered about what sorts of situations, possibly fraught with danger or filled with adventure, we would face during the days ahead. The first episode came sooner than I expected.

We walked quickly through the forested, snow-laden countryside until about 0300, at which time we came upon the small hamlet, actually a substantial farm complex, that the Partisan commander had told us about earlier. This complex was laid out in an open area with only a few large trees close to some houses that were clustered around one larger, more prosperous-looking house. The snow-covered ground and the brilliantly starlit early morning sky made this gathering of homes and farm buildings appear illuminated by artificial outside light—it seemed almost as bright as day. I remember vividly that the large main house, an impressive two-story home, was painted white with dark green trim. Rolling land sloped up and away from the cluster of houses, barns, and outbuildings toward the thick forest just beyond it.

A rapidly flowing shallow creek ran through the complex about fifteen or twenty yards in front of the main house. There was no bridge over it, just a flat area where wagons could cross. Large flat stepping-stones had been placed in the stream at the flat area to enable people to easily walk across. Once more, we were witnessing a tranquil sight in hostile territory. One could easily visualize what a happy place this farm could be in another time.

As we crossed the stream, passed by the main house, and made our way up the slope to the large barn, our caravan was greeted by twenty or thirty Partisan soldiers, who seemed to come from every direction and gave us the exuberant greetings we had grown used to. Fortunately, everyone seemed to realize that nine of us had been through a difficult previous day and were very much in need of sleep, so the Partisans in charge led the hay cart and those of us following it to the barn, where my crew was dispersed into different parts of the dimly lighted structure—the only illumination was supplied by a few oil lamps.

I wondered about, but did not question, this separation of our crew members. I assumed the Partisans had a reason for splitting us up and soon learned what it was. For some reason—which I was never told and was unable to figure out—I alone was led to the main section of the barn by a tall, husky, attractive female Partisan soldier. She was about five feet, eleven inches tall, about thirty years old, and she appeared indestructible and all-business—very much a soldier in command. She did not speak English, and when she spoke, it was in a gruff voice. She wore the regular Slovenian Partisan uniform and was very impressively armed with an automatic weapon—Russian, I presumed—and scads of ammunition. Two bandoleers full of cartridges looped over her shoulders and crossed her chest. She also carried a sidearm—also Russian—in a full leather clipped holster and a trench knife in a leather sheath on her belt. And—I am not joking—many small hand grenades hung from her belt.

She motioned to the area where she wanted me to sleep, and I sat down at that spot on the abundant soft hay that covered the earthen floor and started to take off my flying boots as she stood over me. As I started to unzip my right boot, she firmly pushed the barrel of her automatic weapon into my chest and said something in a loud, firm voice. It sounded like she wanted me to stop, so I stopped and re-zipped my boot. I could not see whether she had her finger on the trigger of her machine gun, but it didn't matter, as her point was well understood. It was a disconcerting few seconds for me, although I'm sure she was likely being careful not to shoot me.

She could see that I was puzzled by her abrupt action and she sat down beside me to try to explain the reason for it. With more hand signals and sign language, she drew me a picture, explaining why she did not want me to take off my boots. What I understood was that no one took off his shoes or boots while resting because if we were attacked by the Germans while resting bootless, we could be killed or captured while taking the time to put them back on. And if we fled or were captured without our boots in the middle of winter, our chances of survival without injury would be slim. Once I showed that I understood, her gruffness turned into a soft smile, and I had the feeling that she was sorry about frightening me.

There were eleven other female soldiers in the same section of this big barn with me, and they seemed similar to their leader in size, shape, and age, and just as well-equipped for combat as she was. I was teased by the other men on my crew about the somewhat unusual experience of spending part of a night in a big barn with twelve attractive Slovenian women, though the experience was not at all amusing to me.

We greatly deserved a rest, and in no time we were all fast asleep. But only two hours later, the magnificent quietness was shattered by the sound of gunfire from heavy machine guns and rifles, as well as some light mortar rounds that were landing around the compound. My crewmen and I and the small contingent of Partisan soldiers traveling with us had been located by the Germans and were now under a fierce attack by a substantial, tenacious, and well-armed German force. The mortar fire the Germans were directing at us was becoming more accurate by the minute. The ferociousness of war had suddenly arrived at this quiet and comfortable barn.

When we had arrived at this farm, I was told that we would rest here for a time, and I didn't think we'd be here very long; but our rest was much shorter than I had imagined. As quick as a wink, the female Partisan soldiers were up and moving about the barn, gathering the nine of us together. They led my injured crewmen to the hay cart, and at the same time our six guards hitched the two horses to the wagon. Once the four injured men were on board, the guards spirited us out of the large door at the rear of the barn and directed us into the thick forest beyond and, we hoped, to safety.

As soon as we were out of the door, the women went out a door at the front of the barn to take part in the fierce firefight that was taking place beyond the stream in front of the main house. The Germans had not taken the Partisan sentries by surprise as they sneaked up on the area, and the sentries quickly made this attack very costly for them—we were told that the remainder of the Partisan soldiers in the complex had rapidly repositioned themselves for a strong frontal and flank attack on the advancing German troops. The tone of the battle soon changed as the German force fell back, having suffered many casualties.

This was another example of the bravery of the Slovenian Partisans. Their heroic, rapid, and professional actions had undoubtedly saved our lives. I was never able to learn whether any of these men and women lost their lives defending our escape into the forest that early morning, and perhaps it's best that I don't know. This graphic true-life experience at the farm complex had brought to me the reality of what fighting men and women on the ground were required to endure day in and day out.

We could hear the sound of battle for some time as we hastily made our way through the forest. The land began to slope downward and then leveled out somewhat as we made our way out of the forest and onto a small, rutted dirt path. We continued our speedy travel for another twenty minutes or so and then stopped our caravan on the crest of a small hill. It was then about 0615 and still dark; however, from our position at the top of the hill, we could see the dim outline of a small village down below.

At this point, all six of our Partisan guards had a deep discussion about something—something mysterious, apparently, was about to unfold. When they concluded their conference, I found out what they had been hashing out: They had formulated a gutsy plan that sounded like it might be very tricky to carry out. I had been in Slovenia less than twenty-four hours, and already had been exposed, with humble pleasure and surprise, to many marvelous accomplishments achieved by these Partisan friends. So I didn't doubt their ability to succeed in the unusual plan they proposed; in any event, I had little choice but to trust them!

Their plan (as explained to us by the English-speaking Partisan in charge of our guard detail) was to ask a favor of the mayor of this country village. I expressed some doubt and amazement about it, but agreed that we would play our part in the venture and then outlined the plan to my crew members. The Partisan explained that the small village which lay at the bottom of the hill sat on the west side of the Crmosnjicica River, which we must cross in order to continue our journey, and we must cross it before sunup. The village was occupied by a small garrison of German soldiers, and the only way to assure our uninterrupted passage through this little town and across the bridge was to somehow bypass them. We needed the mayor to negotiate our crossing with the German commander.

The Partisans would send one of their men, who knew the mayor, to speak with him and bring him back up the hill where we were waiting, and we would attempt to formulate a plan. They said that the mayor was a Slovenian and a "good guy," and they thought he would be able to work something out with the rather lackadaisical German officer in charge to make it possible for us to get through the town, over the bridge, and on our way.

The plan commenced: The man who knew the mayor went down the hill to visit with him. After about twenty minutes, he reappeared out of the darkness with the mayor. Introductions were made, and the plan was unveiled and agreed upon. The mayor would bribe the German officer in command with American money and cigarettes—a small token for the German commander's kindness—to secure our free passage.

It sounded preposterous, I thought—a bit crazy—but it might work. On the other hand, it might not and we could all be killed! But I thought the Partisans knew what they were doing, and it was imperative that we cross the river here. There were few bridges at all over this river, no boats available, and swimming was out of the question.

Without further delay, I collected $330 from six of our escape kits (each kit contained fifty-five American dollars in Gold Seal notes), and five packs of American cigarettes from the crewmen who still had them. I gave the hush money and cigarettes to the Partisans who would return to town with the mayor and hide in the woods close by while he discussed our scheme with the German officer.

Before they left, I collected some more money and asked the lead man to try to buy some food for all of us. Everyone was hungry, cold, and thirsty. Because they had had no exercise, the crewmen in the hay cart were especially cold in spite of the soft, almost enveloping hay in which they rode. With the assurance that they would do their best to reach terms with the Germans and find something for us to eat, the Partisans and the mayor disappeared down the hill and into the darkness.

After about forty minutes had passed and they hadn't returned, we began to be concerned, but the four guards still with us explained that these things sometimes took some time. After another few minutes, the two guards appeared with the mayor. They were all in good spirits and proclaimed that their mission had been a complete success. The negotiations between the mayor and the German officer had gone well and our safe passage was assured. The Partisans had also obtained some food—several large loaves of very tasty bread, an abundance of cheese, and four bottles of dark red wine. We were starved and greeted our feast with much exuberance. It would fortify us for the adventure that lay ahead.

We quickly shared the food; if we were to perish going through this village, at least we would do it on full stomachs! Then down the hill our caravan traipsed, emboldened by the fine meal, the good wine, and a feeling that we had consummated a good deal with both the mayor and the German commander. We had a lilt in our walk, and we had the necessary cock-sure ability to be able to brazen through our well-planned and rather capricious escapade. Contrary to my philosophy that "discretion is the better part of valor," I never mentioned to any of my crew the apprehension I felt about the whole arrangement.

The little dirt road we were following turned to the right as we reached the bottom of the hill and joined a more substantial road as we approached the village. As our passage through this village was supposed to take place at just before sunrise, we were right on schedule. We had about another quarter mile to travel before we reached the center of the village, and the eastern sky was becoming brighter. We would be across the bridge just before sunup.

As I considered what the German soldiers would think when they saw us, shivers ran up and down my spine, and again I had misgivings about what we were going to do. Picture this: four American Air Corps combat crewmen riding in a hay cart drawn by two large horses driven by two Partisan soldiers. Five other American Air Corps crewmen walking leisurely behind the cart, accompanied by four more heavily armed Partisan soldiers. We Americans are dressed in flight gear, including fleece-lined helmets with earphone cords and plugs dangling to our shoulders. Some of us wear big fleece-lined leather flying boots and others wear GI shoes. Some wear fleece-lined leather jackets and overalls. Four of us have gabardine flight coveralls over our regular officer's uniforms and jackets. We all have electrical cords hanging out of our hip pockets. Most of us wear chest holsters carrying forty-five automatics, webbed belts with three or four extra clips of ammunition in pouches, and sheathed trench knives.

We lacked very little in the way of combat bomber crew outfitting, yet as we walked right into a German-held town, their armed soldiers stood around open fires talking and showing little interest in us. It was another instance when I wish that I had had a camera! While praying this plan worked, I continually wrestled with the thought of possible betrayal and the fact that we could end up full of holes in the middle of the village.

We joined the main road into the village and after a hundred yards or so we came to an intersecting road at its very center where we would turn right and then proceed about a quarter mile to the bridge. It was still not completely light and it was very cold—about thirty degrees. I know that everyone was wishing that this episode was behind us and we were someplace where we could be warm and sleep for a while.

Just before our right turn, we looked down the road to the left and the hair on my head stood straight up. Less than a hundred yards down the road was group of fifteen or twenty German soldiers standing around a very large fire talking and trying to stay warm. Their rifles were stacked in pyramidal clusters close to where they stood; they appeared to be in full battle gear. These were not casual caretakers; they were the same people whose strategic military targets we bombed almost daily—the same type of people who had shot our airplane down. And here we were, a rather large contingent of American and Slovenian fighting men on the opposite side of the war nonchalantly walking past them as though we didn't have a care in the world—as if there were no war!

The Germans continued their conversations and acted as though they did not see us. We turned right and followed the road toward the bridge. The Germans had ignored us, and we also ignored them. We didn't change our pace or give them a second glance; we acted as though our presence there was as normal as the approaching morning.

We tended to the important issue at hand—getting across that bridge and continuing on with our journey to repatriation. For the time being, at least, we were secure and felt that our plan had been successful.

As we neared the bridge, the road began to run closer to the river, and the Partisans encouraged us to quicken our pace. We wondered why there were so few people to be seen in this small river town. Those we had seen ignored us completely, and the town was almost deathly quiet. We did see a few villagers in front of buildings on what was probably the main street. They were no more than twenty-five yards from us, but they went about their early morning business and ignored us. I was amazed. It was most unusual—bizarre, to say the least.

We could now see the bridge and the river; the bridge was a fine stone structure of substantial size, and the river flowed rapidly and was larger than I had imagined. I understood now why we needed to cross the river here. Bridges such as this one, still intact, were not plentiful in Slovenia, particularly ones free of German control. Three small elongated arches supported the main structure and roadbed. They were built of large pieces of fieldstone, and a full-length hip-high solid side wall ran along each side of the span. It was very picturesque. Even today it is effortless for me to picture this fine stone bridge and its construction as it spanned the fast moving river.

I remember well the noise the steel rims of the hay cart's wheels made as the cart rolled over the cobblestone and wood surface of the roadbed. I'm sure everyone in the village must have heard us, but our Partisan companions kept motioning to the fellows driving the hay cart to move more quickly and motioned to us to quicken our gait. They didn't seem to care about the noise. It must have taken us four or five minutes to cross the bridge, and we stepped off the other end just as the new day was breaking. Our mission had been accomplished. I didn't understand why our guards had kept hurrying us along; however, I was soon to find out.

Over the Bridge Just in Time

The dirt road beyond the bridge turned to the right (toward Semic) and curved slightly away from the river. On the left side of the little road, opposite the river, was a steeply rising bluff that graduated into a 1500-foot mountain beyond. Our Partisan friends continued to hurry us every step of the way as we continued our travel; why such speed was necessary I still didn't know. But then the reason for our haste was revealed. No more than twelve minutes after we had stepped off the bridge, we heard the familiar muffled rumble of aircraft engines, probably large radial engines. As the engine noise became louder, we Americans were startled— why would aircraft be flying this low in a mountainous area? What were they doing in this river valley?

We all stopped and turned in the direction from which the noise was coming—looking back along the river toward the bridge—and were amazed when we realized what was taking place. Two American Air Force twin-engine medium bombers, which had flown down the wide, curving valley over the river, each made a run on that bridge—one after the other in close trail formation—and destroyed the span with their bombs. After the bomb drop, they pulled up steeply and zoomed out of the valley and into the clear blue sky above. They were soon out of sight and hearing range. Their mission had been precise, quick, and successfully completed. That bridge was no longer usable to the Germans or anyone else.

When I asked the Partisan leader about the destruction of the bridge, he simply said that the operation had been planned in advance, both on our behalf and also to somewhat isolate the German garrison in the small town we had just successfully traveled through. He seemed rather unconcerned about the entire incident and pointed out that our safety had been enhanced by the bridge being knocked out. To me, it was a classic operation, with timing I would characterize as perfect—very professional.

I also realized then why the Partisans had constantly urged us to walk faster. Being caught on the town side of the bridge after it had been destroyed would have caused untold problems. Because we had crossed in time and the bomb run had been so well performed, the enemy could not easily catch up to us since there were no other bridges for many miles in either direction.

Our route now took us away from the river at about a forty-five degree angle to the left—a southeasterly course. The narrow road soon led us away from the larger hills close to the river and into a rolling terrain with more medium and small hills visible ahead. The road was bordered on each side by woodland. I suspected that it was selected by our guides because the woods offered us protection. When we occasionally heard aircraft close by, we dashed into the dense trees. It seemed that the Germans were still trying to find us, as ME-109's kept flying over at a very low altitude.

After two hours of tolerably fast walking, we started climbing a moderately steep hill. All of us, including the two horses, were beginning to show signs of the wear and tear of rapid travel, and we were pleased to finally reach the top of the hill. We were not only tired, but also hungry, despite the bread and wine we'd had earlier, and we had no idea when, or from where, our next meal would come. The green powdered eggs, fried Spam, burned toast with grape jelly, and the thick black GI coffee served at our officers' mess was beginning to sound like a royal meal.

The weather wasn't cooperating either. The sky, once filled with scattered cumulus clouds with some sun in between, was becoming overcast, and large snowflakes were beginning to fall. Our Partisan companions would not let us eat snow to ease our thirst, of course, because of its detrimental effects, and small streams from which we could drink had become scarce. We hoped to reach a spot soon where we could melt some snow for drinking. The horses had been fed some grain when we stopped above the river village, but they, too, needed food again.

The forest thinned as we reached the top of the hill, and our caravan came to an expanse of somewhat clear land perhaps half a city block in size. Scattered around the periphery were four or five burned-out houses. All that remained of them were stone chimneys and small portions of houses that had been built of stone. It was a sad and desolate picture. Snow was now falling heavily. The flakes seemed as large as saucers, and the cold and quiet imparted an eerie feeling to this ruined little community. The Partisans, evidently steeled to realities such as this, showed little emotion. They had but one purpose in mind—to quickly deliver us, all in one piece, to our destination farther south in Slovenia.

We continued slowly and cautiously to the center of the open area, where a few large trees grew, and came to a stop. Our guards fanned out, rapidly checked the area of the charred houses, and then returned to where we were waiting. I was not sure if they had heard something we didn't or knew something that we were unaware of. However, they now seemed to be satisfied that all was well, and we proceeded toward the far side of the clearing where the forest started again.

I'm sure my crew members felt as I did—that perhaps now we would stop and rest for a while. Surely when we reached the wooded area at the far side of the clearing we'd be able to take a break. But what was in store for us was not rest but another surprise: As we approached the far edge of the clearing, we saw, standing quietly by the tall trees, two splendid horses very similar to those that had been pulling the hay cart for the past nine or so hours. They were tethered to a tree, bridled, and ready to be hooked up to the hay cart. They were patiently standing there in the snow, just waiting for us to arrive—an astounding picture! We Americans were intrigued and amazed by this, but the Partisans were business as usual— very matter of fact. The soldiers methodically unhitched the tired horses, tied them to a tree, hitched the new team to the hay cart, and off into the woods we trudged. Our leaders once again set us walking at a fast clip. They must have had another schedule to satisfy, and now, with two fresh and spirited horses, there was no holding them back. These rugged fellows never seemed to tire.

Walking through the forest on the narrow trail (barely wide enough for the hay-cart), I continually thought about just how large and tall all these trees were. They were magnificent. I mused that some of these same type of trees were those into which I so violently crashed in my parachute at such a low altitude, and they had probably saved my life.

The countryside now sloped away from the more mountainous terrain and the land was more open. There were still some high hills—perhaps 1800 feet up to almost 3000 feet. As we traveled in what seemed to be a south-southeasterly direction, we came upon several small streams that we drank from and easily forded. The Partisans seemed to know this part of the country very well.

We had changed the horses at about 1015. At about 1115, our small country road broadened and we entered an area that was more heavily populated. We frequently saw small hamlets in the distance, so I expected to see more Slovenian farm people, larger villages or towns, and perhaps even more Germans. (It seemed to me that a bit more caution might be in vogue here.) Within a few minutes, we came upon a small group of Partisan soldiers who had set up a roadblock at the intersection of the narrow road we were on and another road of equal size. On a bank about twenty feet high to one side of the road they had dug a position for a machine gun emplacement. To my surprise, in this emplacement was a complete twin fifty-caliber machine gun top turret from a B-17 set up on a heavy wooden structure; the gunner stood on a wooden platform beneath the turret.

We learned that this turret had been removed from a B-17 that had crash-landed in the area. The Partisans told us that they had recovered hundreds of rounds of fifty-caliber ammunition from this one B-17, and more from other B-17s and B-24s that had crash-landed nearby. This installation was well-situated and equipped to carry on a sustained fight. The guns could be turned 360 degrees laterally and 180 degrees in elevation. My crew members and I were very impressed with the work the Partisans had done putting this turret together and told them so. They had located tremendous fire power here!

Another surprise was that they knew we were coming! Again there had been communication between Partisans in different areas, yet we never saw evidence of any sort of communication network. How did they know when we would arrive?

After they thanked us for our interest in their work, we bade them good-bye and continued southeastward. I have since been told that this roadblock was on the outskirts of the town of Semic, which was the Slovenian Courier Post TV-6.

Our group arrived at Semic about 1145 and then spent an enjoyable fifteen minutes or so meeting and chatting with some of the Partisan officers who were in charge of the sizeable headquarters post there. We were given some food and some very tasty hot coffee. We needed the short period of rest and relaxation as much as we needed the food.

Just as we were finishing our meal and relaxing a bit, we were greeted with another happy surprise! Our tenth crew member, armor gunner Duane Berthelson, had also reached Semic. He was escorted by two Partisan soldiers from the same brigade as the guards traveling with us. They had been with him since he was rescued and hurriedly spirited him away from the Germans, who were trying to find him in the area where he had landed. I knew they must have been traveling rapidly to be able to link up with us here, and found out that his guards had been able to move faster than we did since they had no hay cart to be concerned with and could manage a more direct route with many shortcuts. I also learned that bringing us all together here at Semic before proceeding southward to Cerkvisce was another part of the Partisan Command and Control network's plan.

Duane looked well, but tired and hungry. The hunger was soon taken care of, but he would be able to rest for only a few minutes, as the Partisans had us scheduled to leave in a short while. We were elated to see him and to learn that he was safe and would be continuing to Cerkvisce with us. It was a real joy for me, in particular, to have another "family member" returned to us safe and sound, as I had secretly been concerned about his well-being from the outset of our journey southward.

Ten happy bomber crewmen and our six Partisan guards set out from Semic around 1220 and continued our trip, heading in a southerly direction through a lovely almost-open valley with little snow on the ground. As we walked, we commented on the formidable mountain ranges—2500 to 4000 feet, we thought—well to the west of our route. Seeing these large mountains reminded me of how fortunate the timing of my men's exits was; a later jump time could very well have placed us all in much higher terrain and possibly in a more dangerous circumstance. It had been a stroke of good luck!

I had been told at Semic that we would be following a route to the south, through the small towns of Gornja Paka and Lokve. Lokve was one of the most important Partisan headquarter posts in this area, and from there we would proceed southeast around the outskirts of the city of Crnomelj, and then walk the final leg of our journey to Cerkvisce. This, I realized, had been the destination of our group from our very first day in Slovenia.

I have learned from research done at the Slovenian Archives in Ljubjana that Semic was the primary place in central Slovenia where Allied airmen who had bailed out or crash-landed their airplanes were taken. From Semic, they were then routed south through Gornja Paka and Lokve and finally to Cerkvisce. Most of these men were eventually flown back to Italy from the aerodrome at Krasinec by the Balkan Air Force's supply and re-supply aircraft.

This last segment of our travel, from Crnomelj to Cerkvisce, would take us almost due east instead of the usual south or southeast. Cerkvisce is tucked away in pastoral rolling country a little more than four miles

A copy of my Yugoslavian passport. (Slovenian)

west of the large Kolpa River, which marks the border between Slovenia and Croatia.

We reached Lokve at 1330 and were taken to the Partisan headquarters building there for some quick processing. Amazingly, most of the necessary paperwork, such as a Slovenian passport for each of us, had already been taken care of by the time we arrived—another case of excellent advance planning! With everything in order, we departed the Lokve headquarters at 1530 on our way to Cerkvisce via Crnomelj.

This leg of our walk took us through some heavily wooded areas, with no view of hamlets or villages—just forest and undulating countryside. We passed northeast of Crnomelj, where the forests thinned for a while and then became dense again as we proceeded due east. As we walked away from Crnomelj, the land became much more rolling. We walked up and down many small, low hills and forded several shallow streams. There was more snow on the ground, particularly in the heavily wooded areas, and that made walking more tiring.

Our Partisan guards always seemed to know exactly where we were as they led us on trails and small rutted roads. We knew that most of these trails were obscure and unknown to outsiders, which gave us an additional measure of safety during our passage.

The commanding officer had mentioned to me when we departed Lokve that he expected us to arrive at Cerkvisce at about 1830. Lo and behold, as we walked out of a rather dense forest into an open stretch of country, there, about half a mile ahead of us, was the little hamlet of Cerkvisce, and the time was about 1815. By this time none of us doubted the Partisans' time estimates; we had learned that the pace they set for us was predicated on being somewhere at a particular time, and it always seemed to work out.

When we arrived at Cerkvisce, our guards conversed with some Partisan soldiers and farm people, who came from everywhere to greet us. They also knew we would arrive when we did. I was told that we would proceed on to the Kolpa River to meet up with a Partisan company contingent that was encamped there. The Partisan soldiers at the river had been advised that we would be arriving about dinnertime, and they were preparing a meal for us, the ingredients having been graciously provided by the local farm people. We stopped only momentarily at Cerkvisce.

I wondered, as I had in similar situations before, about the logic of leaving this pleasant little village—where I was certain we could find a warm barn to sleep in for the night—just as the day was waning and darkness was nearly upon us. But this was another case where the partisans had fully formulated a plan for our travels south, and moving on from this little hamlet was part of that plan. This decision had evidently been made much earlier, at the Headquarters Post TV-15, well before the nine of us left that post. In fact, the Partisans had planned our route, our stopovers, the bridge incident, and the trip to our final destination in great detail, but at no time did they apprise me of the big picture. We simply followed our escorts and completely trusted their judgment.

Now, many years later, I fully realize, because of the thorough research that has been done on my behalf by my Slovenian friend Matija Zganjar in Ljubljana, that the people with whom we associated in Slovenia actually knew from Friday, March 9, 1945, that the long-range plan was to fly the ten of us out of Slovenia from the aerodrome at Krasinec, to Italy on Sunday, March 11, 1945, in a Balkan Air Force C-47. What vision! Even today, I am very touched when I think about how diligent, unselfish, and charmingly protective all of these people were in regard to ten young Americans. Each day of our short stay in Slovenia was underscored by the many wonderful things these fine people did for us. They were always thinking of us and about our welfare.

As we left Cerkvisce in darkness at close to 1840, we expected our trek to the river to take about forty-five minutes. At about 1920, we were greeted by the first Partisan sentry as he emerged from the shadows of the tree line. He was stationed a hundred yards or so west of his company's encampment, and he greeted our guards and us as though we were a family he had not seen in years arriving for a visit. I had become accustomed to this sort of happy welcoming ceremony, and enthusiastically enjoyed them, sentimentalist that I am.

This happy fellow led us to the encampment, where there was another greeting ceremony. Thirty or forty Partisan soldiers, all heavily armed, were in this contingent. I wondered why this formidable group was camped here by the rapid flowing Kolpa River which had to be well over one hundred yards wide at this point. I later learned that it was because of this area's central location and its proximity to both Cerkvisce and the aerodrome at Krasinec that they had chosen this spot, and they had evidently used this same place for previous encampments. The next day, I discovered their role in the scheme of things.

The night was crisply cold, with bright starlight—another pleasant night (unlike many other very dark nights I had become accustomed to in other parts of the world). There were several good-size fires scattered around the encampment to help people stay warm, and in the area farthest from the river, there were three fires where cooks were preparing an evening meal for more than fifty hungry people. These Partisans were men of all ages, including young boys; no women were in the contingent, however.

We were introduced to the commander, his officers, and noncoms. The officer in command spoke English very well, as did several of his accompanying officers. He explained to me that our evening meal was almost ready to be served and that we would spend the night with them here by the river, about thirty yards from the river's edge. He told me that he knew we would arrive and had been expecting us almost exactly when we showed up. I knew better at this point than to think otherwise!

In a short while, my crew and I enjoyed a fine dinner, our best Slovenian meal thus far. Everyone ate heartily and enjoyed the good food that had graciously been provided by the families of Cerkvisce. It was a wonderful treat consisting of a pot roast type of meat, boiled potatoes, boiled cabbage, and warm bread and hot coffee.

Shortly after we finished, a Partisan courier arrived and addressed the C.O., who was seated on the ground in the large circle of men who had eaten together. He handed the commander a note, saluted, and then went to the area where the cooks were still finishing their meal so he, too, could eat. The note was from British Air Force Flight Officer McGregor, of the Allied Mission at Podzemelj, requesting that I have a courier (one of my crewmen) at their covert location at 0900 Sunday, March 11, 1945, to find out whether the Balkan Air Force C-47 supply mission airplanes would be arriving that day. If these aircraft were scheduled to arrive, it was possible that the ten of us could be flown to the military hospital in Bari, Italy, on a return flight.

The C.O. had asked the Partisan courier to report to him after he finished his dinner. In a short time he joined us, and I asked him to please advise Flight Officer McGregor that we would all indeed be at his location in the morning, prior to 0900, and I thanked him (through the C.O.) for his help in these communications. Podzemelj was about a one-hour-and-thirty-minute trudge from Cerkvisce to the north. The commander

The note written by flight officer McGregor.

said that he had been aware that McGregor's note to me would be arriving sometime this evening, and he would guide us to their location in the morning after we had eaten breakfast.

I told him I had noticed the lights and activities of a small town directly across the river from where we were camped. I could see some people moving about who I thought might be military, even though it was nighttime—was I correct? He explained that there was a very small contingent of German military men garrisoned on the Croatian side of the river, but they knew the Slovenians in the encampment had more strength than they did and wouldn't bother us. He said that there were no Slovenian or Croatian people in that town any more—only German military. The German troops had little or no backup in the immediate area and were alone, so they never provoked a fight by coming across the river. He said, "They leave us alone, so we leave them alone. This little village is of no importance to us at present."

I asked whether the Germans ever sent a soldier or two across the river to reconnoiter the area, and he said that this rarely happened. My curiosity was somewhat satisfied, and my crew and I gathered around a large fire and conversed for a while before lying down on the cold ground to sleep. The only insulation between us and the somewhat snowy ground was a thick layer of straw supplied by local farmers. Fortunately, there was less snow here than we had dealt with farther north; less even than at Cerkvisce, only forty minutes or so west of here. Our night sleeping on the ground would not be a problem. There was no wind to speak of and the temperature was a little above freezing. By 2100, most of us were sound asleep.

Before the C.O. and I turned in for the night, we discussed the security precautions around the camp perimeter. He told me where guards would be positioned along the river's edge and the warnings he would give them. Ten soldiers were in this detail—five for the first four-hour watch and five for the second. He gathered the men—they actually looked like young boys, perhaps fourteen to sixteen years old and underfed, tired, and tattered—and I'll never forget watching him brief them on their positions and duties and position them in the tall grass seven or eight yards from the water and twenty yards apart. He told me that he had instructed them most emphatically to stay awake, because the Germans could possibly send men across the river to check on us during the night, and if they fell asleep, they could be caught by surprise. Unfortunately, the worst-case scenario took place sometime during that night—the Germans crossed the river while two sentries were asleep.

About 0530—well before daylight—we were awakened by loud conversations and startled exclamations. Two of the young sentries had been killed during the night while they slept at their posts! The C.O. said German soldiers had ventured by small boat across the river in the dark of night, apparently to find out our size and strength and the reasons for a large military presence on this side of the river. They had come upon these two young sleeping sentries and silently killed them. This was another of those terrible tragedies of the war of occupation that the Slovenian people endured daily. None of us heard a sound or were aware that the Germans had been creeping around the periphery of our encampment during the night. The intruders didn't bother anything or anyone else.

This was another occurrence that I could not have envisioned taking place—how naive I was! I was deeply affected by the incident. In spite of the sadness this morning, breakfast was under way. I don't remember exactly what we ate, as I could not move my thoughts away from the tragic deaths of those two young boys.

After breakfast, our caravan was escorted north to the S.O.E. (Special Operations Executive) Mission by the C.O. of the Partisan battle group. We arrived at about 0830 and were introduced to the British S.O.E. officer in charge, Major Peter Moore, and to Royal Air Force Flight Officer McGregor. After our introduction, I filled Major Moore in on our trip. He said that he had wondered from the outset how quickly our group would be able to travel here.

Moore was a delightful fellow who had been subjecting himself and his group to the constant danger of his task for several years in German-occupied Yugoslavia. Flight Officer McGregor was not of the same happy disposition. He was difficult at times and would not cooperate on some issues, one of which was that I wanted to let the 15th Air Force at Bari know that all ten of us were alive and in relatively good condition, and also to ask headquarters to notify the 483rd Bomb Group of our status. McGregor felt that transmitting this information was not vital, and he would not allow me to use his radio. We were somewhat disappointed about this; however, I did not press him on the subject.

Much to our consternation, the major had received a message stating that no supply airplanes would be landing today; however, one C-47 would fly an airdrop mission over this area in the late morning at the regular drop zone.

18

Day Number 3—Sunday, March 11, 1945

The Airdrop Mission and Supply Recovery

We were asked if we would help with the airdrop recovery to relieve some of the Partisans for other tasks, and all ambulatory members of my crew volunteered. Some of the Partisan soldiers escorted the hay cart containing my injured men back to Cerkivsce, where they could rest in one of the large barns we had seen the afternoon before. We would all be quartered in this barn until we could be flown out to the military hospital in Bari, which might not be for a few days—airdrop supply was a day-to-day operation whose schedule depended on many variables.

Six of us joined the Partisan recovery team and proceeded to the airdrop zone northeast of Podzemelj, about three miles away near the hamlet of Otok. Our odd-looking contingent consisted of four small hay wagons—each drawn by one horse and driven by one Partisan—six Partisans who were experienced at airdrop recovery, and the six of us. We were all smiling and upbeat—we anticipated having some fun as we accomplished our assigned mission (another occasion when a camera could have recorded war humor photographs of the century).

Keep in mind that this was still hostile territory—a country occupied by active and belligerent Germans—so although we treated this recovery operation almost like a walk in the park, we were still cautious. When we reached the drop zone, the drivers parked their wagons among the large trees to one side of a small cleared area. The leader of the Partisan recovery group instructed my crewmen and I to lay out an eight-inch-wide red ribbon around the periphery of the zone and to make a large X in the center to tell the supply pilots where to make the drop.

The drop was to occur within ten minutes, so we waited back in the trees for the C-47 to make its high flyby, which would alert us to its subsequent low-altitude pass. In a few minutes, we heard the familiar sound of the Pratt and Whitney radial engines, and as we emerged from the trees, we saw the Douglas C-47 flying overhead at about eight thousand feet and surmised that it would make its inbound pass in a southwesterly heading and drop its cargo in about six minutes.

The Partisans explained that the cargo drop would be from treetop level. This was a surprise to me, as I had not seen an air supply drop from anything less than around 800 feet. When I asked about the altitude, the leader said they did not use parachutes in these drops because of the German troops in the immediate area. The supplies would be dropped in crush-proof baskets made of very thick woven wicker. He said that they rarely received damaged supplies in a basket drop like this, although the baskets took on all sorts of strange shapes as they crashed into the ground, bouncing and rolling along the surface as they hit. He suggested that we watch them fall and land from the tree line to get a firsthand look at them doing their weird dance along the ground.

Almost before we heard it flying above us, the C-47 dropped its cargo. It really was at treetop level, just barely skimming the branches—no more than sixty to eighty feet off the ground. In a matter of seconds the wicker baskets had landed dead center—what an odd, noisy, and humorous sight—like an episode in a cartoon. The airplane was gone in a flash, and quiet returned to the area.

The small wagons were rapidly deployed from under the trees, and we all hastily loaded the baskets into them. The Partisans were nimble-footed and worked with considerable speed. As we loaded the wagons, other Partisans were busy rolling up the red ribbons, tying the big rolls securely, and putting them on board. We were told to vacate the area immediately—minutes and even seconds counted. We must disappear into the forest well before the arrival of a German patrol, which would most likely be searching this location soon—they had probably seen the C-47 flyby. So we scurried quietly away and returned to the SOE Mission's secluded compound. My crewmen and I did not wait to see the baskets unpacked in the well-hidden underground storage area, but the British major told us that the supplies dropped were usually medicines and other hospital provisions, blankets, a few construction tools, some types of military supplies, small arms ammunition, and some other items.

We six who had participated in the recovery returned to the barn at Cerkvisce a little after noon, just in time for a very light lunch of bread, cheese, and coffee served by the barn's owners. After our snack, we filled one of our leather helmets with straw, tied it securely with twine, and got in a half hour or so of touch football. We needed some fun and mental stimulus, with nothing serious hinging on the outcome. This attempt at play gave us the relaxing activator we needed.

The air was fresh and the sunshine warm, we'd had some food and exercise, and the group was somewhat relaxed, so it was time for a nap. The barn was warm and quiet, and we retired to its soft hay and soon fell asleep—something we'd be unable to do for a day or so. Our slumber was broken by the owner of the barn announcing that a small dinner was awaiting us in the kitchen, the food graciously provided by the ladies from the other homes in the hamlet. From what I could gather, these wonderful people provided meals on a rotating basis. Although the plan called for us to be provided one meal a day, they tried to see that we had something to eat at least twice a day, since they looked upon us as growing boys.

Because of the German occupation, food was very scarce and the Germans sometimes took food to nourish themselves. To compensate, we ate very little. We sat in the kitchen, which was quite large—we'd call it a "great room" in a modern American home. I'll always remember the room because of its color—bright green—but another feature was also memorable: the two cookstoves. One was a typical iron wood-burning stove/oven unit similar to what many of our families had cooked and baked with not too many years before. The other was a very large Dutch oven that was evidently the pride and joy of the lady of the house, as she showed it to us with much happiness. The fact that her dear husband had constructed it for her made it even more special.

This large oven had been constructed in one corner of the room. Its cook top was made of large red firebrick, as was the straight rear portion of the back of the oven, which actually became part of its chimney. The firebox was well below the cook top. Two steel swinging doors closed off the main cooking section of the oven and the firebox. The doors had heavy steel hinge pins that were pointed so that the doors could easily be removed. Soon I learned, to my amazement, that this oven served a function even more important than cooking, and after the visitors from the other farmhouses had left, the owners of the house explained what it was. The Partisan soldiers who were still in the kitchen knew about this second function, and they helped to explain and demonstrate it.

Our host revealed that he had built the stove to mask the presence of a secret room. He and a couple of the soldiers dismantled the cooking base, portions of the rear chimney section, and the front area. Brick by brick, they removed the main structure of the oven to reveal that a person could step up, over, and through the center of the large opening and into a secret room behind it that was large enough to conceal eight to ten people. The oven was very cleverly designed and could quickly be dismantled and reassembled. Our hosts told us that if they were hiding British or American military people in the secret room, and German patrols were nearby, they built a fire in the firebox and had food cooking on the stove in case their home was inspected.

After our host and a few Partisan soldiers reassembled the stove, my crewmen and I were escorted to the barn to rest, and we all dozed off quickly. Even our Partisan guards took a nap, and as the big horses that had pulled the hay cart had been unbridled, put in stalls and fed, they seemed to be napping along with the rest of us.

It's a Small World

Later that evening, about 1910, while we were in the barn keeping warm and relaxing, a Partisan courier arrived with a request for me. He spoke English with some difficulty; however, I understood his request. The language difficulties we experienced in Slovenia were not really much of a problem. We certainly didn't expect the Slovenians to speak English—after all, we were in their country and we knew that none of us could make even the slightest attempt to speak their language. It made me feel somewhat inadequate not to be able to communicate with these gallant people in their native tongue. Happily, we were almost always able to find Slovenians who could speak and understand English. It was also fortunate that Bob Mahan, my bombardier, spoke and understood French, and Joe Pirrone, my engineer and top gunner, spoke Italian, so they helped to communicate on several occasions.

The courier asked Pirrone and me to accompany him on a forty-minute walk to meet someone who wanted to talk with us. This was a very unusual request, and had we not been in the care of other Partisan soldiers, I would have been more suspicious about going with this one. After all, the Germans were crafty about capturing American airmen, and even though the Slovenian Partisans were strong in this area and had pacified some of it quite well, the Germans were still continually active.

For about thirty-five minutes, Joe and I followed the soldier on a small path through a heavily wooded area covered with about eight inches of snow. There was very little of the usual glow from the clear starlit night above us because the forest was so dense and the snow did not provide much illumination, so walking was difficult. This did not bother our guide—he plowed through the snow as though it were springtime.

Joe and I, tired from the hike, were pleased when we finally arrived at our destination—a small, thatched-roof house. Our guide led us up to the house and ushered us inside without even a knock on the door, which we felt was rather odd. He said he'd return in about an hour to lead us back to the barn, and, with that said, he departed.

The inside of the little house was dark except for the glow of a few small oil lamps and candles scattered about the main living area, and the soft light of a fire in the fireplace at the far end of the room. I called out gently, "Hello, is anyone home?" and a slight, soft voice answered, "Yes, please come over by the fireplace." We walked across the room and were amazed to find, sitting in a large upholstered wingback chair facing the fire, a small white-haired woman who appeared to be about seventy years old.

She welcomed us and asked us to be seated near her so that we could converse, relax, and stay warm. She spoke English perfectly—no accent at all—which, along with the unusual surroundings, captivated us. She introduced herself to us, but her name has long ago escaped me. She asked Joe his full name and where he was from in the States. He answered, "Joseph F. Pirrone, Tech Sergeant, 36 Cornwall Avenue, Mount Vernon, New York." Next she asked whether he had an uncle who owned and operated a butcher shop at an address she gave in Mount Vernon, and whether there was an apartment over the butcher shop. Joe answered affirmatively. Finally she said, "I thought so. I know your uncle and his wife well. I lived in that apartment for quite a few years." She explained that she had left Mount Vernon to visit her family here in Slovenia prior to Hitler's invasion of Yugoslavia and that because of the rapid occupation of Slovenia, she had become trapped and was not permitted to return to the United States.

Joe and I looked at each another in astonishment. This uncanny setting, the odd meeting, and the revelation of this woman's relationship with someone in Joe's family was almost more than we could wrestle with, but it made perfect sense. I could see that Joe was quite emotional about the situation—a natural reaction, I thought, as this woman was practically a relative.

The three of us chatted about such things as the German occupation of her native country, her life here in Slovenia, and our situation with the Germans and the Slovenian Partisans under the leadership of Marshall Tito. She knew all about our airplane, our being forced to leave it, and that four of our crewmen had been injured and could not walk well on their own. She was relieved and happy to know that we were all alive and safe. She and Joe talked for a while about Joe's uncle, fond memories of their family, and Joe's childhood days in Mount Vernon. Time was flying by, and tomorrow was supposed to be a busy day, so at 2200 I suggested that we return to our barn and turn in for the night. She gave us each a hug and a kiss on the cheek and told us that all the people of Slovenia considered us their friends and their heroes. She wished us Godspeed on our journey home.

We found out that many of the people here who spoke English—or their families—had lived in the United States but had returned to Slovenia before the war and then could not return after the war broke out.

As we walked out the front door of our friend's lovely little home, we found our guide huddled on the front porch waiting for us. We were concerned that he might have been cold and that we had caused him to wait much longer than we had originally anticipated. He graciously told us he had stayed warm on the front porch, out of the night air, and that he had enjoyed the rest while he was waiting. As Joe and I walked back to the barn, we wondered about this lovely woman. Would she be able to survive the Nazi occupation of her country and one day return to the United States?

As we told our story to the rest of the crew, they sat entranced—as if they were watching a mystery movie. I have thought of this woman—and of Joe Pirrone—hundreds of times since that classic adventure in the Slovenian forest on Sunday, March 11, 1945.

During our short stay in Slovenia, we learned that information about allied military personnel who were hidden by the Partisans and others in the area was being passed to some people outside the inner circle of command on a need-to-know-basis. The Slovenians were staunchly loyal to one another and knew whom they could share information with. Joe and I surmised that the Partisan soldier who guided us to this woman's home, or another (probably high-ranking) Partisan, was related to her, and that he shared information about us—particularly about Joe—with her.

The area where our experiences took place was very remote and sparsely populated. Houses were scattered in ones, twos, and threes, with no apparent reason for their locations. As this woman apparently lived alone, we felt that the house where we visited her had always been a family home, and that her family had been longtime residents of the area. We did wonder about her safety. However, we realized that for her to have been briefed about us, she must have connections to the inner circle of Partisan hierarchy and was surely well-protected.

19

Day Number 4—Monday, March 12, 1945

A Disappointing Development

Our breakfast the next morning was an early one. The farmer in whose barn we were quartered roused us out of the hay—literally—at 0600 and led us into his wife's big green kitchen for coffee and hot bread with honey. During our second cup, another contingent of Partisan soldiers arrived to escort us to Podzemolj, where the British major and Flight Officer McGregor were stationed. We left the farmhouse just before 0700 with our four injured crew members in the hay cart, two big horses pulling the cart, two drivers, and four other Partisans, for a more than one-and-a-half-hour walk to the north. The major and McGregor were waiting for us. Again, I was amused that this little group at Podzemolj, supposedly very secret and secluded, was always easy for us to locate. Perhaps it was because we were considered "good guys."

We would be working with the Balkan Air Force. The Balkan Air Force (BAF) was formed in June 1944 at the Italian port of Bari on the so-called Aegean Sea. Bari was the center for the Inter-Service Allied Headquarters. It became the Balkan Command Coordinating Authority for Land, Sea, Air, and Special Operations in the Aegean and Ionian Seas.

The BAF's first commander was Air Vice-Marshall W. Elliot. An air component of eight squadrons and one flight of aircraft supplied the Yugoslavian Partisans, starting in May 1942, and gave them direct air support, starting in late 1943. The BAF's history includes supplying the Italian Partisans and Missions for SOE and American OSS in the Balkans, Poland, and Southeast Europe.

Men from Greece, Italy, Poland, South Africa, the United Kingdom, the United States, the Union of Soviet Socialist Republics, and Yugoslavia participated in the BAF's air component, which operated fifteen types of aircraft and had flown 38,340 sorties by May 1945. The BAF flew more than 19,000 wounded men and women out of Yugoslavia to military hospitals controlled by the Allies. Force 399, the principal force, ran special operations in Yugoslavia and Albania under the Command of Brigadier General Fitzroy McLean, who was attached to Tito's headquarters.

The major advised me that the Balkan Air Force C-47 supply planes would arrive about 1100 at the grass airstrip by the river to the south-southwest (about a fifty-minute walk). This long, narrow grass airstrip, which paralleled the River Kolpa, was referred to as the Karsinec Aerodrome by the Partisans. When it was not being used for airplane landings and takeoffs, a few cattle grazed on it and kept the grass at an acceptable level.

Our group of crewmen and Partisans continued from Podzemolj to the airstrip. Major Moore, McGregor, and their people would follow in half an hour's time with several farm wagons full of wounded Partisan soldiers who would be flown out for treatment and rehabilitation at the American Military Hospital in Bari, Italy. Once strong and healthy again, they would be returned to Slovenia to continue the Partisan struggle to liberate their country from the Germans. We never saw or heard about these wounded men or women until shortly before supply mission airplanes were to land. Then they would appear at the airstrip—seemingly out of nowhere—in wagons and carts.

I have since learned that the central hospital of the Partisans was located about twenty-five miles north-northeast of Krasinec in the small town of Gor Suhor, adjacent to the border of Slovenia and Croatia, and this was why the aerodrome at Krasinec was used so extensively to evacuate wounded Partisans. It was also the airstrip from which many downed Allied airmen—escapees and evades, as well as escaped prisoners of war—were repatriated back to Italy.

The wagons and carts carrying the wounded Partisans were also used to transport supplies brought by the planes. The supplies were immediately hauled away to hidden cave complexes and other secret locations nearby.

This airstrip at Karsinec, located in a long, wide valley, is bordered by hills 800 to 1700 feet high, with the higher ones mostly on the Croatian side of the river. The hills to the east-southeast, south, and southwest are on the Slovenian side. Both of these natural features—the river on one side and the hills around the others—enhanced the airstrip's security and also protected it somewhat from immediate peripheral hostile interference. Its location made it ideal for very rapid in-and-out supply flights. The length of the runway was ample for the C-47's (about 5000 feet, I estimated), and its width was more than wide enough for landing and taxiing while the airplanes were on the aerodrome.

When our group arrived at the airstrip, we immediately began preparing it for the arrival of inbound planes by intermittently lining each side and the ends of the runway with wide red ribbon similar to what we had used during the airdrop the day before. Today's exercise took many big rolls of ribbon and the efforts of many people because the landing area was so long. After laying down the ribbon, we built a grand bonfire at the southern end of the strip. The movement of the smoke from this fire was used by the incoming pilots as a guide to wind direction and velocity (for planning their approach and landing).

As 1100 approached, the number of people gathered at the landing site continued to grow. More than forty heavily armed Partisan soldiers arrived on the scene as a unit—probably as a protective combat team. They appeared to be the same men we had spent the night with at the river, and were no doubt positioned here for defense of the landing area if it were needed. I supposed that all of the British major's SOE Mission team was also in attendance, along with Flight Officer McGregor and his people. The little grass airstrip was beginning to look like the grounds of an air-show rather than a Partisan resupply exercise in an enemy-occupied country.

A few minutes before 1100, four British Spitfire fighter aircraft flew over the strip and began to make wide circular patterns around the aerodrome area. Two flew in circular patterns to the left at about 2000 feet, and the other two flew in similar patterns to the right at about 3000 feet. They were there to provide top cover for the approaches and landings of the C-47's, and also for the unloading and reloading processes. Their flight was beautiful and reassuring to watch.

Almost immediately after the Spitfires arrived, the first of five C-47's appeared over one of the higher hills to the south-southeast and made a left-hand turn to the east of the field to land. Immediately thereafter, the other four made the same left-hand approach, setting up for their landing sequence. The width of the grass runway was sufficient to permit each C-47 to land, taxi back up the side of the area, and park along it near the approach end even as the other airplanes continued their landings. This procedure placed each plane in an uncomplicated and clear position for an expeditious taxi and takeoff immediately after it was unloaded and reloaded.

Within a few minutes, each of the C-47's had made its approach and landing, and parked at a forty-five-degree angle at the edge of the runway. As soon as the propellers had ceased rotating, the big side cargo doors were opened and the offloading of both men and materiel began in earnest as the loadmaster of each airplane supervised and directed. In no time at all, two or three large horse-drawn farm wagons were lined up behind the port side of each plane, ready to be loaded. The offloading was done quickly, and as each wagon was packed, it was pulled around the airplane's left wing, across the landing strip, and off into the seclusion and protection of the forest.

As soon as the offloading was done, the disabled Partisan soldiers' wagons and carts were pulled up to the airplanes, and the wounded men and women were assisted on board. Most of them could not walk and some were on stretchers—it was a pitiful and saddening sight.

My crew and I waited for our time to board with Major Moore and Doctor Pintaric—the Partisan military's principal medical doctor of this region—at the approach end of the landing area. The idea that we might not be given the green light to board one of these planes never entered my mind. However, the shock of reality was about to hit. As we stood there talking, the senior loadmaster, who was evidently in charge of the entire operation, approached Major Moore. He advised him that the loading of the aircraft had been completed, and due to the large number of wounded and disabled Partisans, there was no space on board any of the airplanes for the ten of us. We would have to wait until the next supply flight, probably at 1100 the next morning, and he thought that enough space would be available on one of the airplanes so that we could all fly out together.

The expression of disappointment on his kind face showed us that he was troubled by this news, and the major expressed his frustration both by his expression and in his words. He knew that we would be crushed by not being able to leave today, but we tried to digest the bad news as bravely as possible. We realized the difficulties the Partisan commanders and their medical staffs faced in trying to care for their wounded compatriots, and we were acutely aware that these many battle casualties were in dire need of surgical and medical care that was not available here.

The Partisan medical facilities in Slovenia and elsewhere in Yugoslavia were small because they had to be kept hidden from the Germans, whose search-and-destroy missions involving medical facilities were a top priority in their effort to deplete Partisan forces. The so-called "hospitals" were small medical units consisting of a few doctors and nurses or orderlies, and few medical supplies. They might be hidden in craggy mountain caves, sometimes high in the cold mountains, or concealed in cold and poorly lighted dug-out hillsides. The American Military Hospital in Bari was one of the few complete medical facilities in the area that could provide the care seriously wounded patients needed.

My crew and I, though disappointed that we'd have to wait another day before we could leave, were more than willing to give up our ten spots on an outgoing plane—we were in relatively good physical condition, and our spirits were high. We remained near the runway and watched the C-47's take off after quickly completing their run-up checks. The Spitfires headed out with them toward the Adriatic Sea and Italy beyond. As I witnessed the cargo planes' takeoffs, I appreciated the heavy load each carried—some of them were barely able to lift off by the end of the grass strip. As they became airborne, their flat climb further indicated their struggle with a difficult flight. But once their airspeed increased, their flight was as graceful as an American eagle. As I watched them leave, for a fleeting moment I thought, "There goes my chance for a refreshing shower, with soap and hot water." I knew that it would be necessary to spend another day living with the fleas and lice that inhabited our bodies. There was no getting around it, but we could stand it.

After the planes left, it was decided that my crew and I would return to our barn in Cerkvisce, and perhaps our Slovenian host and hostess would persuade us to eat a little lunch with them. Our favorite hay cart, with its grand horses and two friendly Partisan drivers, was readied for my disabled crewmen, and we set out for Cerkvisce, our Partisan guards walking along with us. When we arrived at the barn, our host and some of his neighbors greeted us. They were surprised to see us and disappointed for us because we had been unable to fly out with the supply planes. However, as expected, they asked us to have some lunch with them. We ate very little, knowing that they had little themselves, and retired to the barn for a rest shortly after noon.

About 1300, our sleep was interrupted by a very large Partisan soldier—an officer of considerable rank sporting a very large Russian automatic weapon—who indicated he wished to speak with me. He spoke some English, so I understood his message with only a small amount of difficulty.

The Rendezvous ... A Long Walk Worthwhile

From what I could gather, this soldier was requesting that I follow him to a rendezvous with family members of a local high-ranking Slovenian civil official. The family's complex of homes was about a forty-minute walk from Cerkvisce, and we would leave any time I was ready, if I were in agreement. He said that he would escort me to this home, wait for me, and then return me to the barn. I agreed to accept—refusing would be a slap in the face to the people who had extended the invitation. Nevertheless, anyone who has been involved in the type of clandestine existence and operations that we had been over the past few days can understand my reluctance to go. I was, frankly, quite leery about it, especially after one of my crewmen said in jest while we were discussing it, "You could get shot, and you're too young to die!" On the other hand, I did trust the soldier who had delivered the invitation and who would escort me. The owner of the barn in which we were quartered knew him, and I considered this sort of a "security clearance" for the adventure.

So the large Partisan courier and I commenced our journey through the forest just before 1400 at a pace that an Olympian sprinter might use. We hiked—on what seemed to be an upward slope—through about six inches of snow. Fortunately for me, the big fellow cut a substantial path for me to follow, but although he spoke to me once in a while and smiled often, he didn't tell me where we were going. At about 1450 we arrived at a settlement—a welcome conclusion to our trek up the hill. The grouping of large, well-constructed wooden buildings was impressive. There were several homes, barns, and associated structures, one-story barracks-type buildings, and what appeared to be an office or administration building. Most of the structures were located among the large trees of the forest, but the barns and other outbuildings were in a somewhat cleared area. I was surprised to see that all the buildings had wooden roofs, not the usual thatched roofs that I had become accustomed to seeing in Slovenia. It was quite beautiful and reminded me of a wintry movie scene.

The building I was taken to was rather large and long, and the roof had three-foot-wide eaves all the way around. A covered entrance with a substantial door protruded from the center of one of the long sides, and a few steps led up to it. The design and construction of the building intrigued me—it was very well done. The building appeared to have two main sections—which perhaps contained two separate living quarters. It reminded me of a type of duplex in the United States that had a large entryway in the center that separated two side wings. Multi-paned windows provided light on all four sides.

My companion opened the door for me and beckoned me to enter. A Partisan guard with a Russian machine gun stood just inside and immediately stood at attention as we entered. My companion smiled at him, they exchanged a few words, and then the guard left the building. In the hallway we had entered was a long table with a glowing oil lamp on it and a large wooden bench in front of it—for what reason, I can't say (perhaps a place where a guard could relax and stay warm while on duty). My guide motioned for me to follow him down the short hall where a door lead to the left side of the building. He gently knocked on it three distinct times. A soft voice answered, and my guide said something in return. He then motioned for me to open the door and go inside. Needless to say, I was very curious about these strange goings-on, but also wary.

As I grasped the knob to open the door, he smiled and gave me a soft salute. Then he turned, walked down the hall to the entry door, and left the building. The door I opened led into a small hallway, and as I slowly walked down it, I saw another door leading to a large bedroom on the right. Farther down was another door that I assumed led to another bedroom or perhaps a bathroom. When I came to the end of the hall, I found myself in a very large, well-appointed living room. There was a grand stone fireplace on the right side of the room which was constructed with a long raised hearth that extended four feet on each side of the fireplace opening and was high enough to be used for sitting. The room also contained a kitchen and a small dining area, and there were large blocks of curtained windows on my left and at the end of the room directly across from me. The windows, of course, were all closed, but the front windows' curtains were partially drawn, allowing warm afternoon sunshine into the room and making it feel relaxing and cheerful. The fire in the fireplace, which warmed the entire room, added to the ambience and tranquility of the setting. The ceiling was made of wooden planks supported by evenly spaced heavy wooden support beams. The floor was also of wooden planks that were about ten inches wide and partially covered by some rough-textured, hand-woven rugs. The furniture—some wooden and some upholstered—was attractive and included a large, comfortable-looking sofa facing the fireplace. The overall atmosphere of the room was not what one would expect in the rural countryside of an area of conflict. Despite the comfort I felt, I was still most skeptical about what was taking place. Could this be some sort of trap?

While examining this fascinating room and wondering why I had been brought here, I had completely ignored its most interesting feature—the person who was waiting there to greet me! Anyone observing me would have thought me demented for not immediately noticing a lovely young woman in her mid-twenties standing before a substantial wooden table on the left side of the room. She was very pretty and wore what I imagined to be the Slovenian native dress—a full white blouse, a colorful above-the-ankle skirt, a multi-colored vest, woolen stockings, and somewhat heavy leather shoes. I noticed that her light brown hair was braided and her eyes were green, but it was the quality of her voice that struck me first.

She spoke to me in her language as I removed my helmet, gloves and heavy leather jacket, and, bowing slightly, she stretched out her arms to welcome me into her home. The aura of doom and mistrust I had been harboring quickly fled! We walked toward each other and touched our outstretched hands together. She motioned for me to sit with her on the sofa facing the fireplace and continued to attempt to converse with me as we were bathed in the warm glow of the fire. She spoke only a few phrases of English—and, unfortunately, I spoke not a word of her language. What an impossible situation!

She was feminine and beautiful, and I was unclean and, I'm certain, did not exude pleasant scents. I was dingy, tired, hungry, and still very concerned about what this engaging encounter meant and where exactly it was supposed to lead, although I was starting to get the message! Although I was gratified that the powers-that-be had chosen to allow me to visit with this lovely woman, no matter how deeply I endeavored to view this visit in its intended light, I felt out of place here. It may sound puritanical, but I was embarrassed and felt very unsaintly—I was certainly no prize and absolutely no hero! My hostess and I sat together before the fire for about thirty minutes, trying to converse and enjoying some hot tea and cake. After an hour or so, I somehow explained to her that I needed to return to my fellow crewmen.

It was obvious that she wanted me to stay and, from what I could gather, have a bath, dinner, and a good night's sleep. Leaving this captivating person was most difficult, but it was what I had to do. We walked to the door, where I held her hand, thanked her for the very pleasant visit and our tea and cake together, and departed, with the distinct impression that we were both a little sad to see our friendship end so quickly and abruptly.

The Partisan officer who had escorted me was waiting inside the building by the entrance door, sitting on the long bench. He stood as I came out of the room and walked down the hall toward him. As I extended

my hand to shake hands, he looked at me questioningly and then nod-
ded as I motioned in the direction we would travel on our return to
Cerkvisce. He didn't question my hasty departure; I had the feeling he
understood my reasons well enough. When I asked him who had set up
this tête-à-tête, he just said it was a friendly gesture by someone who
wished me well. I let it go at that.

Throughout the return trip, I wondered whether I would ever see
and visit with that very intriguing young woman again. She had made a
firm imprint on my young mind in the short time we had spent together.
We reached the big barn about 1700 and were greeted by all my crewmen, who were surprised that we had returned so quickly.

After this encounter was over, I often wondered why my guide had
not revealed to me beforehand what the mysterious rendezvous was all
about. Perhaps he thought I'd refuse the invitation if I knew the true
nature of the arrangement. If that was his notion, he was correct—I would
have declined.

My crew was amazed when I told them of my cozy meeting with the
appealing young lady and about her home, its furnishing, and its surroundings, and offered some good-natured teasing and bantering on the
subject, but it was not excessive—they knew only too well that even though
I was a hard-nosed leader, I was also a gentleman.

An Enjoyable Evening with a Good Egg

Just about the time everyone was wondering whether there would be
any dinner, another Partisan soldier—a non-commissioned officer—came
into the barn, along with the barn's owner, to see me. Although he spoke
only broken English, he knew French, so translation was done by Bob
Mahan. He and Bob conversed for a few minutes and Bob then turned
to me to explain the fellow's message, which was that I had been invited
for dinner this very evening. He knew somehow that my day so far had
been very active, and he expressed hope that I would be able to accept.

My dinner companion would be one of the high ranking officers in
the region, and the dinner was to be at his quarters in the eastern outskirts of Crnomelj, about six miles north of Cerkvisce. The journey would
take "only" two hours of walking—not a difficult walk, according to this
gentleman. These Partisan fighters seemed to feel that any walk was an
easy walk, no matter its length, but in my view, a two-hour walk at night
was a long walk, especially with my damaged right foot arch.

Although the Partisan did not at first say who this officer was, I was becoming more trusting of the Slovenians' nice gestures, and accepted the invitation. For the second time that day I said "so long" to my crew and trudged off into the forest to an unknown destination and an uncertain adventure. It was only when we were en route that my guide made an effort to fill me in on the identity my host—from what I could understand, he was a Russian colonel who was the liaison officer in charge of the Russian mission in Slovenia.

We left at about 1715, which meant that we would arrive a little after 1900, which translated into dinner about 1930. Thinking optimistically, I surmised that I would be on my way back to our barn and some good rest by 2215. As we walked, my guide told me more about the Russian officer: He was attached to the central Communist command, which held sway over the entire group of surrounding countries in Southeastern Europe and, of course, the Russian/Slovenian Mission at Crnomelj.

When we approached the house, the guard, a rough-looking fellow, said very little to my escort, which seemed odd, as these soldiers were usually very friendly toward one another. The guard opened the front door of the house, which led to a hallway with a door at the opposite end. As I entered the door, my guide told me that he would wait for me close by to escort me back to my quarters. I thanked him and he walked to one of the other buildings—to keep warm, I hoped.

The guard who took me inside may have been Russian, not Slovenian, although his uniform was not a Russian one that I recognized. He knocked on the inner hall door, opened it, and ushered me into the foyer of the living room just as my host—Colonel Boris Bogomolov—came forward from where he had been standing in front of the fireplace to greet me. I removed my helmet and gloves and we shook hands.

In rather good English, with a heavy Russian (I thought) accent, he welcomed me to his home. I removed my heavy jacket, and as I looked around the room, I was surprised to find that he did not have elaborate personal living quarters. Although the one-story home was of good size, it had a thatched roof and stone main structure much like Slovenian houses in the area. There was a combination living/dining room, with a large stone fireplace in the living room portion. The room was overly filled with large pieces of furniture upholstered in earth-tone canvas—light tans, light grays, soft greens, and mild rusts. It was rather nice; I had expected something more drab.

Bogomolov put his arm around my back and invited me to sit by the fire. He told me that I had displayed great courage in getting my aircraft to Slovenia and that he was very happy that I had accepted his dinner invitation. He knew that my crewmen and I were eager to move on with our journey and be repatriated back to Italy, so he was afraid that I would not have time to fit in a dinner visit at a later date. He seemed to know all about the damage to our bomber, the crew parachuting into Slovenia, the crash on the slope, and my narrow escape—in other words, he knew the whole story. Someone had obviously briefed him thoroughly about us and our experiences.

In front of a roaring fire, we talked about the war; the Germans; Hitler (the Mad Man, he called him); and the United States, specifically its ability to produce large quantities of well-made equipment and supplies and its powerful and efficient war machine. Then we sat down at a large wooden table to eat our dinner. My host had uncorked a large bottle of Russian vodka just after I had arrived and had been drinking the liquor from a large wine glass. There were many other unopened bottles of vodka on the service table and additional wine glasses, but no ice. He offered me a drink before dinner, but I declined, as I was in no condition to drink any sort of alcohol. One drink and I would have been on my ear. I wanted my head to be as clear as possible since I saw—as my host consumed more and more vodka—that the conversation was leaning toward politics and ideologies. I was sure that he'd eventually want to talk about Communism, the United States, and possibly even enter into a Cold War–type discussion (the Cold War was beginning to show signs of taking shape even back then).

Dinner was served by a soldier and several middle-aged women who also appeared to be Russian. The food was very plain, but tasty and well-prepared: some kind of meat cooked like a pot roast, with potatoes and a root vegetable (probably a rutabaga or turnip). I can remember the taste to this day—very fortifying! Some rather crusty fresh bread was also served, but, of course, there was no gravy or butter. It was the best meal I had eaten in three days, and I told my host how much I was enjoying the food and our meal together.

Near the end of the meal, he brought up the subject of Communism, telling me that it was the best way to govern people, and that our American system of democracy and capitalism was outdated and would surely never endure. He felt that Russia—under Communism—would continue to grow and would surpass the entire world economically in a very short time. One day, he said, Russia might exert influence on most of the world through Communism, with its socialistic economy.

He waited for my reaction to all this talk—one he obviously thought would be of surprise and perhaps displeasure. But I surprised him by looking right at him and smiling. Actually, from the onset of his talk about Communism, I felt that he had been baiting me—I don't think he believed all that Communism hogwash himself! I told him I was sure Russia would not really attempt to follow that philosophy, and doing so would be nonproductive and self-defeating for them. I offered the premise that our two countries were allies and friends, and, above all, we needed to work and fight together to defeat Hitler and his military forces—and bring lasting peace, freedom, and prosperity to all of the European peoples.

A little taken aback by my non-caustic response, he smiled at me and extended his big hand across the table to shake hands. He said that he would always be my friend, lifted his glass full of vodka, and toasted me as a fine American airman and his hero. Then he stood up and walked around the table toward me. I stood up as well and looked at him, not knowing what would happen next—it could have been almost anything. As he approached me, he grasped his cigarette holder, which still held one of the odd-smelling cigarettes he had been smoking. He removed the cigarette from the holder and threw it into the fireplace, held the empty holder out to me, and said, "Please take this. It was carved for me by a dear friend. I am proud of it, and I want you to have it as a personal gift. You, dear fellow, are the man of courage here and a guest of honor in my home and we shall always be friends."

I accepted it, thanked him, and told him that I would always be proud to have such a meaningful gift. I did take a few minutes to explain to him that in our military, we did not have "heroes" as such. The men and women in the American military forces all worked together as a team, and "heroics" was not part of our way of life in combat. Our training and deep respect and care for our fellow soldier, seaman, or airman were the principal virtues we lived and fought by.

We reseated ourselves and finished our dinner while discussing the war in general, the German occupation of Yugoslavia (and particularly Slovenia), and the many other problems caused by the Germans. He was very appreciative of Tito, his Partisan soldiers, and their fine counter-military activities, as well as the American and British special units that operated with the Partisans in Yugoslavia. He praised the American air forces in Italy and England and offered many toasts to their unrelenting bombing attacks on German strategic targets. He expressed amazement that our crew had survived when such devastating damage had been done to our B-17, and he was glad we had all been able to get out alive and relatively uninjured. That some of my crewmen were injured had not escaped him, and he was aware as well that we had been continually pursued by German soldiers. He was pleased that the 15th Air Force's daily bombings were taking a high toll on German industry and petroleum facilities, as well as transportation centers.

As we continued our conversation in front of the crackling fire after dinner, he saw that I was tired and eager to return to my quarters for a good night's sleep. I had left the barn about 1715 and arrived at his house at 1905. We had eaten dinner between 1935 and 2145, and I still had almost two hours of walking to do before I could sleep—no wonder I was tired!

Finally, he said, "I trust you have enjoyed your dinner and our evening together as much as I have—you were very gracious to have accepted my invitation and joined me here for the evening, and I wish you well always." I stood and saluted him, and he stood and returned my salute. We shook hands, he gave me a big bear hug (he was a big fellow), and he smiled and walked to the door with me. As he opened the door, the Russian guard, who had been sitting in the hallway conversing with my Partisan escort, stood at attention, as did the Partisan. We all walked outside onto the snow-covered ground to say our farewells.

As my guide and I walked away into a very cold night, we turned and waved good-bye. As we trudged along, I reminisced about the evening and the Russian officer—he was a good egg and an enjoyable person to have spent time with. But the entire evening seemed somehow unreal, almost as though I had read about it in a book of war stories.

Although it would have been wonderful to have photographs of the dinner, I do still have one tangible memento from it—the beautifully hand-carved wooden cigarette holder the colonel gave me. It's a little over three inches long, and the symbols carved on it include a hammer and sickle, a flag, and some Russian letters. It is one of my most prized possessions and brings back a memory of World War II that will endure throughout all time. I look at it often; each time, I can readily see the gregarious gentleman who presented it to me—and I wonder how his life played out, both during the war and after it ended. I hope that his life has been as full as mine.

My traveling companion and I reached the barn about 2355—and all my crewmen were still awake, eager to hear about my adventure. But first, with Bob Mahan's help, I thanked my escort for his generous care and told him I hoped he had been given some dinner. I'm sure the two and a half hours he spent waiting for me were a real bore. We shook hands, he gave me a big hug, and he went on his way. Then I told my crew about the dinner, and the whole adventure struck them as it did me—very unusual. Someone blew out the oil lamp at 0025, and within minutes we were all sound asleep.

20

Day Number 5—Tuesday, March 13, 1945

Repatriation

At 0630 we were again invited to our host's kitchen for breakfast, and our four regular Partisan guards and the two who drove the hay cart (who had become almost like family) were also there. The plan, I learned, was that after breakfast we would all follow the hay cart to the aerodrome at Krasinec.

After we ate, we thanked our hosts for their kindness—the care, the fine meals, and the use of their quiet, secluded barn and the washing facilities by their well. Other people from Cerkvisce who had helped to feed and care for us were also there to say good-bye and wish us a safe journey back to Italy and a prompt return to our homes and loved ones in the United States. There were plenty of hugs and smiles to go around, as well as some tears. These marvelous people had become like family to us during our very short stay. We never forgot that these gallant people had sheltered the ten of us at what could have been the cost of their own lives if the Germans had found us. They never seemed to give this frightening scenario a second thought.

Once again, our Partisan companions loaded my injured crewmen onto the hay cart, and we all set out for the aerodrome. As we departed, I had mixed emotions. I was extremely happy about going home to our Bomb Group, but I was saddened at leaving my remarkable newfound friends. I wondered what the future would bring for the dear people of Cerkvisce.

We arrived at the grass landing strip of the aerodrome at 1015 and were greeted by the British Major and Flight Officer McGregor. The Major told us that the planes would arrive at 1100 from Bari, and he was sure we would be able to leave with one of them today. Again we helped the Partisans prepare the runway for the impending landings and takeoffs by partially marking it with wide ribbons and starting a bonfire. But 1100 came and went, with no planes in sight, and we wondered what had happened to their usual fail-safe timing. However, we were accustomed to flying machines that were persnickety at times, and to uncooperative weather, so we thought positively and patiently sat on the big boxes and waited. In a few minutes, the familiar sound of aircraft engines made our ears perk up, and soon we could see five C-47's and four Spitfires.

There they were—five Douglas C-47's circling at about four thousand feet over and beyond the hills on the far southeast side of the airstrip, with their four Spitfires a few thousand feet above in their escort role. This heart-warming sight caused me again to become deeply sentimental as this was the day the ten of us had been hoping and waiting for—final repatriation! Further adding to the emotion was the fact that these beautiful American airplanes were built in our own country—and perhaps some were flown by American Air Corps pilots. We were very proud of these facts.

The C-47's landed and rapidly parked at the side of the grass strip for unloading and reloading while the Spitfires flew concentric circular patterns above. As before, carts and wagons came from every direction, some carrying wounded and injured Partisan men and women and some empty, to be filled with the supplies on board the airplanes. Unloading was accomplished very quickly, and patients were loaded—as before, it was a sad sight. Within a few minutes, the Chief Loadmaster approached us and told Major Moore that space had been saved for us on the fourth C-47 in the line, and that the pilot—a British major of the Royal Air Force—expected us to board soon. Our little hay cart was immediately sent to the airplane, and the rest of us followed close behind. Dr. Pintaric, who had been treating the wounds of my crewmen, as well as the injury to my right foot, was on hand to see us off, monitor the loading of his patients, and make a preliminary check of his inbound medical supplies. Dr. Pintaric was a fine doctor and gentleman—a very compassionate person. His job was a most difficult one for varied reasons previously referred to, but this did not deter him from caring for his many patients.

I climbed on board and went to the cockpit to introduce myself to the pilot. He asked me to load my crew as soon as the wounded Partisan men had been loaded, as he would be starting engines shortly. I hurried back to my crew and the others waiting outside the airplane, and then we said good-bye to all our Partisan friends. We gave them our silk maps, escape kits, remaining money (American gold seal notes in five dollar bills), medicine, forty-five-caliber Colt automatics (with extra ammo clips and leather holsters), webbed green belts, and trench knives.

I presented my forty-five and its extra ammo clips, holster, belt, knife, escape kits, and medicine to Dr. Pintaric. We regretted that we did not have more medical supplies to offer him, but he was elated with his gifts. We had tears in our eyes as we hugged and shook hands with all of our friends and saviors. They will be in our hearts until the end of time.

Just before we boarded, the leader of our escort group—a noncommissioned officer—presented me with a gift from him and our other five Partisans escorts. It was a battle knife (a type of trench knife) he had made himself. It is ten and one-half inches long, and its aluminum sheath— made from the sheeting of a crashed bomber—is about seven inches long. The bayonet-style blade is six and one-quarter inches long, and the grip— made of animal horn—is fastened at the hand protector by a copper band. The butt end is fitted with heavy round aluminum plates that secure the grip to the shank of the blade. This knife is a work of art, and from what I was told, it had been tried and proven in actual combat. This wonderful gift and the tenderness of its presentation brought tears to my eyes, and it graces the top of my bedroom credenza to this day.

It saddened me to say good-bye to Major Peter Moore—and to leave him in such a dangerous place—although I understood his devotion to helping the Slovenian Partisan cause in any way he could. Flight Officer McGregor was more gracious at this time than before, and he too wished us well as we prepared to board the C-47.

When we were advised that we could board, we hurried to take our places among the badly wounded Partisan soldiers on the cabin floor. The floor of this airplane is constructed of long, corrugated aluminum panels running from front to back, and it was sobering to find blood in many of these corrugations. The C-47 is a tail-low airplane, and blood flowed from the forward part of the cabin to the tail from the wounds of the badly wounded Partisan soldiers who lined each side of the airplane, with their heads toward the sides of the fuselage and their feet toward the center. Some of them had only one foot; some had none. Others had lost one or both legs. We were devastated to see them. These fine men had endured the worst hardships of war in an area where there was insufficient medical care for severe injuries. They showed no sign of the terrible pain they must be in. They were real heroes, and we tried to do anything we could to make their flight to Bari easier. Seeing them made us realize how lucky we were to be in one piece.

Once all of us were on board, the cargo door was secured and we started our taxi for takeoff behind the number three plane. Then we were rolling down the runway, and soon all five airplanes were airborne, climbing out of the river valley in trail and leaving our dear friends, the ground war in Slovenia, and the enemy behind.

In less than two hours we were in Bari. After landing, we taxied to the hospital receiving portion of the airfield ramp, where scores of olive drab ambulances awaited our arrival. As we disembarked, the ten of us were met by officers and men of the 15th Air Force, Fifth Wing, and were immediately taken to the American Military Hospital, where we were deloused and defleaed, our clothes were burned, and—after a long hot shower—were issued pajamas, heavy terry cloth bathrobes, and slippers. Then my injured crewmen were given preliminary treatment for their injuries. Once again, we felt like human beings! We were given a light meal in our respective quiet and darkened hospital rooms and were left alone to sleep in great beds with clean white sheets, pillowcases, and warm white blankets.

In a few hours, my sleep was interrupted by a hospital nurse, who advised me that my copilot, bombardier, navigator, and I were now to have some coffee or tea, milk, and a light snack before meeting with some 5th Wing Intelligence Officers for a debriefing session. The session lasted about an hour and covered our entire mission—from March 9 through our five-day sojourn in Slovenia. We were told that they would meet with us again the next day to review more of our experiences.

During the session, I found out that no one had informed the 483rd Bomb Group that we were safe in Bari, although I had the feeling that our bomb group's C.O. was aware that we were flown out of Slovenia to Bari and were in the hospital there. When the session was over, we were served a delicious early dinner in our rooms, and this set us up for a full night's sleep.

21

The Return

Day Number 6—Wednesday, March 14, 1945:
Getting Back to Normal

After breakfast the next morning, we each had a more thorough physical examination than the ones we'd received when we arrived. And, of course, the injured crewmen would be treated intensively and readied for the trip back to our Bomb Group, where they would fully recover before being returned to flying status. After the examinations, my three officers and I were again debriefed, this time in more depth.

After lunch and a nap, I was informed that we had passed our physicals and that we would be released from the hospital the next morning. After our official release, I could call our Squadron Commander and the Operations Officer at the 817th Bomb Squadron to request transportation back to our base. This bit of information was music to my ears!

On the morning of our second day in the hospital, I inquired about calling my squadron commander at the 817th Bomb Squadron to advise him of our status. I was informed by the hospital C.O. that he requested I wait until the final diagnosis of our crewmen's injuries were made, and also when the official security/intelligence clearance had been obtained for us to return to base.

Day Number 7—Thursday, March 15, 1945:
Our Homecoming Day

My entire crew, I was told, breakfasted in their rooms at 0700 and had been issued new uniforms (courtesy of the U.S. Army Air Corps). Our official release from the hospital would take place at 1100, after which I could call my Bomb Group. Sporting my new olive drab officer's outfit, I went to the communications room and used the field phone to call the Operations Office of the 817th Bomb Squadron. The phone was answered by Lieutenant George Hong, my original copilot, who was ecstatic. Actually, he was almost speechless, since he, along with everyone else in the Bomb Group, thought we were either down somewhere in the Austrian Alps or had managed to fly to Hungary (portions of which at that time were under Russian control).

I explained that we had been in Bari in the hospital for a few days after returning from Yugoslavia, and had now been released to return to our base. He said he'd obtain permission from our squadron's CO to use one of our B-17s to fly to Bari and bring us back to Sterparone. I waited on the phone while George spoke to our Squadron CO. He was told to take the "weather ship" to Bari to bring us back to Sterparone. He told me they'd be in Bari at 1500. That would allow them time to prepare the plane and fly here while I arranged transportation from the hospital to the air base and enjoyed one more good—and large—hospital lunch in the mess hall.

Lieutenant Bob Keno, my original bombardier, happened to be in the office speaking with George at the time my field phone call to Operations was made, and received the good news of our survival. Later he told me he had always felt that we would return.

At 1455, George taxied the weather ship off the runway and onto the ramp—a moving sight for all of us. We were almost overcome with emotion—we had survived! We had lived to fly another day! Anyone who served his country in combat and experienced the satisfaction of winning—of success—and the exaltation produced by the pride you have in your country, and the military organization to which you belong, can understand all the wonderful feelings I experienced watching that beautiful B-17 taxiing toward me that day ...

When George, Bob, our plane's crew chief, and the other well-wishers jumped from the rear entry door to greet us, we had a regular old-home-week celebration. Our hugs, handshakes and cheers must have continued for twenty minutes before we all piled on board to fly "home." With the engines started, and clearance from the control tower to taxi, George made our run-up and take-off checks. Within a very few minutes we were airborne and climbing northwest, bound for the area of San Severo and our base at Sterparone.

When we arrived, we were surprised by a big crowd and a celebration.

Officers of B-17 "Je Reviens" en route to rest camp on Isle of Capri after Missionn 34 for Logan and Metz. *Rear, left to right:* 1st Lt. Leslie Anton, Co-Pilot; 1st Lt. Edward F. Logan, Jr., Pilot. *Bottom, left to right:* 1st Lt. Robert Mahan, Bombardier; 1st Lt. Robert (Jim) Metz, Navigator.

Edward's certificate—Isle of Capri Rest Center.

When George parked the B-17, we saw a welcoming group of more than seventy-five enthusiastic friends. Everyone from the 817th Squadron was there—from pilots, navigators, and bombardiers to maintenance people and administrative ground personnel. We celebrated with snacks from the mess hall, GI beer, and other treats for an hour, after which we retired to our respective tent homes to let the reality of being back sink in.

When you are shot down, your group family goes into almost a state of shock. I had experienced this sadness myself when men I knew had been lost. But this time, it was I who had fallen from the formation and had caused my friends to worry and grieve. Now I was able to observe the happiness from the other side. Thoughts of the stirring events and the many wonderful people who were involved with my thirty-fourth mission will stay in my mind forever.

As for me, I had one more mission to fly to complete my combat tour of duty—thirty-five credited combat missions. Then I would return to my family and home. The war would, I hoped, be over for me; as an "Escapee and Evadee," I could choose where I wanted to be—either in or out of the U.S. Army Air Corps.

```
                            OPERATIONS
                    817th Bombardment Squadron (H)
                    Office of the Operations Officer
                                                        March 28, 1945.

SUBJECT:  Mission Record.

TO    :  All Concerned.

      1.  Enclosed herewith is the Mission Record of 1st Lt. Edward F. Logan, Jr.
O-827017.
```

| | | | | TOTAL | TOTAL |
DATE	TARGET	MISSION	HOURS	MISSIONS	HOURS
10-10-44	Treviso M/Y	1	5:10	1 1	5:10
10-11-44	Vienna O/R	2	6:45	2 3	11:55
10-13-44	Blechhammer O/R	3	8:10	3 5	20:05
10-14-44	Blechhammer O/R	4	8:20	4 7	28:25
10-16-44	Skoda Arm Wks	5	8:00	5 9	36:25
10-20-44	Brux O/R	6	8:45	6 11	45:10
10-23-44	Skoda A/W	7	8:50	7 13	54:00
* 10-29-44	RED ROVER·PILSEN,CZECHOSLOVAKIA-A/W	7A	4:20	-- --	58:20
11-7-44	Maribor S M/Y	8	6:00	8	64:20
11-16-44	Insbrook M/Y	9	7:20	9	71:40
11-18-44	Korneuburg O/R	10	7:20	10	79:00
11-19-44	Ferrara RRB	11	6:15	11	85:15
11-22-44	Munich M/Y	12	7:30	12	92:45
11-24-44	Linz O/R	13	7:00	13	99:45
12-11-44	Moosbierbaum O/R	14	8:00	14	107:45
12-17-44	Blechhammer O/R	15	8:10	15	115:55
12-18-44	Odertal O/R	16	8:25	16	124:20
12-19-44	Blechhammer O/R	17	8:30	17	132:50
12-25-44	Brux O/R	18	8:00	18	140:50
12-27-44	Linz M/Y	19	7:05	19	147:55
12-29-44	Insbruck M/Y	20	8:30	20	156:25
1-15-45	Vienna S-E M/Y	21	7:25	21	163:50
1-21-45	Lobau O/R	22	7:10	22	171:00
2-5-45	Regensburg O/R	23	7:40	23	178:40
2-13-45	Vienna S-E Depot	24	6:00	24	184:40
2-15-45	Vienna S-E Good Yard	25	6:05	25	190:45
2-17-45	Linz Benzol Plant	26	6:45	26	197:30
2-19-45	Bruck M/Y	27	7:00	27	204:30
2-21-45	Vienna Yards & Shop	28	6:35	28	211:05
* 2-23-45	RED ROVER - WORGL,AUSTRIA - MARSHALING Y.	28A	2:40	--	213:45
2-24-45	Graz M/Y	29	6:30	29	220:15
2-27-45	Augsburg M/Y	30	7:00	30	227:15
3-1-45	Moosbierbaum O/R	31	6:40	31	233:55
3-4-45	Sopron M/Y	32	7:00	32	240:55
3-8-45	Hegyashalom M/Y	33	6:20	33	247:15
3-9-45	Graz Main Sta.	34	6:00	34	253:15
3-25-45	Prague A/D	35	7:00	35	260:15

```
                                              C.E. Talman,
                                              Section Chief.
```

```
* RED ROVER MISSIONS — NO MISSION CREDIT
  1/2 FLIGHT TIME CREDIT
  E.F.L.
```

Missions record for 1st Lt. Edward F. Logan, Jr.

Tour of Missions Complete

Yes, I did fly my thirty-fifth mission to complete my tour of duty. After returning to Sterparone from Bari, my three other officers and I were sent to the Isle of Capri Rest Center for a week. Shortly after we returned, I was privileged to lead the 483rd Bomb Group on a very successful mission to strike a large German Aerodrome at Prague, Czecho-

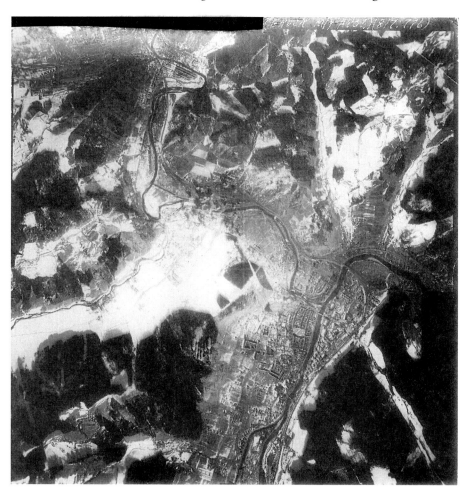

Bomb strike photograph of the Bruck, Austria, marshalling yards showing some bombs hitting the target and a "salvo" of seven one-thousand-pound bombs just released from my airplane en route to the marshalling yards. This cluster of seven bombs can be seen at the lower center of the picture. Mission No. 27 — February 19, 1945. This photo gives a clear view of the Mur River.

Bomb strike photograph of the Graz, Austria, marshalling yards and shops showing numerous bomb strikes on the target. Mission No. 29—February 24, 1945. Their antiaircraft gunners there missed me on this mission.

slovakia, on March 25, 1945. I have often reflected back on that last mission. It was a very satisfying experience which I am happy I was given the opportunity to complete.

Motivation for this strike was clear. Allied intelligence saw that the Luftwaffe had moved a large number of all types of their aircraft from Silesia to the two airfields adjacent to Prague because of the broad advance of the Russians in that region. With this large number of

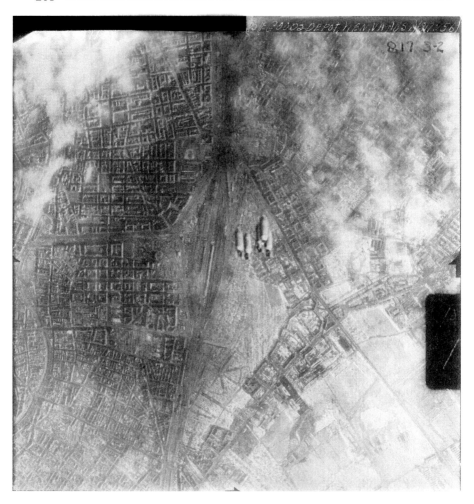

Bomb strike photograph of the Vienna, Austria, southeast goods depot showing a salvo of six two-thousand-pound bombs leaving my airplane en route to the target. Usually, every other two-thousand-pound bomb was fitted with a "booby trap" fuse or a delayed actions fuse to delay repair of the target. Mission No. 21—January 13, 1945.

aircraft in one area, it was a perfect opportunity to deal a severe blow to the Luftwaffe.

Here I was, leading my Group's bombing formation and a portion of the Fifth Wing of the Fifteenth Air Force. As an Escapee and Evadee, I felt as a bomber pilot I was finally completing the goal I had initially set for myself nearly three years earlier. Even with the threat of being attacked

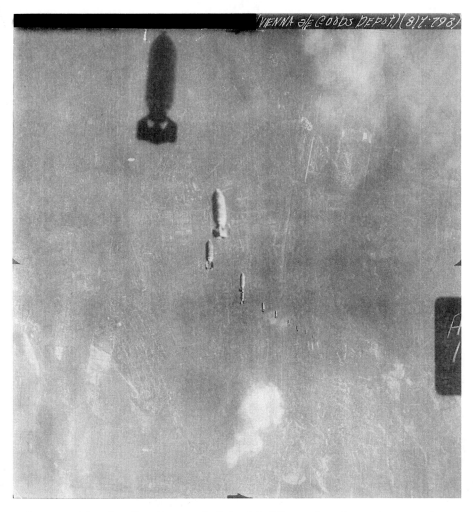

An unusual bomb strike photograph. It is of the Vienna, Austria, southeast goods depot showing eleven of the twelve five-hundred-pound bombs which have fallen from the bomb bay of my airplane en route to the target. The actual target is not visible at this point in the picture. Mission no. 24—February 13, 1945.

by German interceptors flying to and from the target, and being shot at by enemy antiaircraft gunners throughout the mission, I approached this last bombing mission with a sense of relaxed optimism and positive thoughts.

Every long-range high-altitude combat mission is full of dangerous situations and many unforeseen problems. Each of us approached these bombing missions with a natural concern and a subconscious apprehension

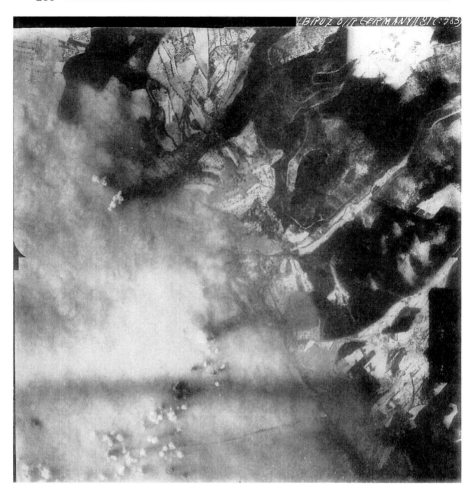

Bomb strike photograph of the Brux, Germany, oil refinery (beneath a stratus cloud cover) showing numerous bomb strikes of the previous squadron and some bombs hitting the target from our lead squadron. We were striking this target using our "Mickey," or radar equipment. Mission no. 6—October 20, 1944.

as to the outcome of the day. However, this mission, the last day of bombing, stirred more of the usual anxious thoughts in me.

The weather for this day was to be at its best—clear from takeoff to the target and return. On the takeoff, as lead airplane, I had the first crack at the clear cool morning air, and, after collecting my flock (consisting of the other three squadrons), we headed out over the assembling beacon at Lake Lesina and climbed to our target in the crystal clear sky. Our fighter escort, the 332nd Fighter Group (the Tuskegee Airmen), was right on

Bomb strike photograph of the Lobau Oil Refinery at Vienna, Austria (target not fully visible in picture), showing heavy damage from our previous squadrons' incendiary bombs dropped on the oil refinery and two of six canisters of incendiary bombs leaving my airplane's bomb bay en route to the target. These bomb canisters—long metal containers—would come apart in sections well below the airplane, and the many incendiaries would be released as the canisters came apart. Mission no. 22—January 21, 1945.

time. They filled the sky above us flying those wonderful silver "Mustangs" with their red tails and red propeller spinners—a magnificent display of protective fighter cover.

As we approached Prague from the southeast, over Hungary, we sighted German fighters in the distance, preparing for their attack on our

A B-17 of the 840th Bomb Squadron (yellow cowlings and red rudder) at its hard-stand, minus any armament (machine guns and turrets), standing ready for a long-range high-performance special operations flight.

formations. At the same instant, the 332nd was maneuvering to respond to their attacks and aggressively dove into the German fighter formations before they could penetrate our bomber formations. The aerial dogfight continued as we dropped our bomb loads on the two large Aerodromes near the city of Prague, and continued even as we flew away from the target area. The Tuskegee Airmen shot down three German twin engine ME-262 jet fighters that day. The 31st Fighter Group, who was also in the battle, shot down four ME-262 jet fighters during the battle. Later reports confirmed that neither had sustained any losses.

The gunners of our bombers were credited with shooting down an additional six ME-262s, an ME-109 and an ME-410 twin engine fighter bomber. The antiaircraft fire we encountered in and around the targets was moderate to heavy. Many B-17s were damaged by the enemy fighters and ground fire, but, fortunately, none were shot down.

Suffice to say, I was relieved and happy to park my airplane on its hardstand after the mission and shut down its engines, knowing my combat flying was complete. Sitting there in the cockpit as those wonderful engines' propellers stopped turning, my thoughts drifted back to "Je Reviens" and the last picture in my mind of that classic airplane—up there on the mountain slope, severely damaged, twisted, bent and burning in its final moments. My heart was a little heavy and my eyes a little teary, but I chose to remember that she was a gallant bomber. I shall never forget that beautiful new silver "flying fortress."

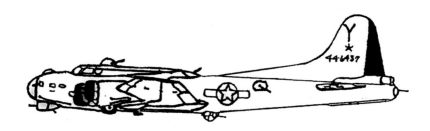

"JE REVIENS"

5TH WING 15TH AIR FORCE
483RD BOMB GROUP (H), 817TH BOMB SQD.
ITALY – 1944-1945

Epilogue

My Wingmen's Story

When my crew and I returned to our Bomb Group at Sterparone after we were released from the hospital, our fellow pilots told us that there had been some interesting and rather odd speculation about what had happened to us on March 9. Both of the pilots who were flying as my wingmen told me that at the instant our squadron released its bombs, they realized we had been struck by antiaircraft fire, but they didn't realize at first how serious the damage was and continued to fly on my wings, trying to maintain our three-plane formation. They watched as our airplane began a slightly lifting slow roll to the left—sort of a very large barrel roll—after we were hit. They continued on my wings for a few seconds before they realized that the roll was not planned—my plane was rolling over on its own. Then they broke formation and moved up and away from me.

This transpired so rapidly that neither of the wingmen was aware of the amount of damage we had sustained. They were able to observe that we were trailing gasoline from behind the left wing and that the left wing was smoking heavily. And they could see that the number one and number two engines had been damaged and were inoperative. However, from their vantage point and the fact that our airplane had started spinning downward, they didn't know what other damage we had sustained.

After returning to the United States from Italy, I had quiet times—while sailing my boat on Biscayne Bay—to reflect on the events of my thirty-fourth mission and place them in their proper perspective. When

I returned to the 483rd Bomb Group and spoke to my wingmen from that mission about their observations, they told me they had thought I might have headed for northwestern Hungary, because by the time I had recovered from the spin and gained control of the plane, we were about eighteen miles southeast of Graz and heading southeast—in the direction of Hungary. Their tail-gunners had reported seeing us flying on this course.

As readers know, I did not consider flying to Hungary. It was not an option for at least three reasons. First, the battle lines of the German and Russian forces in Hungary were very fluid, so attempting to parachute or crash-land behind Russian lines could have been a disaster—either side could have fired on us. Second, we 15th Air Force airmen knew that some Russian military commanders did not show great concern for downed Americans, some of whom endured many months of intense hardship with the Russian military while endeavoring to rejoin with American or British forces. Some never made it back—they simply vanished. Third, we had heard that some Americans had been captured by the Germans and sent to POW camps or even executed. I felt that the part of south central Slovenia where the friendly Yugoslavian Partisans were most active would be the best area for me to try to reach. Returning to Italy from there would be much easier than returning from Hungary.

Recorded History of This Mission

As far as the 483rd Bomb Group was concerned, we were MIA. Ten crewmen and their aircraft, number G44–6437, were "Missing in Action." This loss was noted in the Daily Operations Report of 9 March, 1945–First Wave, produced by the 483rd Bomb Group's Statistical Office. It was also listed in the 15th Air Force Mission Report (3–9–45, 1740—483rd Group, Graz M/Y Austria and in the Headquarters, Fifth Wing [US] Supplemental Missing Information Report) of March 9, 1945, as a Special Narrative.

These various official presumptions were just that—suppositions. What actually happened to us that day no one knew—except, of course, for those of us on board—until we returned to Bari and were debriefed.

The Headquarters people of the 15th Air Force, 5th Wing, told me that they were surprised to see us when we arrived at Bari. They said that they didn't know we were headed back to our base until the crew flying our C-47 notified them by radio en route from Yugoslavia that they were carrying ten American B-17 crewmen who would require medical attention.

It is not surprising to me that the Bomb Group was not aware that we had survived our ordeal. Usually, when a crew and its airplane are lost on a bombing mission they are listed as MIA, because no one in the other planes on the mission can say for certain just what happened to them. However, if witnesses see an airplane take a direct hit and fall out of formation in flames, or if they see a plane explode, lose a wing, or lose a tail section—and no parachutes leave the plane—the crew is usually listed as KIA (killed in action).

When a four-engine heavy bomber is so severely damaged that it rolls over on its back into a spiraling dive or spin, the airplane usually does not recover, and most of the crewmen cannot parachute because the centrifugal force of the downward spiral is so fierce that they cannot reach an exit. This is another case where the crew is listed as KIA.

I always entertained the belief that when we missed flying out on March 11th that Major Moore might have radioed the British O.E.S. in Bari that we were under his wing—so to speak—and would be returning to Bari on an available supply mission aircraft soon. Bari knew where we were.

Fifty years after this bombing mission, some interesting facts were discovered about it:

Twenty-one B-17s were scheduled for the first wave of this mission; however, not all of them actually attacked the target.

Twenty of the twenty-one took off on schedule.

One was delayed and made a late departure; however, it could not overtake the main group formation, so it returned to base and landed with its twelve bombs still on board.

Another B-17, which flew over the target in its proper place in the formation, experienced a bomb rack release malfunction and could not drop its bombs. The bombs remained in the shackles after the plane left the target area. While crossing the Adriatic Sea as it returned to base in formation, it was able to jettison six of the bombs into the Adriatic and returned to the base with the other six still on board.

The 483rd Bomb Group's Daily Operations Report for this mission states that a total of 252 500-pound bombs were carried on the twenty-one B-17s that flew in the first wave, but only 216 were dropped on the target (Graz). Six were jettisoned and 18 were returned to the base. In light of this summary, it is safe to say that our 12 were counted as part of the 216 successfully dropped.

The Daily Operations Report for the second wave reveals that four minutes after the first wave dropped its bombs, all twenty-one of the second wave B-17s dropped their bomb loads on the target—252 bombs—on the railway marshalling yards at Graz, with no difficulties encountered. The report also states that they experienced the same intensity of antiaircraft fire that we did and probably were shot at as they flew past Bruck on their way to Graz.

Appendix A: Citations Received by Edward F. Logan, Jr.

MEDITERRANEAN THEATER OF OPERATIONS

—————— · · ——————

15th AIR FORCE, FIFTH WING
483rd BOMB GROUP (H)
817th BOMB SQUADRON

ITALY: 1944–1945

1st LIEUTENANT EDWARD F. LOGAN, JR.
USAAC—SERIAL NUMBER A.O. 807017
- CITATIONS Received -

—————— · · ——————

* DISTINGUISHED FLYING CROSS WITH ONE OAK LEAF
   CLUSTER
* AIR MEDAL WITH THREE OAK LEAF CLUSTERS
* ETO RIBBON WITH TWO BATTLE STARS
* PRESIDENTIAL GROUP CITATION WITH ONE STAR
* EUROPEAN—AFRICAN—MIDDLE EAST CAMPAIGN METAL
* VICTORY METAL

Appendix B: Ferry Crews

The Five Ferry Crews Assigned to the 483rd Bomb Group

As this story relates, I was in one of ten crews that ferried B-17s from the United States to England on September 2, 1945. Five of these ten crews were assigned to the 483rd Bomb Group of the Fifteenth Air Force's Fifth Wing in Italy for their tours of combat. Their pilots were Lieutenant Devereaux W. Bush, Lieutenant Henry Carlisle Dent, Captain Walter L. Glass, Jr., Lieutenant William A. Haskins, and me, Lieutenant Edward F. Logan, Jr. Four of them survived their combat missions. Their participation in the air war goes far beyond their first journey together from Hunter Field at Savannah, Georgia, to Valley Wales, England.

LIEUTENANT DEVEREAUX W. BUSH was flying with the 840th Bomb Squadron on a mission to strike the large synthetic oil refinery at Ruhland, Germany, on March 22, 1945, when his B-17 was shot down by a direct hit from an eighty-eight-millimeter antiaircraft shell. No one on the airplane survived; it went down in flames. Bush was nearing the completion of his combat tour when this tragedy occurred.

LIEUTENANT HENRY CARLISLE DENT's B-17 was badly damaged by flak and was struck by the thirty-millimeter cannon fire of German ME-262 jet fighters on this same Ruhland mission of March 22, 1945. In spite of the extensive damage to their B-17, he was able to fly home to the 483rd Bomb Base. His radio operator was killed on this mission. Dent was assigned to and flew with the 817th Bomb Squadron. He ferried a B-17 back to the United States after the war in Europe ended.

CAPTAIN WALTER L. GLASS's B-17 was severely damaged on his first combat mission—to bomb the oil refinery at Vienna, Austria. The damage was caused by the explosion of an eighty-eight-millimeter shell in the fuselage and wing root area on the right side of the plane adjacent to the radio compartment, creating a hole in the fuselage large enough to drive a Jeep through. Two of his crew were killed instantly and two others were seriously wounded. His ball turret gunner (one of the wounded men) was trapped in the ball turret and could not be extracted until they arrived back at the base after the mission. Glass was assigned to and flew with the 815th Bomb Squadron. He ferried a B-17 home to the United States with a group of other B-17s after the war ended in Europe.

LIEUTENANT WILLIAM A. HASKINS completed his thirty-fifth combat mission just a few days after reaching his twenty-first birthday without having experienced serious difficulties during his combat duty. He returned to the United Stated shortly after completing his missions on February 17, 1945.

I have no detailed record of all the combat-related incidents that happened to these first four original ferry crews. However, they probably had to contend with many of the same difficulties the rest of us did while flying our thirty-five bombing missions and "Red Rover" missions.

The Other Five Ferry Crews

I cannot offer an account of the combat tours of the other five crew captains because we became separated at the 8th Air Force Combat Crew Replacement Pool in England. I suspect that most of these men were assigned to the 8th Air Force in England. The pilots of these five crews were: Lieutenant W.S. Cremen, Lieutenant DeFrancesco, Lieutenant Marshall Clyde Dunn, Lieutenant J.V. Galiano, and Lieutenant Gupton.

I do know that Lieutenant Dunn was killed in action while flying his B-17 on a bombing mission. Of the ten original pilots, Marshall Dunn was one of my closest friends. He was one of the seven young men with whom I progressed through the entire Army Air Corps training program, and from the very beginning we were close friends. We started military life together at indoctrination training (boot camp) and went through the Aviation Cadet School Program together. Seven of the original eight who started together graduated from Twin Engine Advanced Flying School at Moody Field in Valdosta, Georgia, as second lieutenants, and one, as you are aware, graduated as a second lieutenant from Bombardier School. Marshall Dunn and I also attended B-17 Transition School and Combat

Training at Avon Park together. From Avon Park we went to Hunter Field, and from there we ferried B-17s to England together.

These men will always be in my memories and thoughts—I deeply admired each and every one of them!

Appendix C:
About the Fifteenth Air Force

Composition in World War II

21 Four-engine Bomb Groups (H); 6 B-17 "Flying Fortress" Groups (Fifth Wing); 15 B-24 "Liberator" Groups; 7 Fighter Groups, 3 P-51 "Mustang" Groups; 3 P-38 "Lightning" Groups (some groups with "Droop Snoot" Pin Point Bombers); 1 P-47 "Thunderbolt" Group (eventually converted to P-51 fighters); 4 Medium Two-Engine Bomber Groups; 3 B-26 "Marauder" Groups; 1 B-25 "Mitchell" Group, 1 Photo Reconnaissance Group—F-5 Type Aircraft; 1 Special Operations Group—B-17 and B-24 Aircraft; 1 Tactical Reconnaissance Group—B-17 and B-24 Aircraft; 1 Weather Reconnaissance Group—P-38 Aircraft

World War II Statistics

Sorties flown: 148,955 bomber; 87,732 fighter (80 percent were effective). Aircraft lost: 3,400 bombers; 400 fighters. Enemy aircraft destroyed: 1,946. Enemy transport units destroyed: Locomotives: 1,600; Rail cars: 1,400; Motor transport: 800.

Tons of bombs dropped on enemy targets: 303,842 in 12 countries (Italy, Austria, Germany, Romania, Czechoslovak, Poland, Hungary, Yugoslavia, Greece, Egypt, Libya, Tunisia, and others in Europe and Africa), including attacks on 8 capital cities. Rounds of ammunitions expended: 25,150,400. Gallons of fuel consumed: 450,000,000. Casualties: Killed in action: 2,703; Missing in action: 12,359; Wounded in action:

2,553. Awards: Medal of Honor: 2; Distinguished Service Cross: 2; Distinguished Service Medal: 13; Silver Star: 939; Legion of Merit: 46; Distinguished Flying Cross: 11,984; Soldiers Medal: 729; Bronze Star: 2,741; Air Medal: 163,651; Distinguished Unit Citations: 63; French Croix de Guerre with Palm: 2; HQ 15 AF Decorations: none.

The First Forty Years of the Fifteenth Air Force: An Encapsulation

From *Fifteenth Air Force: The First 40 Years, 1943–1983* by the Directorate of Public Affairs, Headquarters Fifteenth Air Force. Courtesy of the Fifteenth Air Force Association, March Air Force Base, California.

At its inception, on October 9, 1943, the Fifteenth Air Force was designated by the United States Joint Chiefs of Staff to become the new large Strategic Air Force that would operate from bases in the Mediterranean Sea Theater. The Fifteenth would conduct its missions in conjunction with the British Royal Air Force's 205th Group in what would be a reshaped Mediterranean Allied Air Force.

The Fifteenth Air Force initially included two experienced Heavy Bomb Groups—the 97th and the 301st—both of which had conducted bombing operations as part of the 12th Air Force under the command of General James Doolittle during the North African campaign of 1942 and 1943. Some units of the veteran 9th Air Force's medium bomber groups that had participated in the North African campaign were also integrated into the newly formed Fifteenth Air Force. General Doolittle was selected to be the first Commander of the Fifteenth, with headquarters in Tunis, Tunisia.

The Fifteenth wasted no time getting started destroying strategic German military targets. It flew its first missions on its day of activation—November 1, 1943—from its base in Tunis. B-17s of the Fifth Bomb Wing attacked two targets in Italy—La Spezia Naval Base and the railroad bridge at Vezzano. On the second day of its new existence, November 2, the Fifteenth flew into Austria to attack the Messerschmitt airframe works, where the famed ME-109 was built, at Wiener Neustadt, Austria. It dropped 312 tons of bombs that day.

On December 1, 1943, the Fifteenth moved from Tunis to permanent headquarters in Bari, Italy, in the Foggia Valley. However, because of prolonged inclement winter weather in southern Italy and numerous engineering problems, the rebuilt aerodrome facilities and the new bomber and fighter bases were not finished on that date, so only a portion of the Fifteenth's now-large fleet of aircraft made the transition.

In spite of the great logistics problems involved in the move, the Fifteenth mounted a bombing attack the day it arrived at the new base: more than one hundred B-17s struck the ball bearing works and marshalling yards at Turin, Italy. That same day, Martin B-26 twin-engine medium bombers carried out three separate attacks on railroad facilities and bridges in north central Italy.

On January 3, Major General Nathan F. Twining was assigned as commander of the Fifteenth, and General James Doolittle was reassigned as commander of the Eighth Air Force in England. General Twining continued to lead the Fifteenth for the duration of the conflict in Europe.

The Fifteenth's first mass bombing attack was made on December 19,1943, penetrating into Germany to strike the Messerschmitt factory located at Augsburg.

In the first few days of January, 1944, the Fifteenth continuously bombed in and around Cassino, Italy, in support of the American ground forces that had been blocked in their advance northward by strong German forces in the area. Its heavy and medium bombers also attacked numerous targets in central Italy during a six-day period, and in the middle of January, in support of the planned Anzio beachhead landing on January 22, 1944, more than six hundred sorties were flown.

During that so-called "Big Week"—February 19 through 25—in a combined operation with the Eighth Air Force, the Fifteenth carried out intensive mass bombing attacks against German aircraft manufacturing complexes throughout southern Germany and Austria. The first day of the Big Week's bombing offensive saw the loss of 14 of the 183 bombers the Fifteenth flew against the target at Regensburg, Germany. During the remainder of the week, the Fifteenth lost 36 more four-engine heavy bombers. On February 25, the Fifteenth flew 400 bombers against the Regensburg aircraft factories. One-hundred-seventy-six of these struck the main target, and the others were dispatched against other targets at a shorter flying range. The Fifteenth lost an average of 6 bombers per mission—a total of 89—during the Big Week.

The Fifteenth again attacked the Cassino area, in conjunction with the Twelfth Air Force, with fierce saturation strikes on March 15, and flew its first 1,000-ton strike of a five-day effort on March 28. This operation was code-named "Operation Strangle" and was designed to block supplies traveling by railroad through northern Italy.

During the spring of 1944, the Fifteenth dropped more than 3,000 tons of bombs on Budapest, Hungary; Bucharest, Romania; Sofia, Bulgaria; the area around Athens, Greece; and the rail and transportation complexes in southern France in preparation for the upcoming cross-channel invasion. Also in the spring, the Fifteenth started attacking the large oil refinery installations at Ploesti, Romania. It continued these attacks into late August 1944. As the destruction of the Ploesti refining complex was completed, the Fifteenth turned it attention to the synthetic-oil producing plants in the German-occupied Silesia area and northwest Czechoslovakia. The output of these facilities was reduced by more than 80 percent by these sustained, accurate bombing missions.

"Operation Frantic" began June 2, 1944. During the operation's shuttle missions, American bombers—escorted by American fighters—departed their American Bomb Group bases in Italy, struck German targets in eastern Europe, and landed at one of three air bases in western Russia when the mission was done. In the first of these missions, B-17s, escorted by P-51 fighters, bombed Debrecen, Hungary. These shuttle operations continued until the middle of September and were stopped then for several reasons—problems that developed with the Russians, the vulnerability of American aircraft to German air attacks while on the ground at the Russian airfields, the inefficiency of the operation as a whole, and other difficulties.

The Fifteenth also participated in "Operation Anvil"—the Allied invasion of southern France—and flew numerous bombing missions in support of the amphibious landings there.

During August of 1944, the Fifteenth was assigned the task of destroying the German V-1 flying bomb manufacturing complexes and their launching sites. Three-hundred-twenty-three of the Fifteenth's heavy bombers unloaded over 773 tons of bombs on the V-1 manufacturing facility at Ober Raderach, Germany.

The Fifteenth used its newly developed "blind bombing" techniques on many of these bombing strikes because the harsh winter conditions in the target areas often did not permit visual bombing. These frequent bombing strikes greatly curtailed German oil production prior to and during the ill-fated Battle of the Bulge in December of 1944.

Crumbling resistance of the German armies in late winter of 1945 saw the Allied ground forces begin to penetrate the borders of Germany itself. On March 24, 1945, the Fifteenth Air Force flew its first bombing mission to attack Berlin, striking the large Daimler-Benz tank factory nearby. Two of the last B-17s shot down in the war were lost on this mission.

The last significant strategic bombing attack conducted by the heavy bombers of the Fifteenth Air Force was flown on March 25, 1945, when they struck the main aerodrome and the still-productive tank works at

Prague, Czechoslovakia. (Note: My last mission—number 35—was to lead the 483rd Bomb Group on this attack.)

On April 15, 1945, the Fifteenth executed the largest bombing operation the Air Force had ever conducted. It was a tactical mission in support of General Mark Clark's breakthrough at Bologna, Italy. (Strategic bombing and tactical bombing are distinctly different: strategic bombing is a mission to destroy a facility vital to the enemy's war effort—such as an oil refinery, an aircraft production plant, a battle tank factory, a railroad network, a bridge or a submarine pen; whereas a tactical bombing mission is one which is carried out in support of a ground army in a battle they are waging.) On this tactical mission, dubbed "Operation Wowser," 1,235 bombers hit the strong points, gun emplacements, and troop concentrations at the Germans' "Gothic Line," which had been in place since the previous September. Bologna was the main anchor of this defensive battle line.

Other missions of the Fifteenth during the spring of this year involved bombing attacks to stop the German forces' escape from northern Italy, dropping food to the inhabitants of that area, and evacuating prisoners of war—in converted B-17s.

The culminating drive by the American Fifth Army—toward the Brenner Pass in the middle of April—was heavily supported by the strike operations of 2,052 Mediterranean Allied Air Force aircraft from April 15 to 18. This extensive aerial campaign represented the most sustained use of heavy bombers ever flown in the Mediterranean Theater of Operations. P-51 Mustang fighters were the last American aircraft to attack the retreating German forces as they moved north toward Verona—bombing and strafing them as they fled.

The Fifth Wing's B-17s flew their final mission—blasting the marshalling yards at Salzburg, Austria—on May 1, 1945. The unconditional surrender by the German command in Italy was signed on May 2, 1945, preceding by only five days the total surrender of the Germans at Reims, France, on May 8, 1945—V-E Day—Victory in Europe by the Allied Forces.

On May 26 General Twining—who had become a three-star general while serving as commander of the Fifteenth Air Force—was reassigned to the United States and soon became commander of the Twentieth Air Force in the Pacific Theater. He was replaced by Brigadier General James A. Mullison, and the Fifteenth's personnel and materiel were redeployed to the United States and the Pacific Theater.

The Fifteenth contributed abundantly to the Allied pursuit of the war in its efforts to destroy Hitler's war machine. The eighteen months during which the Fifteenth flew combat bombing missions from its bases in Italy reveal innumerable accomplishments. Some of the most prominent were destroying about half the entire fuel production capacity of Europe, severely incapacitating the enemy's transportation system in most of Nazi-occupied Europe, and destroying a substantial portion of German fighter aircraft production.

The Fifteenth honed its high-altitude precision bombing to a fine skill. Its heavy bombers placed a high percentage of bomb loads well within the desired thousand-foot circle around the target's center and successfully struck sightless targets (those that were obscured by adverse weather). Strategic bombing by the Fifteenth reduced the effectiveness of the Luftwaffe by limiting its available fuel and materiel. It also added to the breakdown of the German submarine campaign and threw the German war economy into disarray, which led to manpower and materiel shortages.

Besides its unrelenting attacks on the enemy's industry, transportation, communications, oil production and refining, and port facilities, the Fifteenth was also very active in the rescue and repatriation of air crews that had been shot down in enemy territory. No other Air Force recovered as many of its missing pilots and crews, and no other undertook escape activities in as many countries as the Fifteenth did. In more than 300 successful operations, men were brought back safely from Tunisia, Italy, France, Switzerland, Greece, Albania, Bulgaria, Romania, Hungary, Yugoslavia, Poland, Czechoslovakia, Austria, and Germany. By V-E Day, a total of more than 5,900 people had been returned by air, by surface vessels, and on foot through enemy lines.

At the end of World War II, the Fifteenth Air Force was, in its totality, congratulated by General Twining for its splendid performance, high degree of effectiveness, and conscientious devotion to duty.

The Fifteenth Air Force was deactivated on September 15, 1945.

After the war, the Fifteenth was not inactive for long—it was reactivated in the spring of 1946, at which time it became the first operational numbered Air Force in the Strategic Air Command (SAC) as one of three SAC Air Forces serving the United States.

The Fifteenth entered the age of ballistic missiles in September of 1958 when it was assigned responsibility for the new missile program which was then underway.

The Fifteenth Air Force's first forty years of service—1943 to 1983—are replete with successful operations and firsts in every field of participation, in both wartime and peacetime. During those forty years, it flew many types of aircraft from its many bases in the United States and other parts of the world. During World War II it operated B-17s, B-24s, B-25s, B-26s, and single-engine fighters such as the P-38, the P-47, the P-51, and the stabled P-80. In later years it also flew the B-29, B-50, F-86, KC-97, KC-135, KC-10, B-47, B-36, B-52, U-2, SR-71, and the B-1B.

Index

231